STUDY SKILLS FOR TODAY'S COLLEGE STUDENT

STUDY SKILLS FOR TODAY'S COLLEGE STUDENT

Jerold W. Apps

Professor of Adult/Continuing Education

University of Wisconsin—Madison

McGRAW-HILL PUBLISHING COMPANY

New York St. Louis San Francisco Auckland Bogotá Caracas
Hamburg Lisbon London Madrid Mexico Milan Montreal New Delhi
Oklahoma City Paris San Juan São Paulo Singapore Sydney Tokyo Toronto

Material in Chapter 3 about unlearning, challenges for learners, and returning to familiar themes appeared with different titles in *Adult and Continuing Education Today* (Learning Resources Network, Manhattan, Kansas.)

This book was set in Times Roman by the College Composition Unit in cooperation with Monotype Composition Company.
The editors were Lesley Denton and Susan Gamer;
the production supervisor was Denise L. Puryear.
The cover was designed by Rafael Hernandez.
R. R. Donnelley & Sons Company was printer and binder.

STUDY SKILLS FOR TODAY'S COLLEGE STUDENT

2 3 4 5 6 7 8 9 0 DOC DOC 9 5 4 3 2 1 0

ISBN 0-07-002464-2

Library of Congress Cataloging-in-Publication Data

Apps. Jerold W., (date)
Study skills for today's college student / Jerold W. Apps.
p. cm.
Rev. ed of: Study skills for adults returning to school / Jerold W. Apps.
Includes bibliographical references.
ISBN 0-07-002464-2
1. Study, Method of. 2. College student orientation. I. Apps.
Jerold W., (date) Study skills for adults returning to school.
II. Title.
LB2395.A66 1990
378.1'70281—dc20

89-27602

ABOUT
THE AUTHOR

JEROLD W. APPS has been a professor of adult and continuing education at the University of Wisconsin—Madison since 1964. He has taught younger and older students at both the undergraduate and the graduate level at the University of Wisconsin and several other universities. He has also taught many noncredit workshops for adult learners throughout the United States and Canada.

Professor Apps has done research on barriers to learning, and on preferred learning styles of both younger and older college students, for more than a decade.

He is also the author of several books on education and study skills, including *Study Skills for Adults Returning to School* (1978 and 1982), *Improving Your Writing Skills* (1985), *Problems in Continuing Education* (1979), *The Adult Learner on Campus* (1981), *Improving Practice in Continuing Education* (1985), and *Higher Education in a Learning Society* (1988).

His awards include the following: Research to Practice Award, presented by the American Association for Adult and Continuing Education (1982); Outstanding Adult Educator of the Year Award, presented by the Wisconsin Association for Adult and Continuing Education (1987); Best Non-Fiction Book of the Year (1977) and Best Scholarly Book of the Year (1988), presented by the Wisconsin Council for Writers.

Avocationally, he studies rural and local history and speaks and writes on these topics.

For Susan

CONTENTS

PREFACE

I graduated from a small high school in rural Wisconsin, where my graduating class numbered fifteen. The next fall I enrolled in the University of Wisconsin at Madison. In my first few months at the university, I tried to adjust to living in a city, attended classes—most of them larger than my entire high school—and worked at learning how to study. I discovered that I was sorely lacking in such basic study skills as using a library, taking lecture notes, and managing my time. If any books on study skills were available in those days, I didn't know about them.

But my instructors and their teaching assistants helped pull me through my first semester—along with fellow students whose study skills were far more developed than mine and who shared their knowledge about surviving in college, including some shortcuts I have never forgotten.

Ten years after I had received my bachelor's degree, I returned to the university to work on a graduate degree. By then, my study skills were rusty, and I experienced the predictable problems of adjustment, such as juggling a schedule that included work, a wife and three small children, and my studies. I also met some unsympathetic faculty and staff members who couldn't understand why anyone in his early thirties would be coming back to school.

During my career, I have worked as a teacher of adults, and then as a professor. I have worked with older and younger college students for more than 30 years. In the 1970s I began researching adults returning to school. I was trying to describe the barriers returning students face, and to find ways in which colleges and universities could be more responsive to returning students. As a result of that work, I wrote *Study Skills: For Adults Returning to School* (McGraw-Hill, 1978), which was later revised as *Study Skills for Adults Returning to School* (1982).

Many changes have taken place in higher education since I wrote those books. Probably most significant is the fact that the number of returning students has increased to the point where it will soon equal or exceed the number of younger, more traditionally prepared students on many college campuses. I have also noticed that younger and older students have more in common than they once did. Many in both groups are married and have families. Many in both groups are working and studying part time. Many in both groups have left college at some point and returned a semester, a year, or several years later.

Thus, in planning this new version, *Study Skills for Today's College Student,* I decided to consider both groups of students together. But there will, of course, always be differences between younger and older students: for one thing, returning students obviously have more years of life experience to draw on; for another, returning students do have some particular problems. Therefore, the last two chapters of this book, Chapters 21 and 22, are devoted to returning students and the issues that concern them—issues that may differ from those facing younger students.

I gathered materials for this book from several sources. My own research and my years of teaching and counseling students and returning students provided the bulk of the source material. In addition, I reviewed a host of study-skills books, though unfortunately, almost none of them addressed the problems returning students face, and none addressed traditional and returning students together. I have also included some of the text materials and a few of the exercises from *Study Skills for Adults Returning to School.*

This revision is written for both younger and older students, traditionally and untraditionally prepared students, students just out of high school and students who are returning to college studies after an absence of a few months or many years.

I have divided the material into five parts. Part One, You and Your Learning, shows students how they can take charge of their own learning. Information in Part One ranges from assessing study skills to identifying learning styles, learning how to learn, and organizing learning.

Part Two, Improving Your Study Skills, is the core of the book. It has chapters on listening and note-taking; improving writing, reading, and speaking skills; and sharpening the memory. Chapters 13 and 14 are special chapters. Chapter 13 is about how to learn with electronic media, including television, audiotape, and computers; and about studying off campus. Chapter 14 describes a systematic plan for approaching the different disciplines, to make them more accessible.

In Part Three, Resources for Learning, Chapter 15 is about using the modern college library, which usually includes a computerized card catalog as well as access to CD-ROM storage systems and computer database searches. Chapter 17 discusses the many other resources available on college and university campuses today.

Part Four, Developing Life Skills, covers such important topics as time management, how to concentrate, managing stress, and keeping healthy.

As mentioned above, Part Five, Returning to School, is primarily for the returning student. Chapter 21 takes up issues of concern to returning students; Chapter 22 describes topics of concern to graduate students.

An Instructor's Resource Manual is available to adopters. This is an extensive resource for instructors which will help them organize and plan their study-skills courses. It includes a wide variety of exercises and activities, along with material on specific teaching techniques.

I am indebted to many people for the preparation of this book. I particularly want to mention Judy Adrian, a graduate assistant in my department. Judy helped with this project every step of the way, from assisting with literature searches to reading draft after draft of manuscript.

Finally, McGraw-Hill and I would like to thank the following reviewers for their many helpful comments and suggestions: Robyn Browder, Tidewater Community College; Martha DePecol, Adirondack Community College; Marilyn Eanet, Rhode Island College; Diane Geerker, SUNY, Cobleskill; Barbara Haxby, Triton College; Peggy Patterson, University of Guelph; Joseph Raab, University of California, Los Angeles; Ed Rogers, Indian River Community College; and Richard Schmonsky, Columbia Greene Community College.

Jerold W. Apps

TO THE STUDENT: HOW TO USE THIS BOOK

When you enroll or reenroll in a college or university, the experience can be exciting and challenging, but it can also be rather frightening. This book is designed to help make the experience easier and more enjoyable for you.

I've written this book for all college students—those who have recently graduated from high school and are starting higher education for the first time, as well as those who are older and may not have been in school for several years. Some students may have dropped out of college and are now returning. Others may have completed high school and worked for several years and are only now starting a college career. Still others may have completed an undergraduate degree several years ago and are now returning to do graduate work.

FIRST STEPS

After you read this introduction, turn to Chapter 1 and work your way through "Assessing Your Study Skills." How you see yourself as a learner—and especially where you feel you need help—will give you a road map for using this book.

If you need to know more about yourself as a learner, and if you need to learn how to learn, you'll want to spend some time with Chapters 1 through 4.

Starting with Chapter 5, I share detailed, in-depth information about improving basic study skills such as note-taking, listening, writing, reading, speaking, and taking exams. Chapter 13 is a special chapter on learning with electronic media such as computers and videotape. Chapter 14 provides an approach for studying the various disciplines. Chapters 15 and 16 focus on using the library and finding resources for learning.

Chapter 17 begins a section about developing life skills such as time management, concentration, stress management, and keeping healthy.

Chapter 21 is written specifically for returning students, with emphasis on special problems they face. The new graduate student is the subject of Chapter 22.

BAFFLED BY TERMS?

You're not really sure about all the terms associated with colleges and universities? You're not alone. What's a TA? How do assistant, associate, and full professors differ? What's a college credit? What's the difference between auditing a course and taking a course for credit? What's a bursar? A dean? Turn to the Glossary (starting on page 275) for answers to these questions.

CHALLENGES

If you are just beginning a college career or are returning after several years away, you probably believe that survival is your greatest challenge. Many of the ideas I've included in this book will help you survive, and much more. You'll soon discover that you can survive quite well, and then your challenge will be to get the most out of your college experience. You will be challenged to go well beyond memorizing facts. You will learn how to think for yourself—how to question and challenge ideas that your instructors present and ideas that you hear from your fellow students.

There was a time when getting an education meant memorizing the facts associated with various disciplines. The sciences are a good example. As an undergraduate, I spent untold hours memorizing the veins in a frog, for a biology course, and hundreds of chemical formulae for a chemistry course. Some memorization of facts within the disciplines still continues to be important. But research is changing some fields of study so rapidly that simply memorizing facts is of little use: those "facts" will be out of date soon after you've received your degree. Today, you will be challenged to learn the core concepts within each discipline, its organizing principles, and the way in which information is added in that discipline. Thus college learning will give you a foundation for becoming a lifetime learner.

The day is long past when people could rely on a college degree to serve them throughout life. In the modern world, all of us, no matter what career or life work we pursue, will need to keep on learning. The extent to which we can accumulate organizing principles within the disciplines during our formal college years, and the extent to which we can develop sound study skills, will determine how easy and how enjoyable our education can be.

ADJUSTING TO COLLEGE LIFE

For those of you who are enrolling in college directly from high school, this is probably your first experience of living away from home. Not only do you have to adjust to many academic requirements; you may also have to adjust to a roommate, to taking charge of your own personal discipline, to setting your own priorities, and to dealing with many different attitudes, beliefs, and opinions expressed by your fellow students and instructors. You may never have had as much freedom as you have now, but with freedom comes the challenge of organizing and planning your time. If these issues are critical to you now, you'll want to turn to Chapter 17, on time management; Chapter 18, on concentration; and Chapter 19, on stress management.

If you are returning to college several years after high school or a previous college experience, you too are facing an assortment of challenges associated with becoming a student again. I discuss challenges faced by returning students in some depth in Chapter 21.

STUDY SKILLS FOR TODAY'S COLLEGE STUDENT

PART ONE

YOU AND YOUR LEARNING

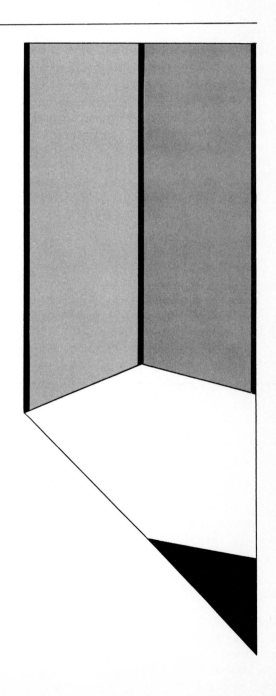

1

ASSESSING YOUR STUDY SKILLS

PRETEST

One way to begin improving your study skills is to identify your present strengths and weaknesses. If you are not sure about your ability in a particular area, or are unclear about what is actually involved in any area, you might want to examine that topic before you fill in the following self-rating chart.

SELF-RATING CHART

Priority		Not a problem	Sometimes a problem	Often a problem	Reference (page numbers)
_____	1 Attitude toward learning	_____	_____	_____	
_____	2 Knowledge of personal learning style	_____	_____	_____	
_____	3 Studying various disciplines	_____	_____	_____	
_____	4 Concentration	_____	_____	_____	
_____	5 Planning learning	_____	_____	_____	
_____	6 Time management	_____	_____	_____	
_____	7 Stress management	_____	_____	_____	
_____	8 Health	_____	_____	_____	
_____	9 Reading speed	_____	_____	_____	
_____	10 Reading comprehension	_____	_____	_____	
_____	11 Reading for different purposes	_____	_____	_____	
_____	12 Overview reading	_____	_____	_____	
_____	13 Marking reading material	_____	_____	_____	

SELF-RATING CHART (*Continued*)

Priority		Not a problem	Sometimes a problem	Often a problem	Reference (page numbers)
_____	14 Taking notes from reading	_____	_____	_____	
_____	15 Writing clearly	_____	_____	_____	
_____	16 Writing a term paper	_____	_____	_____	
_____	17 Writing a book review	_____	_____	_____	
_____	18 Evaluating own writing	_____	_____	_____	
_____	19 Preparing a manuscript	_____	_____	_____	
_____	20 Writing with a word processor	_____	_____	_____	
_____	21 Creative thinking	_____	_____	_____	
_____	22 Problem solving	_____	_____	_____	
_____	23 Critical thinking	_____	_____	_____	
_____	24 Speaking	_____	_____	_____	
_____	25 Taking lecture notes	_____	_____	_____	
_____	26 Listening	_____	_____	_____	
_____	27 Learning from television or video courses	_____	_____	_____	
_____	28 Learning from a computer course	_____	_____	_____	
_____	29 Using a computerized card catalog	_____	_____	_____	
_____	30 Finding learning resources	_____	_____	_____	
_____	31 Selecting a graduate program	_____	_____	_____	

MAKING A STUDY-SKILLS DEVELOPMENT PLAN

Once you have assessed yourself in the various study-skill areas, check off in the "Priority" column those items you consider "often a problem." Using a different symbol, add the items you consider "sometimes a problem."

Using the "Reference" column, you can turn directly to the chapter in this book where each problem is discussed, for tips on how to improve in this area.

You may also want to contact the student services office of your college or university for information about short courses or workshops that may cover areas where you believe you need most help. For example, often a college library will offer short courses and orientation sessions and provide written materials to familiarize students with its resources. The numerous colleges and universities with computerized card catalogs sponsor self-help and orientation sessions to help students become comfortable with the computer as quickly as possible.

Once you have found out what resources are available on your campus to help you improve in your high-priority areas, develop a plan for getting the job done.

Following is a form you can use for a study-skills improvement plan.

STUDY-SKILLS IMPROVEMENT PLAN

Skill to improve	Resources	Time	Assessment
1			
2			
3			

List the highest-priority study skills you identified on your self-rating chart. Then, using the results of your research on what forms of assistance are available, fill in the "Resources" column. Establish a deadline for studying the appropriate material in this book, attending a workshop, going to an orientation session, and so on—whatever is appropriate for the skill you are trying to improve. In the "Assessment" column, note what you would like to achieve in improving each skill.

Let's look at how you might develop your plan. Suppose that you've given "using a computerized card catalog" a high priority. You will discover that this book provides considerable information on that topic, and you might also find that your college library offers a special orientation program at the beginning of each semester. Under "Resources," then, you would list the appropriate pages to study in this book and the dates of the orientation session. You would also want to note the dates when you will practice using the computerized catalog—and the date by which you hope to be at least minimally proficient. Under "Assessment," you would note the skill level you wish to achieve (for example, "able to find call numbers of books by author, subject, or title, unassisted").

Do the same sort of thing for each of your high-priority areas.

KEEPING A STUDY-SKILLS JOURNAL

Keeping a study-skills journal is another technique many students find extremely useful. A journal allows you to write down your thoughts about successes and challenges as you try to sharpen your study skills. This not only gives you a record of your own progress but also may be an enjoyable experience in itself.

A spiral notebook makes a good journal, since having the pages fastened together will keep your notes from floating around and becoming lost. A good way to keep a journal is to draw a line down the right-hand side of the page, about one-quarter in. Write on the wider side of the page, leaving the narrower column blank. Later, you may want to come back and make additional notes in the blank column.

What can you write in a journal? You will probably want to keep a fairly detailed record of the study-skills areas you are trying to improve, the strategies you are using, and—most important—how you feel about the process. A learning plan is a rather straightforward account of the study skills you are trying to improve and your specific plans for improving them; a journal is broader. Here you can write down your frustrations, your joys, and your innermost ideas. And if you are having problems with a particular study skill, you may sometimes find a solution merely by writing about it. A journal helps you draw on your unconscious, where novel solutions to problems are often generated.

By writing in your journal two or three times a week, you will be able to see, as time passes, what progress you are making in sharpening your study skills.

UNDERSTANDING YOUR OWN LEARNING: WHAT FACTORS AFFECT HOW YOU LEARN?

Many factors affect how you learn. Let's consider some of the more important ones.

Your Study Patterns

In addition to assessing your present level of study skills, you may want to reflect on your study patterns, including how much time you devote to studying.

Two researchers, Thomas P. Hogan and Elizabeth Hendrickson, compared the study habits of younger and older college students. They found that older students tend to put in slightly more time than younger students. Students age 25 and older studied about 2¼ hours per credit per week; students 24 and younger, about 1¾ hours per credit per week. Thus for an average load of, say, 12 credits per semester, students are studying between 21 and 27 hours per week, or about 3½ hours per day.

When the students in this research project were asked how they spent their study time, reading the class text was ranked first and reviewing lecture notes second. Preparing class assignments and writing term papers were also ranked high. Both younger and older students studied most often at home or in their dormitories. The university library ranked second as a place to study; for older students, their place of employment ranked fourth.

Another aspect of study patterns is barriers to study. For Hogan and Henderson's respondents, barriers included household tasks, families and roommates, work schedules, noise, and lack of motivation.[1]

How do your study patterns compare with this research? If you're not sure, you may want to keep a study log for 1 or 2 weeks and record the

[1] Thomas P. Hogan and Elizabeth Hendrickson, *The Study Habits of Adult College Students*, University of Wisconsin–Green Bay, Green Bay, Wis., 1983.

results in your journal. You might also want to note where you studied and what barriers got in the way.

Your Age

Age affects how we learn. Research has shown that as we grow older, our reaction time decreases somewhat: it takes us longer to do things. This is also true with learning. But *capacity* to learn is not the same as *speed* of learning, although for many years educators confused the two. Now it is clear that (if they have no major debilitating illnesses) people are able to learn well into their advanced years, even though it takes them longer to learn.

If you are an older student and have been away from formal schooling for several years, you may have already experienced the frustration of wanting to ask your instructor to slow down a bit. And you may well have arranged your schedule so that you can take as long as you need to comprehend what you are learning.

The aging process also affects our ability to see and hear, although the decline in ability varies at different ages and there are different rates for different people. For example, some people require glasses at age 12 and others never; but when we examine large groups of people, research indicates that visual efficiency declines rapidly after age 40. Hearing declines rather gradually from about age 25 to 55, and then somewhat more rapidly. Today, most impairments in seeing and hearing can be corrected quite easily, and thus have little affect on people's ability to learn.

A larger question has to do with intelligence in general: Does intelligence decline, remain the same, or increase with age? Popular opinion tends toward the idea that intelligence declines with age. Is that true?

Such questions are complicated because intelligence is not a unitary concept. Rather than having "an intelligence," each of us has several "intelligences."

Baltes and Schaie conducted research with 500 adults whose ages ranged from 21 to 70. They tested the group over a 7-year period and identified four "dimensions" of intelligence: (1) *crystallized intelligence* (skills acquired from education and from living, such as language, numbers, and inductive reasoning); (2) *cognitive flexibility* (ability to shift one's thinking from one approach to another, as in dealing with antonyms and synonyms); (3) *visualization* (organizing and processing visual materials, as in identifying an incomplete picture); and (4) *visual-motor flexibility* (coordination of visual and motor tasks).

Baltes and Schaie discovered that scores for crystallized and visualization intelligence increased dramatically with age and continued to increase to age 70 (the age of their oldest subjects). Cognitive flexibility remained constant. Only scores of visual-motor intelligence decreased with age.[2] Schaie, reporting on more recent studies, notes, "We can now conclude that on abilities where speed is not of primary importance, there is very little change in intellectual function for an individual throughout adulthood."[3]

A research project in the Soviet Union, involving a sample of 2300 adults aged 18 to 40, examined memory, thinking, and attentiveness. The researchers concluded that from ages 18 to 25, memory, attentiveness, and thinking ability may rise *and* decline. Attentiveness was rather stable in subjects from age 18 to 21, but from age 22 to 25 it went up and down. Attentiveness peaked between ages 26 and 40 (this research did not include subjects over 40).

Dusan Savicevic, a Yugoslavian educator who summarized the research, said,

> The significance of the Soviet investigations is that they give a new image of the potentialities for intellectual development in adults aged eighteen to forty. They have shown that the exercise of intellectual functions, which is attained through learning and education, is the main builder of strength, of skill development,...Not only do the results point to the possibility of learning during the adult years, but from them it follows that learning and development are absolutely essential to the maintenance of [human beings] and the development of their skills.[4]

All students bring their own life experiences to the classroom, and these experiences influence how they learn. Older students, by virtue of their age, bring more experience. Sometimes, these experiences get in the way when they are trying to learn new things.

Life-span development research helps us understand how we change throughout life, in a more or less predictable fashion. Erik Erikson, for example, divides human life into eight stages of ego development and describes each stage in terms of what happens if people are successful or unsuccessful in working through the tensions that characterize it. According to Erikson, in early adulthood we must resolve a tension between intimacy and isolation: that is, between commitment to others and avoidance of commitment. During middle adulthood, there is a tension between generativity and stagnation, or productivity (for oneself and

---

[2] P. B. Baltes and K. W. Schaie, "The Myth of the Twilight Years," *Psychology Today*, Vol. 7, pp. 35–40, March 1974.

[3] K. Warner Schaie, "Adult Changes in Adult Intelligence," in D. S. Woodruff and J. E. Birren (eds.), *Aging: Scientific Perspectives and Social Issues*, Brooks/Cole, Monterey, Calif., 1983, pp. 144–145.

[4] Dusan M. Savicevic, *The Man and Life-Long Education*, Republicki zavod za Unapredivanie Skolstva, Titograd, 1983.

others) and nonproductivity—excessive self-love and egocentricity. In late adulthood, there is a tension between integrity and despair. Integrity includes appreciation of one's continuity with the past, present, and future—a sense of completeness; despair implies having found no meaning in life and losing faith in ourselves and others.[5]

Robert Havighurst identified developmental tasks in six life stages: (1) infancy and early childhood, (2) middle childhood, (3) adolescence, (4) early adulthood, (5) middle age, and (6) later maturity. Examples of developmental tasks for early adulthood include finding a mate and getting started in an occupation; examples for middle age include achieving adult civic and social responsibility and adjusting to aging parents.[6]

Erikson and Havighurst are only two examples of life-span research. Developmental studies like theirs help us understand how we change as we age, though the findings are not universally accepted. Some people argue that not everyone goes through the various stages these researchers describe. (In particular, the concept of a midlife crisis has been questioned.) Yet, dramatic changes do occur in many adults' lives, and these changes influence not only how they learn but also their reasons for learning. For example, unhappiness with one's job or career is often a compelling reason for returning to college—the intent is to learn new skills and move into a new career.

Your Culture

College students today are more and more culturally diverse. The cultural mix includes many international students, plus greater numbers of Hispanics, African Americans, Asians, Native Americans, and other racial and ethnic groups. At many institutions minorities account for 10 percent of the student body; in some cases, more than 30 percent of the students are members of minority groups. Moreover, many colleges and universities are now making special efforts to increase minority enrollments.

Where you grew up—on a farm, in a small town, in another country, or in the center of a large city—affects how you see the world and thus how you learn. Each of us is a reflection of a personal history which has implications for our learning. How you see things is often referred to as your *world view;* it includes your beliefs about other people, about how society works, about what is good and bad or right and wrong, about how things ought to be done—even about what foods to eat, and so on. The

---

[5] Erik H. Erikson, *Childhood and Society,* 2d ed., Norton, New York, 1963, pp. 247–274.
[6] Robert J. Havighurst, *Developmental Tasks and Education,* 3d ed., McKay, New York, 1972.

meaning you extract from a passage in a textbook, what you hear when an instructor lectures, what you see on a videotape—all these are influenced by your world view.

You may be unaware of many of the beliefs you hold. They are so much a part of your life, so much a part of your makeup, that you never call them into question. And it is upsetting when your world view is questioned. Yet the college experience often brings your fundamental beliefs to the surface, to be examined and acted on.

Your Social Situation

Your social situation influences your learning. One area in which the effects of social situation are felt is part-time learning. As many as 75 percent of students 25 and older, and up to 85 percent of those 35 and older, study part time. Younger students are also studying part-time in increasing numbers.

In addition to enrolling for several credits at a college or university, many students are raising families, working full time or part time at a job, and participating in community activities. They might be called *concurrent students*. Their college course work is but one of many responsibilities that compete for their attention. A family—such as a spouse and children—will often directly influence a student's learning. Worrying about a sick child while taking an examination, or trying to smooth over an argument with a spouse about finances while trying to write a final paper for a course, can dramatically affect performance.

Part-time students have a particular set of needs. These students generally do not have time to become involved in campus activities, particularly social activities. Part-time students must have quick and easy access to library facilities, and these facilities must be available at times (such as weekends and late in the evening) when the students are not working.

The reasons why part-time students have enrolled in college are often special as well. Most part-time students of whatever age are attending college for job-related reasons. Many older students are making career changes; others are continuing their education in order to advance in their present jobs. In fact, it is difficult to think of a modern career in which learning is not a requirement of the job.

Your Self-Concept

Your self-concept influences how you learn. Students who have been out of school for several years and are returning often have a poor self-image with regard to their ability to perform, particularly in competition with younger students. Returning students worry that they will say something stupid in class, and that other students will therefore think less of them. Many returning students fear that their rusty study skills will cause them to fall behind. And many students, of every age, fear failure in general.

On the other hand, many returning students—especially part-time students, believe that they can accomplish far more than is humanly possible. They are highly motivated, and often they do accomplish a great deal; but many become frustrated when they cannot accomplish more.

Your Gender

In recent years, many researchers have been exploring gender differences. Do women learn differently from men? Are the experiences of women during youth and adolescence sufficiently different from men's so that their world view is different?

This kind of research is quite new: only recently have developmental studies focused on women. The vast majority of the research over the years concentrated on men, and generalizations were drawn from it about both men and women. As Belenky and her associates report,

> When scientists turn to the study of women, they typically look for ways in which women conform to or diverge from patterns found in the study of men. With the Western tradition of dividing human nature into dual but parallel streams, attributes traditionally associated with the feminine tend to be ignored. Thus we have learned a great deal about the development of autonomy and independence, abstract critical thought, and the unfolding of a morality of rights and justice in both men and women. We have learned less about the development of interdependence, intimacy, nurturance, and contextual thought.[7]

Belenky and her associates talk about the need for women to develop their own voice, a voice that will be consistent with women's development and not merely a reflection of men's development:

> To learn to speak in a unique and authentic voice, women must "jump outside" the frames and systems authorities provide and create their own frame.... [Women must begin] to reclaim the self by attempting to integrate knowledge that they felt intuitively was personally important with knowledge they learned from others.[8]

Women, and men, must learn how to put themselves into what they are learning.

---

[7] Mary Field Belenky, Blythe McVicker Clinchy, Nancy Rule Goldberger, and Jill Mattuck Tarule, *Women's Ways of Knowing*, Basic Books, New York, 1986, pp. 6–7.
[8] Ibid., p. 134.

SUMMARY

- To improve your study skills, start with an assessment of yourself. Once you have done that, and assigned priorities to the study skills you need to improve, you can create a study-skills development plan.
- A study-skills journal can give you insight about difficulties you may be having with particular study skills, and it will provide a record of progress. It can also provide insightful solutions for study-skills problems.
- Examining your study patterns (how much time you study, where you study, and what prevents you from studying) can be extremely useful.
- Who you are affects how you learn. Your age has an affect. As we grow older, certain natural functions slow down, including functions relating to learning. But research indicates that we are able to learn well into late life.
- Where you were born, the community where you grew up, and your generation affect how you see the world and how you learn. The beliefs you hold, in large measure, come to you from your culture.
- Your social circumstances (such as whether or not you are working full-time and studying part-time and whether or not you have a family to support) influence your learning.
- Your self-concept—what you think of yourself as a person and as a student—affects your learning.
- Your gender may also make a difference in how you learn.

2

DISCOVERING YOUR LEARNING STYLE

People differ in how they think, how they organize, how they solve problems, and what they do with information—and in how they learn.

For example, some people like to start with the big picture, an overview, and then proceed to finding out more about the parts. Others start with the details, and then put them together to form the big picture. The first group might be called *whole-part* learners and the second group *part-whole* learners.

People's learning styles differ in many other ways as well. Some of us learn in a well-organized, systematic, linear way: we plan what we want to learn and then proceed to learn it. But some of us learn in a much more intuitive, unorganized fashion.

Some of us learn best when we can discuss with others whatever it is we are studying. Others prefer to learn alone and find that we learn best when we can sit back and contemplate what we have been studying, away from the stimulus of others. In fact, some "lone learners" say that interaction with others tends to confuse rather than clarify.

I may learn a skill best by watching someone demonstrate it, but you may find that you must do the required manipulation yourself in order to learn. You may be one of those who can pick up an instruction book and immediately be able to follow it to put something together; but I may consider most instruction books so much gobbledygook and know that trial and error works best for me. (Whole-part learners usually find that unless they can see an object completed, or at least a picture of it, step-by-step instructions aren't all that helpful.)

13

Many of us learn best when we can see as well as hear someone discuss and describe what we are learning. Many of us learn well by watching a television program or a videotape. But some of us prefer an audiotape. (An audiotape played on a tape deck in a car is often a convenient way of learning, particularly for people who spend considerable time in their cars.)

You may prefer to learn in a lecture hall, with other students all around you and a good lecturer presenting material in an exciting and well-organized way. Or you may prefer to learn by reading and then discussing what you have read with two or three other people, in an informal setting where each person's ideas can be put on the table for examination.

Some people want to be told what to do at every stage in the learning process. They learn best, they say, when they have a carefully developed course syllabus, with readings indicated and topics listed systematically. Others prefer more freedom to move around when they are learning; although they want some structure, they also want to explore topics that may not be listed in the syllabus.

COGNITIVE STYLES

It is clear, then, that we learn differently. Psychologists use the term *cognitive styles* for these various approaches to learning. The noun corresponding to the adjective *cognitive* is *cognition,* which has been described as

> about how people take in information, how they recode and remember it, how they make decisions, how they transform their internal knowledge states, and how they translate these states into behavioral outputs.[1]

In talking about how people learn, we can also use a simpler term—*learning styles.* Robert Smith defines learning styles as "the individual's characteristic ways of processing information, feeling, and behaving in learning situations."[2]

Identifying Cognitive Styles:
Learning-Style Inventories

Several learning-style inventories have been developed, to help learners and researchers understand more about individuals' preferences. The

[1] R. Lachman, J. Lachman, and E. Butterfield, *Cognitive Psychology and Information Processing,* Erlbaum, Hillsdale, N.J., 1979, p. 99.
[2] Robert M. Smith, *Learning How to Learn,* Cambridge, New York, 1982, p. 24.

more popular inventories include the Embedded Figures Test, Kolb's Learning Style Inventory, the Canfield Learning Styles Inventory, the Grasha-Reichman Student Learning Styles Questionnaire, and the Myers-Briggs Type Indicator.

Different learning-style inventories measure different aspects of learning. For instance, one measures how well a person learns from experience; another evaluates preference for structure (that is, how information is presented and what learning situation is desired); and a third assesses preference for competitive on collaborative learning environment.

One of the older inventories was developed by Witkins and introduced in 1954. It differentiates people who look at things in a "global" way from those who look at things more analytically. The two ways of perceiving objects and situations are called *field-dependent* and *field-independent*, respectively.

> The field-independent person is likely to deal with elements independent of their background whereas the field-dependent person deals with the total field or situation. The field-independent person consistently approaches a wide variety of tasks and situations in an analytical way, separating elements from background. The field-dependent individual approaches situations in a global way, seeing the whole instead of the parts.[3]

Witkins's research turned up interesting information that goes beyond how individuals learn:

> Field dependents are not likely to differentiate even themselves sharply from the surrounding field. They, more than field independents, are sensitive to what other people are doing and thinking and are dependent on others for their own orientation.[4]

Learning-style inventories and the learning-styles approach in general do not make judgments about "right" and "wrong" ways of learning. Learners are different, but no particular way of learning is wrong.

Nor does this approach tell us exactly how each of us acquires a particular cognitive or learning style. Researchers studying cognitive styles say that there may be a genetic component to how we learn. But they also say that our learning preferences are largely a product of how we have been taught and how we have learned in the past:

> In general...people probably learn habitual ways of responding to their environment early in life. These habits, spontaneously applied without conscious choice, determine one's cognitive style.[5]

---

[3] K. Patricia Cross, *Accent on Learning*, Jossey-Bass, San Francisco, Calif., 1976, pp. 116–117.
[4] Ibid., p. 118.
[5] Ibid., p. 119.

Applying Cognitive Styles: Flexible Learning

Responding to the Learning Situation Psychologists believe that it is possible for people to learn which cognitive style to apply in any given situation. Thus, even though we all have a preferred learning style that we probably acquired in childhood, we can also learn to use other styles as we face new learning situations. For example, your learning preference may be to look at the broad picture before examining the parts; but in learning some things you may find it more useful to start with the parts. This can be a conscious choice.

Two keys are involved here. First, we must be aware of our current predominant learning style. Second, we must know of another approach for learning a particular thing—an approach that some people say will work better. With these two pieces of information, we can make the necessary adjustments so that we can learn most effectively.

Responding to the Instructor Not only are there ways of responding flexibly to particular learning situations, such as specific subjects (science, English literature, mathematics, and so on); there are also ways of responding flexibly to how information is provided. Flexible learning is especially important for responding to instructors.

Traditional instructors Traditional instructors try to help students acquire information as efficiently and effectively as possible. They may use a variety of teaching methods. Some will lecture almost entirely. Many will combine lecturing with various kinds of audiovisual materials; some will lecture with electronic media such as videotape. How the material in a course is covered, and exactly what material is covered, will be seen by a traditional instructor as her or his responsibility. The student's responsibility is to "learn the material."

Facilitative instructors The facilitative instructor wants students to understand what they are learning, to make sense of it, and to tie it in with their own experience. A facilitative instructor is less concerned than a traditional instructor with simply covering the material. But facilitative instructors, like traditional instructors, use a variety of teaching approaches, including lectures and audiovisual and electronic media. Facilitative instructors will also use small-group discussions from time to time, believing that discussions with peers are one way to enhance understanding.

If you are a learner who likes to have ideas laid out for you neatly, in a well-organized fashion, you will probably respond better to traditional instructors. And you have almost certainly encountered many traditional instructors, since there are far more of them than facilitative instructors. But occasionally in your college courses you will have facilitative instructors; and if you are to make the most out the learning situation, some adjustment of your learning style will be required.

A facilitative instructor will expect you to organize what you are learning, and to show that you understand how it relates to your life—to your job or to your previous experience, for example. You may also have to make decisions about what you want to learn; facilitative instructors frequently offer you choices rather than a firm schedule. Facilitative instructors generally have high expectations for your learning, but that learning will often be more individualized than it is in a traditional classroom. Thus it will be more difficult for you to compare what you are learning with what your classmates are learning. Facilitative instructors are more interested in what *individuals* learn—and whether their learning fits who they are, what their backgrounds have been, and what their present situation is—than in having everyone learn the same thing.

If you are most comfortable in classrooms where everyone is learning the same thing at the same rate, you may be frustrated in a facilitative classroom, where you may have to decide what you will learn and how fast you will learn it. That is why responding flexibly is so important.

Assessing Your Cognitive Style: Learning-Style Preferences

How do you learn best? Below is a simple assessment chart designed to help you identify your own preferences for learning. It will help you to understand three broad aspects, or dimensions, of your learning preferences: (1) how you prefer to receive information, (2) what your relationship to your instructors is, and (3) how you prefer to process information. (This chart is not designed to replace the more sophisticated learning-style inventories. If you are interested in taking one of these inventories, to learn more about your learning preferences, contact the student services department at your college or university.)

LEARNING-STYLE ASSESSMENT CHART

Rank each of the items listed, with 1 meaning "least preferred" and 5 "most preferred."

Preferred method of receiving information		Rank			
Books and journal articles	1	2	3	4	5
Live lectures without visuals	1	2	3	4	5
Live lectures with visuals	1	2	3	4	5
Audiotapes	1	2	3	4	5
Videotapes	1	2	3	4	5
Self-directed computer instruction	1	2	3	4	5
Television	1	2	3	4	5
Small-group discussions	1	2	3	4	5
Large-group discussions	1	2	3	4	5

LEARNING-STYLE ASSESSMENT CHART (*Continued*)

Rank each of the items listed, with 1 meaning "least preferred" and 5 "most preferred."

Relationship to instructor		Rank			
I expect the instructor to tell me what to learn.	1	2	3	4	5
I expect the instructor to structure my learning for me.	1	2	3	4	5
I see the instructor as a guide to my learning, but I want to be in charge.	1	2	3	4	5
The amount of direction I expect from the instructor depends on the subject I am learning, and how new it is to me.	1	2	3	4	5

Preferred approach to processing information		Rank			
I begin with parts and build up to the whole.	1	2	3	4	5
I try to understand the whole, then work on understanding the parts.	1	2	3	4	5
I prefer to reflect on information by myself.	1	2	3	4	5
I prefer to work with other learners when possible.	1	2	3	4	5
I enjoy competing with other learners.	1	2	3	4	5
I like to process information in terms of solving some problem.	1	2	3	4	5
I like to try out information to see if I can apply it.	1	2	3	4	5
I like to relate new information to my experience.	1	2	3	4	5
I like to relate new information to information I already know.	1	2	3	4	5

OTHER FACTORS INFLUENCING YOUR LEARNING

Attitudinal Factors

Your learning style obviously influences how you learn, and knowing something about your preferred learning style and how to adjust it to particular learning situations will enhance your learning. But other powerful attitudinal factors also influence how you learn. These factors include *interest, motivation, fear,* and *self concept.*

Interest   It's tough to learn something that you aren't interested in learning. We've all had such experiences, and it takes an extraordinary amount of discipline to work our way through courses in which we have little or no interest but which are required for a degree.

But interest is not necessarily fixed and unchanging. Sometimes we are surprised. The first few weeks of a course may be dull, dull, and then something happens. It may be the instructor's personality that grabs us. Or it may be the subject matter itself; once we began to understand it, we develop an interest in it.

Motivation   Motivation, of course, often goes along with interest: if we are interested in something, we will be motivated to learn it. Sometimes, though, motivation is separate from interest. We may be motivated to learn something simply because we know we have to learn it in order to pass a test, or a course. Motivation may also be "sugar-coated": there are rewards for learning, and we learn in order to achieve them. (For instance, you may work for an employer who gives an automatic increase in salary when you complete a certain number of college credits.)

The value of motivation that is not based on interest is doubtful, however. To have a lasting affect, motivation must relate to your interests and to your long-term goals.

Fear   Fear strikes many learners, young and old alike. When I advise returning students to take a course in statistics, I often see their knuckles turn white and beads of perspiration appear on their foreheads as soon as I've said the word *statistics*. Statistics involves mathematics, of course, and for many students—particularly returning students who have not taken formal mathematics for several years—mathematics is something to be feared. These students will do almost anything to avoid it.

Yet, in my experience, the vast majority of these students do very well in mathematics and statistics courses, once they get through the first few class sessions—perhaps the first examination—and discover that they are as competent as the next person. Those who overcome their fear of mathematics most quickly are those who develop a study program, which often includes some remedial work. Their fear disappears as they develop confidence.

Self-Concept   Self-concept also affects learning. If you believe that you are not a good student, then the first snag you encounter in learning will reinforce that belief; it will be what I call a "told you so" situation. ("I told you I wasn't a good student.")

Developing strong study skills, overcoming fears (such as "mathematics anxiety"), and building confidence as a learner by taking the college experience a day at a time—all these will improve your self-confidence about learning. And developing a strong self-concept makes the entire learning process easier. As the noted psychologist Carl Rogers wrote,

It is only when the person decides, "I am someone; I am someone worth being; I am committed to being myself," that changes become possible.[6]

Physiology: "Whole-Brain" Learning[7]

Whole-brain activity is another factor affecting learning. You've probably read about, perhaps even studied, "whole-brain" psychology. Books have been written on whole-brain writing, whole-brain painting, whole-brain thinking in everyday activities, and so on. Many of the ideas presented in these books are controversial, and often the books themselves are superficial. But the basic concept of whole-brain activity, in my judgment, is sound, and should be considered as we think about how to improve our learning.

Research indicates that the left brain and right brain have different functions, and which side of your brain is dominant will affect how you do things.

The left brain is the systematic, analytic side. It is objective, rational, concerned about time and efficiency, interested in detail, and language-oriented. Left-brain activity is ordered, sequential, and tidy.

The right side of the brain is visual, intuitive, and concerned with feelings. It wants to see "big pictures"; it is concerned with patterns more than with details. It is concerned with bringing things together, seeing the relationship of larger concepts to each other.

According to researchers, in each of us one side of the brain tends to predominate and right-brain–left-brain theory can help us understand more about learning. For example, consider people who want to start learning by seeing "big pictures" and interrelationships, and people who prefer to start with pieces and then systematically combine them. The former approach reflects right-brain predominance; the latter represents left-brain predominance.

Of course, the two sides of the brain do not operate independently. In a sense, the two sides "talk" to each other. For instance, the right side is often the creator of new ideas and new ways of looking at things. The left side is the judge, critically examining these creations. Often its judgments are made prematurely, before the right brain's creation has had an opportunity for expression. The left brain will say, "That's a dumb idea; where did it come from?" And many of us listen to the left brain more

---

[6] Carl Rogers, *Freedom to Learn*, Merrill, Columbus, Ohio, 1983, p. 278.
[7] The material in this section is based on the following sources: Henriette Anne Klauser, *Writing on Both Sides of the Brain*, Harper and Row, New York, 1986; Sally Springer and George Deutsch, *Left Brain, Right Brain*, Freeman, San Francisco, Calif., 1981; and Tony Buzan, *Use Both Sides of Your Brain*, Dutton, New York, 1976. These books will also be of interest to readers who want to explore the topic further.

often than to the right brain. One reason for this may be that western cultures tend to favor analytical, logical, linear thinking—the kind of thinking that is characteristic of the left brain.

But ideally, in learning—as in many other areas of life—we want to have a healthy mix of right-brain and left-brain activity, not one side operating at the expense of the other. In learning, and in life, there is often a need for creativity, for new ways of seeing and doing. The right brain, if given the chance, can help us greatly. If encouraged, it can help us relate new learning to old learning, in ways we may not have thought possible because they do not seem "logical" or "systematic." Also, it is through right-brain activity that we often acquire insight, the "aha!" or breakthrough experience that comes to us in a flash, often when we least expect it.

Recently, I bought a new portable computer. I had the usual, predictable troubles in setting it up and making it do, at least minimally, what I wanted to do. But I was also trying to figure out a way of tying it to my larger office computer. I had studied all the instructions about how to "cable one computer to another"; I had talked to several people who were supposed to be experts; and I still couldn't figure it out. I was doing everything right, supposedly, but still the cross-computer communication would not work. A few days later—after I had abandoned the problem in total frustration—while I was chopping wood in my back yard, it occurred to me that maybe I had fastened the cable to the wrong port on my computer. I hurried into the house to have a look. At first, my insight appeared to be wrong. According to the markings on the computer, the cable was fastened to the right port. But in a few minutes, I discovered that the markings for two of the ports had been switched. My insight was correct.

All of us, from time to time, run into snags in learning. Allowing the right side of the brain to help us is a practical way to work through some of these snags. But right-brain activity goes beyond problem solving. It can help us develop new ways of thinking, new ways of organizing, and new ways making sense of what we are learning.

Time pressures and anxiety often become barriers to right-brain activity. One strategy that helps me get over these barriers when I am writing is this: I try to finish a draft of project a few days before the deadline; then I go on to something else and come back to the project a day or so before it is due. I find that I have a new perspective on the project, and usually I discover that I have new ideas for additions and revisions. The "time off" has allowed my right brain to make its contribution.

I also try to withhold judgment from the left brain when the right brain is creating new ideas. I try to follow a rule that has long been used in group brainstorming—no comment on an idea, no matter how stupid or impractical it may appear at first glance; save judgments for a later time. Following this rule, I create a kind of "internal dialogue." I allow my creative and judgmental sides to debate with each other. But I also create a jury that watches over the debate to make sure that both sides have equal influence. For instance, when my creative side comes up with a new idea, my judgment side immediately wants to work it over, and often to squelch it before it is completely expressed. The conversation in my head goes something like this.

> *Creative side*: "How about this for a new way of thinking about the relationship of the Civil War to the agricultural economy of the upper midwest?"
>
> *Judge*: "Where did that come from? That idea will never be accepted. Nobody has ever thought about it that way. Aren't you taking a risk here? Who needs risks when you're working for a grade?"
>
> *Jury*: "Wait a minute. Let's at least give the creative side a chance to develop the idea a bit more. There's plenty of time later to evaluate it. Let's give it a chance; let's see where it goes."

Most of us carry on internal dialogues like this one; but sometimes we haven't developed a jury to watch over the discussion, to make sure that both sides have a fair hearing.

Another technique I use, to make sure that my creative side is expressed, is writing new ideas in a journal, or diary. That way they will at least be recorded, even though I may later discard them. I have also found that the process of writing itself often helps me to discover new ideas.

SUMMARY

- Understanding how you prefer to learn can help you in several ways. It will also remind you that learners are different, and that although you may learn differently from your friend, your learning approach may be equally effective.
- Learners differ in several fundamental ways. Some prefer to start with the "big picture" and then examine the parts. Others prefer to start with the parts and build to the big picture. Some people prefer to learn in a linear way: they plan what they are going to do and then do it, systematically and carefully. Others are nonlinear learners: they jump into a learning situation in a much more intuitive fashion. Some learners prefer to work alone; others enjoy and gain much from interaction with others. Some learners prefer lectures; others prefer visual presentations such as films and videotapes.

- Researchers use the term *cognitive styles* for differences in how we absorb information and make sense out of it. Educators, building on cognitive research, have developed learning-style inventories to help students understand more about their own approaches to learning.
- Flexibility is important for learners, who must respond to different situations and different instructors.
- Facilitative instructors involve students and draw on students' experiences. Traditional instructors (who are in the majority) concentrate on the topic they are teaching, with the intention that the information will be covered and the students will learn it. Students need to make adjustments if their own preferred learning style conflicts with the instructor's.
- A learning-style assessment chart can help you understand more about how you learn. Some students will want to contact their student services department, in order to take more sophisticated learning-style inventories.
- In addition to learning styles, your interests, motivations, fears, and self-concept influence your learning.
- Whole-brain activity is also an important factor in learning.

3

LEARNING
HOW TO LEARN

You can learn how to learn. And you can do it at any age. You can also take a major role in planning your own learning. Of course, from time to time you will call on others to help you in your planning. For example, you will probably want others to help you if you are beginning study in an area that is new to you; you would expect your course instructor to organize your learning for you and show you where to start, how to proceed, and what the standards for success are. But even in new areas, with some guidelines, you can take part in planning.

Learning how to learn means taking charge of your learning. It is a helpful skill not only as you enroll in courses and classes, but also as you pursue lifelong learning. Robert Smith, an educational researcher, says that the person who has learned how to learn knows

> how to take control of his or her own learning, how to develop a personal learning plan, how to diagnose strengths and weaknesses as a learner, how to chart a learning style, how to overcome personal blocks to learning...[and] the conditions under which [students] learn best.[1]

In order to learn how to learn, it is important to understand what learning is and how it takes place. Let's start with several definitions of learning and then look at the process of learning.

[1] Robert M. Smith, *Learning How to Learn*, Cambridge, New York, 1982.

24

WHAT IS LEARNING?

You might suppose that educators can readily define learning and, as a group, agree on the definition. But this is not the case. Learning is something of a mystery, and researchers continue to explore what it is and what exactly happens when a person learns.

Situational Definitions:
Formal, Nonformal, and Informal Learning

One way to understand learning is in terms of the different situations where it occurs. *Formal learning* occurs when learning is organized into classes and courses, and credits, grades, or both are given. All your schooling, from the day you first set foot in kindergarten to your college years and graduate work, would be considered formal learning. Formal learning is organized and structured; you generally know what to expect, and you know when a particular course begins and ends. Generally, someone other than yourself decides if you have met the standards that have been established.

Nonformal learning is not for credit. But it is planned and organized. It may take the form of a weekend workshop, a 3-day conference, or a semester-long noncredit course. People who participate in an employer's in-service training program are also experiencing nonformal learning. In nonformal learning, success is usually assessed by both you and some outside person, but it is sometimes assessed entirely by you. After attending a workshop, for example, you may be asked to write or explain what you learned from it.

Informal learning occurs in day-to-day living. Someone at work shows you how to fix your car radio. You watch a television program, and it causes you to think about what you saw. You attend a play with your spouse or a friend, and the two of you talk far into the night about what it means. Informal learning can also occur in conjunction with formal or nonformal learning. For instance, as you become acquainted with foreign students in your classes, you learn much about how they think, what is important to them, and how they see the world—and you begin think about your own beliefs in new ways. Unfortunately, our society tends not to place much value on informal learning. Thus many of us feel that what we learn in our travels or on the job or from our families is not as important as learning that has a course number and a grade attached to it.

Functional Definitions: Levels of Learning

For some college students, learning means simply memorizing facts, repeating them back on an examination, earning as high a grade as possible, and then going on to the next topic. For them, an education is a collection of facts. But this is a rather low level of learning, and—since much factual information is soon outdated or forgotten—it is of limited value in the long run.

Drawing on the work of Jurgen Habermas,[2] I suggest three higher levels of learning, or more valuable outcomes for learning: (1) practical learning, (2) learning for meaning, and (3) learning for empowerment. Each of them goes beyond memorization of facts, although memorization is often involved.

Practical Learning   Practical learning means accumulating necessary information and developing appropriate skills in order to carry out a particular task. Let's say you are studying how to use a computer for word processing. Practical learning would involve learning how to use a particular kind of computer software—how to "boot" it and how to produce certain elements such as paragraphs. Your learning is focused on a specific, highly definable task or outcome.

One kind of practical learning is described as *competency-based;* that is, specific abilities are defined as the outcomes of learning. Learning to use word-processing software would fall into this category.

Practical learning is appropriate in many learning situations, but not all. In some situations, learning for meaning or for empowerment is necessary.

Learning for Meaning   Learning for meaning does not emphasize developing a skill or acquiring information for the purpose of performing a task. Instead, it emphasizes gaining meaning from what you are studying.

For instance, if you are studying World War II, in addition to learning facts you could reflect on the meaning of the war for the future world economy, political boundaries, international relations, and so on. If you are studying John Steinbeck in a literature course, you could focus on the themes he develops in *East of Eden,* and on how these themes relate both to biblical roots and to present-day situations.

Thus the outcome of learning for meaning is not a skill, or some form of competence—although you could argue that learning how to derive meaning from factual or hypothetical situations is one kind of skill. Learning for meaning is more a matter of understanding and developing a new attitude toward something, or a new perspective on it.

In practical learning, students and instructors can usually agree on the extent to which the objectives have been met, but in learning for meaning

---

[2] Jurgen Habermas, *Knowledge and Human Interests,* Beacon, Boston, Mass., 1972.

there is more of a personal dimension. The meaning you derive from some historical event or series of events, for instance, may be quite different from what your fellow students or your instructor will derive. (That does not make your meaning right or wrong, of course.) Learning for meaning, then, can be a more individualized approach to learning, in which your own experiences and thoughts—and your biases and prejudices—are evoked as you examine material. In learning for meaning, your own world view becomes important.

Learning for Empowerment   Learning for empowerment is sometimes called *liberation, emancipatory,* or *transformative* learning. It is even more personal than learning for meaning, for its goal is to help learners take more control over their lives. Learning for empowerment involves questioning and examining assumptions—looking in new ways at familiar ideas and patterns of thought. Roger von Oech, a specialist in creativity, says

> We all need an occasional whack on the side of the head to shake us out of routine patterns, to force us to rethink our problems, and to stimulate us to ask new questions that may lead to other answers.[3]

Learning for empowerment can be unsought or sought. In some of your courses, your instructor will raise questions, and your fellow students will challenge you and what you believe. This is certainly one way to become aware of new ideas and approaches, though it is often uncomfortable.

But you can also deliberately seek out new ideas. For example, you can start by asking yourself, "What if...?" "What if I wrote the first draft of a term paper, nonstop, without including any footnotes, and merely saying what I thought about the assignment?" At another level, you could ask yourself, "What would I need to know if I became president of company X?" You can always ask the fundamental question, "What am I doing?" There is an old story of two bricklayers who were asked by a passerby what they were doing. The first one answered, "Laying bricks," wondering why the passerby had bothered to ask. The second bricklayer replied, "I'm building a cathedral." Which are you doing, laying bricks or building a cathedral?

Not only is learning for empowerment personal; it also has considerable depth. It assumes that you have certain information, which may have been gained from various kinds of practical learning; and that you are able to derive meaning from what you are learning. Above all, it enables you to take charge of your learning and of the actions that result from learning.

[3] Roger von Oech, *A Whack on the Side of the Head,* Warner, New York, 1983, p. 12.

HOW DOES LEARNING TAKE PLACE?

Learning Is Living—and Lifelong

Many people would like to separate learning from living, but that is impossible, for in many respects they are the same. As we live, we learn. Learning is unavoidable. And as we learn, we live; how could it be otherwise? If learning is living and vice versa, then learning is, of course, lifelong. Learning is something we do from the first to the last moment of our lives.

Some people still believe that the only reason for learning is to prepare for life, and that you can then lead your life without further learning. A returning student once told me, "When I finished my baccalaureate, it was my firm belief that I would never set foot in a classroom again; that I was completely prepared for my career; and that I would not change my career, nor would my chosen career betray me and require me to participate in additional education." When the student told me this, not only had he changed careers, but after several years out of school he was enrolled in a master's degree program.

True, much of elementary, secondary, and higher education is focused on preparing for the future. But the day has long passed when it is even possible to suppose that what you learn from your formal schooling will be all that is necessary. Some fields, such as engineering and computer science, are changing so rapidly that as much of half of the information acquired by undergraduate students will be obsolete in about 5 years. Also, most people will changes jobs several times during their working years, and in most instances considerable learning is required for each change.

"Lifelong learning" has truly become a slogan for today. Throughout your life, you will constantly mix formal, nonformal, and informal learning. By planning your own learning—that is, by learning how to learn—you can more easily keep up to date in your job, make career shifts when they are appropriate, and meet the many challenges of an ever-changing society. And you will discover, as you become comfortable in taking charge of your learning, that not all of it will relate to work or to survival in a complex world. You can learn for the fun of it, for the sheer joy that comes from exploring new areas of interest and developing new skills, and for the satisfaction that comes from knowing something you didn't know before.

Learning Involves Doing

Most people who study learning and write about it agree that learning is an active process. We do not learn effectively by sitting on the sidelines;

we must be involved. Effective learners generally immerse themselves in what they are learning, wrestling with the ideas presented, comparing new ideas with ideas they already hold, searching for possible applications, and questioning opinions and positions.

What you read, hear, and observe furnishes you with information. But it remains merely a collection of information until you do something with it. Isaac Watts wrote,

> Reading and conversation may acquaint us with many truths and with many arguments to support them, but it is our own study and reasoning that must determine whether these propositions are true, and whether these arguments are just and solid. . . . It is meditation and study that transfers and conveys the notions and sentiments of others to ourselves, so as to make them properly our own. It is our own judgment upon them, as well as our memory of them that makes them become our own property.[4]

Learning Involves Change

Although educators have trouble agreeing on a definition of learning, they do appear to agree on one point: When you have learned, you have changed. Perhaps they agree on this because it seems so obvious. If you have learned how to write with a word processor, you clearly have changed. After studying the history of a country, you have more information about that country, and probably some different attitudes as well. You have changed.

The changes that result from learning are sometimes only superficial: you have some new information that you didn't have before. But such changes can also be far-reaching and profound: you may have been forced to examine some of your basic beliefs; perhaps your world view has been challenged and you are making fundamental changes in what you believe.

Some changes occur slowly and gradually: developing public speaking skills, for example, or coming to understand Sartre's views on existentialism. Some changes occur with lightning speed, as when you suddenly have an insight about a problem that you couldn't solve.

Learning Often Requires Unlearning

When Unlearning Is Needed   The older you grow and the more experience you accumulate, the more likely is it that you will have to unlearn

---

[4] Isaac Watts, quoted in Noel Entwistle, *Styles of Learning and Teaching,* Wiley, New York, 1981, p. 32.

some things before you can learn others. For instance, you may have learned something which most people believed at the time, but which research has since disproved. Or you may have learned something incorrectly and only later become aware that what you learned was wrong. Most probably, you have learned something without going into it very deeply; and later, when you explore it more thoroughly, you find that you must change some earlier conclusions. For example, sometimes you reach a conclusion on the basis of a single experience, but later you discover that this experience was the exception rather than the rule. All these situations require unlearning—letting go of old ways of thinking, doing, and believing.

I remember clearly learning to use an electric typewriter. I had typed on an old L. C. Smith manual for 20 years and admittedly had fallen in love with the machine. From time to time I sent it off for repairs, and it always came back as good as new. But one day it was returned with a note saying that it couldn't be repaired, and that I ought retire it and think about buying an electric typewriter. No one typed on a manual anymore.

So I began using a fancy electric machine that hummed along and produced a beautiful typewritten page, except that an *l* would sometimes appear mysteriously, and too often five *a*'s would string across the page.

I clearly had some new learning to accomplish and some old learning to get rid of. I had to quit dragging my fingers on the keyboard and stop pounding the keys—that is, I needed some new skills. And I also had to change my attitude. I had the idea that anyone who wrote material that was worth anything wrote it on a manual typewriter. Maybe it was the romantic in me. Maybe I just didn't want to face this new technology that was grabbing everyone else by the neck and not letting go. In any case, I had an attitude problem as well as a skill problem. And for each problem I had new things to learn and old things to unlearn.

At the time I didn't realize how difficult the unlearning process could be. After the first hour at my new electric typewriter, I vowed I would toss the thing into Lake Mendota, which was just down the hill from my office. Once I had rid my life of that humming, uncontrollable hunk of gray metal, I would search for another L.C. Smith, or at least another manual machine. Thinking back on that experience (and I'm embarrassed to admit it was only a few years ago), I now have a better sense of what was happening. I was faced with unlearning.

Why Unlearning Is Difficult Unlearning may sound easy, but most of it falls into the same category as trying to stop smoking—which is indeed one kind of unlearning. The unlearner goes through a mourning process because an old idea, an old attitude, or an old skill must be abandoned.

Not only is there a sense of loss, but leaving something behind and replacing it with something new goes counter to what most of us believe is right. We tend to believe in building on existing ideas, knowledge, attitudes, and skills rather than replacing them.

William Bridges wrote,

> The reality that is left behind...is not just a picture on the wall. It is a sense of which way is up and which way is down; it is a sense of which way is forward and which way is backward. It is, in short, a way of orienting oneself and of moving forward into the future.... The old sense of life as "going somewhere" breaks down, and we feel like shipwrecked sailors on some existential atoll.[5]

The Process of Unlearning What is actually involved in unlearning—this difficult process of leaving something behind and replacing it with something new?

Unlearning has four phases:

1 *Becoming aware*—realizing that something is wrong, that there is a certain discomfort in one's life, that an old idea or an old skill is not serving as well as it once did.
2 *Exploring alternatives*—searching for a new way of doing something, a new answer, a new concept, a new way of organizing one's world view. This may be accomplished by formal, nonformal, or informal means.
3 *Transition*—leaving the old behind and adopting the new. Within this third phase is a "neutral zone" where we are questioning the old but have not yet accepted the new.
4 *Integration*—becoming comfortable with the new idea, the new assumption, or the new skill, and acting on it. Integration means making the new learning a part of you, just as what you unlearned was once a part of you.

In this process, the transition phase (phase 3) is particularly important. It is in this phase—and especially in the "neutral zone"—that much of our mourning for old skills and ideas takes place. The neutral zone is critical because there is always a danger of slipping back into the comfort of old ideas and thus missing the opportunities offered by the new and untried.

How can you help yourself get through the transition phase, and particularly the neutral zone? One important way is simply to realize that it occurs, that you will mourn your old ideas and your old ways of doing things, and that this takes time. The process can't be speeded up or made more efficient.

[5] William Bridges, *Transitions*, Addison-Wesley, Reading, Mass., 1980, p. 102.

Unlearning may seem to be a loss, or a step backward. But to move ahead, to gain, you sometimes must move back and lose. In many instances, unless you move back by unlearning, you will be prevented from moving ahead.

Learning Is Often a Challenge

Some years ago, while working on a graduate degree, I enrolled in a creative writing course, a noncredit adventure offered by the extension division of the university where I was studying. At the time, I was writing my dissertation.

Walking into the classroom on the first evening, I felt extremely anxious. Who were these people—twenty or so of them—sitting quietly, waiting for the class to begin? And who was this instructor, now writing a series of items on the blackboard? I eased into my place at a desk (during the daytime hours, this was a "regular" English classroom) and opened my notebook. An older, gray-haired woman sitting next to me smiled. I nervously smiled back.

"Well, it's about time to start," the instructor said, turning to the class. He was a relaxed, middle-aged man with a soft voice. "I want to find out who is here," he said, glancing around the class and smiling. "Give us your name, and mention what you've published or have in process."

That did it. I felt like slinking out of the room. I could say, if the instructor noticed me leaving, that I'd come to the wrong classroom, that I was really looking for the lecture on Shakespeare's minor works. How could I mention my mostly noncreative dissertation as a "work in process"? And I was sure that my published efforts didn't match what I knew I would hear my classmates mention. A trickle of perspiration went down my back. The woman next to me smiled again. I smiled back again, feebly.

But I was surprised. At least half of the people in the group hadn't published anything. A few had worked on church newsletters and the like. One had published a poem—in 1939. One had published a book—on growing earthworms, I believe.

I began to feel more comfortable. The instructor gave no more recognition to the published writers than he did to the rest of us. He made each of us feel comfortable, in his own quiet, encouraging way. At the end of the class, he gave us an assignment: 1000 words on something from our childhood. Easy enough, I thought. I banged out the piece in a half-hour and turned it in two nights later, when the class met again.

By the third class session, I was feeling quite comfortable, and even a little cocky. No problem here, I thought; I can crank out this creative writing with little effort. Then I looked at my paper on childhood memories, which the instructor had just returned. There were red marks in the margins and between the sentences. There were red arrows and lines and circles, leading from this paragraph to that one. Words were crossed out. Sentences were crossed out. Paragraphs were crossed out. I'd been ambushed.

I folded the paper in half and returned to my desk, staring straight ahead, fearful that the smiling woman would want to ask about my work. But out of the corner of my eye, I noticed that she was also staring straight ahead.

The poet Appollinaire Guillaume (1880–1918) wrote:

Come to the edge, he said.
They said: we are afraid.
Come to the edge, he said.
They came.
He pushed them...and they flew.

I know now what my instructor was doing: he was challenging me, pushing me. But first he needed to get my attention—and he had certainly done so.

Marilyn Ferguson has observed that

The optimum environment for learning offers security enough to encourage exploration and effort, excitement enough to push us onward....We trust the teachers who give us stress, pain, or drudgery when we need it. And we resent those who push us for their own ego,...or take us into the deep water when we're frightened of the shallow.[6]

And Stephen Brookfield has noted,

The teacher of adults...is not always engaged in a warm and wholly satisfying attempt to assist adults in their innate drive to achieve self-actualization. Analyzing assumptions, challenging previously accepted and internalized beliefs and values, considering the validity of alternative behaviors or social forms— all these acts are at times uncomfortable and all involve pain.[7]

To fly, we sometimes need a push. At the time we may not like it; we may resent it; we will usually resist it. But without the nudge, whatever form it takes, many learners will continue to trudge along the dusty roads of life, never feeling the exhilaration of soaring.

---

[6] Marilyn Ferguson, *The Aquarian Conspiracy*, Tarcher, Los Angeles, Calif., 1980, p. 293.
[7] Stephen D. Brookfield, *Understanding and Facilitating Adult Learning*, Jossey-Bass, San Francisco, Calif., 1986, p. 125.

Learning Often Returns to Familiar Themes

The Spanish philosopher Ortega says that we learn in a spiral fashion, coming back to the same interests and concerns time and again, rather than learning something once and never again returning to it. For Ortega, learning is moving forward, more or less, but the movement is in broad circles, or in a spiral, not in a straight line.[8]

You can probably find examples in your own life of Ortega's idea. For instance, if you enjoyed painting as a child, there will probably be times in your life when you come back to painting and learn about it once more.

For three of my books, I collaborated with an artist who prepared the watercolor illustrations and black-and-white pencil sketches. When he began working on the first of my books, this man had not painted for nearly 35 years. He had learned the rudiments of watercolor as a youth, when he was studying to become an architect; and while he was in college, he had won a scholarship to study watercolor in France. But his profession was architecture, and for 35 years he practiced it, giving no attention to watercolor painting, though his profession did require him to keep his basic drawing techniques sharpened. Upon his retirement, at age 70, he wanted to take up watercolor again. And he did, enrolling in classes and becoming involved in a good deal of self-education. By illustrating books, he was able to place his work before the public, and this gave him great personal satisfaction. Ortega would say that my colleague was spiraling. He was returning once more to a learning interest even though it had been dormant for many years.

Each of us, I believe, has a series of "learning themes" that thread through our lives. Sometimes we are well aware of them and work out lifelong learning plans that support them. For instance, I study rural history, and I continue to read, attend lectures, and talk with people about it—in short, I do whatever will help me learn more. But I am convinced that some learning themes are unconscious. We are not aware of them, and yet they influence the learning experiences with which we become involved.

Each time we return to a learning theme, we are challenged to probe it as deeply as we can. And we should also think about new life themes. Some of these may grow out of existing themes; some may be entirely new, but we will return to them periodically from now on.

A lifetime of learning involves exploring new areas and new challenges; it also involves returning to old friends, old themes that we can make richer and more significant.

[8] J. Ortega y Gasset, *What Is Philosophy?* Norton, New York, 1960.

SUMMARY

- We can all learn how to learn—generally by improving the approaches we already use.
- Educators describe learning in several ways. It may be classified as formal (organized into courses with grades and credits), nonformal (organized but without credits), and informal (obtained from day-to-day living).
- Learning can occur at various levels. I describe three: practical learning (gaining new knowledge and skills), learning for meaning (gaining understanding), and learning for empowerment (examining old ways of thinking and old attitudes).
- Learning can also be described as a process, which is lifelong. When people learn, they change.
- Learning often requires unlearning—setting aside old ways of thinking and doing and replacing them with something new.
- The process of unlearning consists of becoming aware, exploring alternatives, making a transition, and integrating the new.
- Learning is often challenging; and it often returns to familiar themes.

4

ORGANIZING
YOUR LEARNING

Malcolm Knowles, a prominent educator, says, "It is a tragic fact that most of us only know how to be taught; we haven't learned how to learn."[1] Formal schooling focuses almost entirely on *being taught*. Students have little input or involvement in the process.

But it is possible, and very important, for students to become actively involved in their own education. In this chapter, I discuss two approaches for organizing your learning: linear and nonlinear. Which one you choose will depend on you, on your personal interests, and on what you are learning.

LINEAR APPROACH

The linear approach has three phases: (1) planning, (2) doing, and (3) evaluating. In the simplest terms, first you decide what you want to learn, then you do it, and finally you determine how effective you have been.

Phase 1: Planning

In the planning phase, you determine the problem you need to solve or the question you want to answer—that is, you identify the learning needs you have, and how you plan to meet these needs.

[1] Malcolm Knowles, *Self-Directed Learning,* Association Press, New York, 1975, p. 14.

Learning needs exist at various levels. You may have determined that you need an advanced degree to progress in your career. Or you may have decided to change careers, and your new work requires new knowledge or new skills. If you have just completed high school, you may consider college as a point of entry into a career; or you may not be certain about what work you want to pursue, and you see college as a place where you can sort things out. At another level, you may simply see a need to acquire or sharpen a specific skill, such as using a computer for desktop publishing.

As you plan what it is you want to learn, you develop a learning agenda which includes learning objectives—specific things you want to accomplish. If you want to learn how to do word processing on a micro-computer, you might include on a written agenda, "I want to learn how to use word-processing software to prepare manuscripts for publication." If you are returning to school to progress in your career, you might identify specific skills and knowledge that you need for advancement.

Some of you will enter college programs where there are a number of required courses. Do not think of required courses as somehow "opposed" to your own learning plan. Many curricula have choices within required areas, and almost every curriculum has a considerable number of credits that you may select on the basis of your own interests. For example, if you are required to earn 25 science credits, several courses may be listed from which you can choose. And even for a course that is absolutely required, you can still develop a learning plan, specifying what you want to get out of it.

You should realize, too, that once you begin a learning plan, whether it is brief or extensive, you may change many of your learning objectives along the way. Systematically planning your learning doesn't mean that change is impossible. The entire process should be flexible, so that your learning will be effective and will achieve your purposes.

Once you have determined your learning objectives, you are ready to ask, "How can I meet these objectives? Where are the resources that will help me?"

For some learning objectives, a library book may be the only resource you need. For others, 4 or more years of college-level work may be necessary. In between these two extremes, there are objectives that can be met by specific courses, workshops, independent study programs, and "resource people."

Often, an objective can be met by a combination of activities. At the same time as you are taking a formal course for credit, you may want to talk to experts or supplement your credit work with a noncredit program. Today, almost every college and university has an outreach or extension department that offers a host of noncredit courses, workshops, conferences, and institutes, usually at very reasonable rates. Many of these programs are in areas such as public speaking, writing, and interpersonal relationships.

Phase 2: Doing

The "doing" phase of linear learning involves two kinds of activities: (1) finding learning resources, and (2) sharpening your learning skills.

You enroll in classes; you take part in independent study; you talk with resource people. At this point, the various study skills that this book discusses can be put to good use. Your goal is to be an effective and efficient learner. You want to get as much as possible from the learning activities you have selected. Part of the responsibility is yours. If you are pursuing formal course work, you must know how to use the various learning resources available on the campus, such as the library and its staff. Your reading, writing, thinking, and study skills must be honed to a sharpness that allows you to learn effectively and confidently.

Phase 3: Evaluation

In a sense, it is inappropriate to describe evaluation as the "third phase" of the linear approach to learning. Evaluation actually goes on all the time, in every phase. When you ask yourself if your learning objectives continue to be appropriate, you are evaluating. When you make a judgment about an instructor or a course, or decide to drop a course because it is not directly related to your needs or because the instructor does not meet your expectations, you are evaluating. When you "overview" a book and decide that for your purposes you need not read any more of it, you are evaluating. When you work through two or three exercises of a computer-assisted course and decide that you can learn the material better by reading a book, you are evaluating.

In addition to this ongoing evaluation, however, evaluation should also occur at the end of a learning project, or at designated points along the way, such as the completion of a course within a degree program. In this sense, evaluation is indeed phase 3 of learning.

When you have completed a course, you want to judge whether or not your learning objectives have been met. You want to determine if you have gained the skills and knowledge you needed to gain. You want to ascertain how effective you have been as a learner.

Here we must stop for a moment and consider a conflict. Who should evaluate your learning? From the wording I have used above, you have probably inferred that evaluation is *your* responsibility. Yet many people believe that in formal learning situations, it is the instructor who has the sole responsibility for evaluating students' learning. Evaluation by the instructor is, of course, the traditional approach; it involves grades, curves, comparisons, and competition among students.

In these few paragraphs, I am not going to resolve the issue of who should evaluate students' performance. But I believe that both the instructor and the student have a role in evaluating learning. You must determine if a course has met your personal objectives. The instructor determines whether you have met certain standards. For example, suppose that you are preparing for a profession: elementary school teaching. Among elementary teachers and administrators, teacher-training programs, and state licensing boards, there is general agreement on what skills and knowledge elementary teachers need, and on what level of skills and knowledge will meet specified standards. When you enter a teacher-training program, certification and licensing requirements will dictate, in large measure, how your learning is evaluated. But there is still room for you to examine what you are learning from your own perspective, to see if it measures up to your personal standards.

Unfortunately, standards and certification requirements for many professions and many degree programs have left the impression among educators that students have no role in evaluating learning. But even in rather tightly controlled areas, such as professional preparation programs, you can still evaluate your courses, the resources you are using for learning, and your progress toward your own goals. And you can take action: you can drop courses, select different resources, and make adjustments in your course schedule. Generally, you can do much more than you may think you can in response to your own evaluation.

NONLINEAR APPROACH

The linear approach has a beginning, a middle, and an end, with specific activities planned along the way. The nonlinear approach is less organized.

The nonlinear approach works particularly well if your learning needs are broad. Some young people and returning students enter college without a clear set of goals. They do not know what they want from the experience, and they don't know what profession or career they want to pursue. Many other learners are not interested in working for a degree; they are interested in a topic but may not have a clear sense of exactly what they want to learn or how to learn it.

What do these students do? They plunge in. They sign up for a course and see where it takes them. They talk to people about their interests.

These students may not have a long-range learning plan in mind, but their "nonplan" is really another kind of plan—a nonlinear plan.

A nonlinear plan doesn't have the structure or the characteristics of the linear plan. It doesn't look as neat and tidy. It may include more false starts and restarts. It may include more dropped courses and more changes in majors.

But such searching is a valid approach to figuring out what you are and what you want to learn. The important principle is this: Sometimes you don't know what you want to learn, or need to learn, until you are in the midst of a learning activity. If this is where you are, then take the plunge—enroll in a course. And don't apologize to anyone for not having a clear long-range plan.

Nonlinear learning has some definite advantages. For one thing, much exciting, important learning occurs in unplanned situations, when we don't expect it. A nonlinear learner is open to such situations and can take full advantage of them when they occur. Moreover, nonlinear learning can be very stimulating. Always knowing exactly where you are going and how you are going to get there can lack excitement and occasionally can be downright boring. Nonlinear learning is certainly not boring; surprises turn up often.

On the other hand, how much nonlinear learning a person can afford, in terms of time and money, is an important consideration, particularly if nonlinear learning is the predominant approach.

On balance, we should not discount the value of nonlinear learning. And we should also recognize that from time to time, in the middle of a well-prepared linear plan, we may want to enroll in a course we hadn't intended to take, or do something we hadn't planned. We may be surprised at what we gain.

SUMMARY

- The linear and nonlinear approaches are two ways of organizing your learning.
- Linear learning has three phases: planning, doing, and evaluating. These steps are planned beforehand and carefully developed.
- Nonlinear learning has little structure. It is appropriate for students who are not yet sure of their learning direction—and also for linear learners who want to explore or have fun.

PART TWO
IMPROVING YOUR STUDY SKILLS

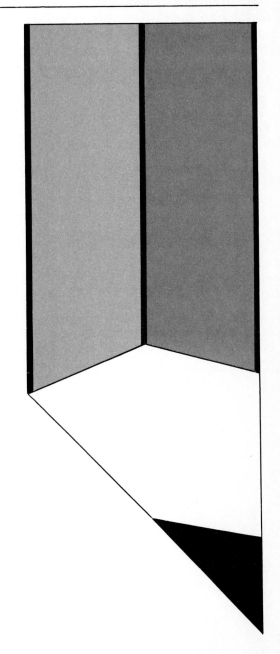

5

LISTENING AND NOTE-TAKING

Even with today's new electronic learning aids, such as computers and videotapes, you'll still find most instructors lecturing to their classes. The size of a lecture class will vary, from twenty or thirty students in a classroom to several hundred students in an auditorium. As a student in a lecture course, your task is to hear what is said and keep a record of the important points. As you are well aware, the content of lectures often becomes the content of examinations; therefore, developing listening and note-taking skills is critical. Unless you have carefully written notes and pay attention to them, within 2 weeks you will probably forget about 80 percent of what you've heard in a lecture. Within 4 weeks, you will have forgotten nearly 95 percent.[1]

Listening is a skill we learn early in life, and most of us think we're quite good at listening. But research indicates that most people listen at only about 25 percent of capacity unless they have had some specific training in listening skills.[2] Why do we have problems with listening, and how can we learn to listen better?

PROBLEMS WITH LISTENING TO LECTURES

The following list describes common reasons for difficulties students have in listening to lectures. Do any of these descriptions apply to you?

[1] John Langan, *Reading and Study Skills,* 4th ed. McGraw-Hill, New York, 1990, p. 103.
[2] Judy Glenn Kilpatrick, "Listening Instruction: Awareness, Identification and Practice," ERIC, ED 257162, 1985, p. 3.

1 *You may simply not be able to hear the lecturer.* Older students often notice that they do not hear as well as they did when they were younger. But younger students, too, may experience difficulty hearing when they are in a large group and are some distance away from the speaker.

2 *You may find the topic uninteresting.* You may become bored during a lecture, or you may decide that a topic is boring and tune out even before the lecture begins.

3 *You may be distracted by the lecturer's mannerisms.* An instructor may say "ah" or "you know" every few seconds, or tug at one ear, or constantly rustle lecture notes. Good listeners learn to ignore the package and focus on the contents—but many students have trouble doing this.

4 *You may be giving too much attention to certain details or specific points.* For example, let's say that you are a returning student and a veteran of the war in Vietnam; if the lecturer mentions war, your mind may leave the lecture room and return to your wartime experience. For another example, let's suppose that the lecturer makes a point with which you disagree; if you are upset by this, you may hear nothing else for the next 5 minutes.

5 *You may tend to concentrate on facts rather than ideas.* If you have difficulty distinguishing what is important from what is not important, you may concentrate only on the facts that are being presented and fail to see the "big picture."

6 *You may be taking too many notes.* If you try to write down everything the lecturer says, you will be so busy writing that you won't have time to listen. (This point is related to the preceding one.)

7 *You may have a poor self-concept with regard to your listening skills.* You might be remembering a parent's words, "Why don't you listen for a change?" or a friend's comment, "You're not listening to me." As a result, you may lack confidence in your ability to listen.

8 *You may have difficulty concentrating.* You can hear about four times faster than a lecturer can talk. This means that you have some valuable "thought time" which can be used for thinking about what the lecturer is saying—how the ideas relate to each other, for instance, and how the lecture relates to your reading. But you may find your mind wandering to other things: what you'll do this weekend, what you'll have for dinner, whether your boss really approves of your going back to school. When you start paying attention to the lecture again, you will probably have missed several important points.

9 *You may be focusing on the irrelevant.* Students usually enjoy a lecturer's stories and jokes and perk up when the lecturer shares a per-

sonal experience. In fact, lecturers often use asides, such as personal experiences and stories, to maintain interest. But such asides should not be confused with the primary content of the lecture. Poor listeners often want to be entertained, and they concentrate on the entertaining parts of a lecture. Good listeners learn to concentrate on the important points.

10   *You may tend to tune out difficult material.* Poor listeners stop listening when the going gets tough, when the lecturer begins discussing something they find difficult to understand. They stop taking notes, sit back, and wait for easier material. Also, some students are put off by vocabulary they don't understand. They ignore unfamiliar terms rather than jotting them down. This kind of tuning out can be disastrous at exam time.

11   *You may listen poorly at certain times of the day.* For some people, lectures that take place late in the day, or in the evening, are extremely difficult. These students are exhausted from a busy day and find it difficult not only to concentrate but even to stay awake. Many returning students have this problem, but most of them can learn to overcome fatigue by carefully developing their listening skills.

TIPS FOR IMPROVING LISTENING

Take Notes

Concentrating on taking notes forces you to listen to the speaker. A system for note-taking is described later in this chapter.

Listen for Ideas

Ideas represent the framework of a lecture. The lecturer presents facts and other evidence to fill in and support ideas. Most lecturers will include no more than four or five major ideas in a 1-hour lecture (though the actual number will of course depend on the subject matter). Listen for them.

Listen for Signals

To identify main ideas and support material, listen for verbal clues from the lecturer. "In the first place..." is a clue that two or more main points are coming. "On the other hand..." is a clue that the lecturer is about to develop a contrasting argument. "The three points I want to make are..." is a clue to the structure of the lecture.

When lecturers pause and look at the audience, they are often giving you time to write down something they consider important. (Of course, they may pause only because they need to find the next point in their notes, but in this case you can see them sorting through their papers.)

When a lecturer repeats something, this usually means, "Important; you'd better write it down."

Write down any definitions the lecturer provides—they are usually critical. And copy material from visuals, such as overhead transparencies, flip charts, or the chalkboard. Sometimes visuals will already be on a chalkboard or flip chart before the class starts. This is an excellent time to copy the material.

Resist Distractions

Discipline yourself to overlook distractions—the lecturer's personal mannerisms, noises from the street, papers rustling behind you. With practice, it is possible to push all extraneous noise and movement from your consciousness. (I have known people who could study in music practice halls, and in rooms where 50 people were all talking at the same time.) When you are at a lecture, your sole task is to listen to the lecturer.

Keep an Open Mind

Listen to what is said; organize the information; take notes. But withhold your agreement or disagreement until later, when you are reviewing your notes. Attempting to make judgments while the lecturer is speaking will only distract you. As you think about your own reaction to what is said, you will miss valuable information.

Use "Thought Time"

Thought time, as I noted earlier, occurs because your mind works faster than the speaker talks. Use this time to sort out ideas and facts, to organize your notes, and to think about related information.

Study Beforehand

If you are already familiar with a topic and its major ideas from reading beforehand, you will gain much more from the lecture. If you already know the main ideas, you will be able to concentrate on the supporting information and the arguments the lecturer makes. And you will be able to note facts, definitions, and other information that was not included in the readings. A lecturer will often present new information that is not yet in your textbook, or take ideas from the textbook and organize them in a different way. Lecturers sometimes arrive at conclusions different from those of textbook authors, though they may use the same ideas.

Understand How Lectures Are Organized

Most lectures have five kinds of material:

1 *Introduction.* The lecturer uses the introduction to capture your attention, perhaps by sharing a personal experience, commenting on a recent event, mentioning a forthcoming assignment, or explaining the outline of a coming exam.
2 *Announcement of the topic.* The lecturer will usually mention what was covered in the previous session and what will be covered today.
3 *Body of the lecture.* In the body, the lecturer presents the main ideas and develops support for each of them. The lecturer may use a deductive approach, first presenting an idea and then giving the subpoints. Or the lecturer may use an inductive approach, presenting details first and then a generalization. The inductive approach is often used when the lecturer is making an argument that builds on several facts or pieces of evidence.
4 *Summary.* In the summary, the main points are restated. Unfortunately, many students slam their notebooks shut when the lecturer says, "In summary..." and thus miss an opportunity to check their notes to see if they have recorded the same major ideas that the lecturer is now repeating.
5 *Asides.* As I noted above, many lecturers include personal experiences, jokes, and other comments designed to keep you interested and give you a mental break from the "heavy work." Remember that these are only asides. Do not confuse them with the subject of the lecture. Some students enjoy asides so much that they listen primarily for them and pay less attention to the serious content.

TIPS FOR IMPROVING NOTE-TAKING

Why Take Notes?

You have probably worked out some type of system for taking notes when you listen to a lecture. You may carry a notebook to the lecture, or you may write on scrap paper (the back of an envelope, for instance) or in the margins of printed material (such as the syllabus). For some of you, note-taking is not a problem, but others are looking for a better technique.

Since the coming of lightweight cassette tape-recorders with built-in microphones, students sometimes wonder why it is necessary to discuss note-taking at all. Why not simply tape lectures and then listen to the tapes as often as necessary?

Sometimes it does make good sense to record a lecture. If you are enrolled in a course where the content is technical and new to you, you may benefit from recording the lectures. If you are a returning student and haven't been in a classroom for several years, you may want to record the first few lectures until you have regained your confidence.

Generally, however, it is not a good idea to depend on tape-recording as a substitute for note-taking. You may find yourself not listening to lectures but allowing your mind to wander, and you may assume that since the recorder is capturing the information, you need not bother to listen. As a result, you will lose all the lecturer's nonverbal clues; you will probably not gain a sense of how visuals (such as material presented on a screen or chalkboard) fit into the sequence of the lecture; and you will miss the opportunity to interact with material as it is presented, to relate it to your reading and your own experiences. There is also a problem of time: how many students have the time to listen to every lecture twice or more?

For all these reasons, developing an effective system of note-taking is far more useful than tape-recording lectures.

A System for Taking Notes

Before the Lecture   To prepare for note-taking, do these four things:

1   Get a standard large-size looseleaf notebook and 8½- by 11-inch looseleaf paper.
2   Draw a vertical line about 2½ inches from the left side of each sheet and a horizontal line about 2 inches from the bottom, as shown in the illustration on the opposite page.
3   Review your notes from previous lectures, for continuity.
4   Read the assigned material related to the lecture.

During the Lecture   There are two important techniques to use during the lecture.

Record notes logically   Take notes on the right-hand side of the paper in a way that will capture the main ideas of the lecture. Several approaches are possible:

You can list the main points at the left margin, indent the subpoints and supporting material, and indent sub-subpoints and their supporting material even more.

You can also write down the main idea, draw a circle around it, and then, using more lines and circles, connect supporting information, il-

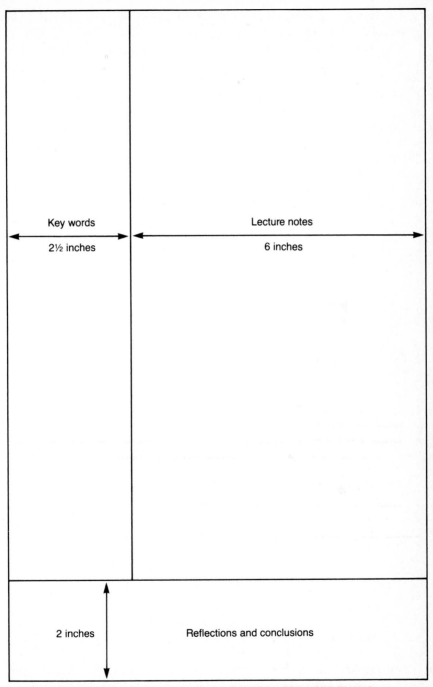

PREPARING YOUR LOOSE-LEAF NOTEBOOK FOR NOTE-TAKING

lustrations, and research material to the major idea. Your note page will show a series of circles, with spokes connecting related ideas.

You might also want to write main ideas in red ink and supporting ideas in another color.

Use whatever system of recording ideas and supporting material is comfortable for you. But don't try to write down everything the lecturer says. That is impossible, and it isn't necessary. Even if you were able to write every spoken word, so much would be irrelevant that you would have difficulty finding the main ideas.

Write legibly   Write your notes so that you will be able to read them later. This may entail practicing a form of printing. It may also require developing a system of abbreviations. When using abbreviations, however, be careful to use only those you are familiar with. Common abbreviations include the following:

and	&
with	w
without	w/o
for example	e.g.
example	ex.
definition	def.
equals	=
does not equal	≠

You will become more efficient if you can learn to write your lecture notes both legibly enough and completely enough so that you don't have to rewrite or type them after each lecture. Although your notes will obviously be neater if you type them, most students do not have the extra time required for typing notes, or for keyboarding them on a word processor.

After the Lecture   Following are some important things to do after a lecture.

Write down key terms   As soon as possible after the lecture, jot down key words and phrases on the left side of your notepaper. Not only does this procedure help you to recall the lecture, but the process of writing significant words and phrases helps fix the information in your mind.

Check your recall   Cover the right side of the notebook page, so that you are looking only at the key words and phrases. Then try to restate the lecture in your own words from these key cues. Uncover the notes to check the accuracy of your work.

Reflect on the meaning of the lecture   Can you think of examples from your own experience, or from your reading, to illustrate the main points of the lecture? Perhaps you will arrive at a conclusion that is different from the lecturer's, or discover that the lecturer has raised some questions which you want to pursue further. On the bottom of your notebook page, in the section reserved for reflections and conclusions, jot down your thoughts and questions.

Reflection can be the most important step in the entire process of listening to a lecture and taking notes, for it is during this step that you are integrating new information: you are relating the new information to what you already know and are trying to give it personal meaning. As I pointed out earlier, learning is much more than memorizing what a lecturer says or what is written in a book or journal; fundamentally, it involves finding out what meaning information has for you.

Review your notes   Occasionally, you should review your notes. As mentioned above, review your notes from the previous lecture before attending the present one. And from time to time during a semester, review all your lecture notes. (One way to do this is to cover the right side of the note pages, as described above, and see if you can recall the content of various lectures.)

Meet with classmates   Meeting with other students in a course is another profitable way to review your notes, check your comprehension, and deepen your understanding. Not only can you review the main points with other students, but you may discover that they have heard points you missed. Also, they may see the relationship among points differently from you. Other students' ideas can be one more resource for you as you try to find meaning in what you are studying.

An Exercise in Note-Taking

Prepare a sheet of notepaper as suggested above. Then ask a friend to read the following selection as if it were a lecture. Ask your friend to read slowly and clearly while you listen and take notes. Don't read the lecture yourself. This sample is much shorter than most actual lectures, but the principles of note-taking are the same.

SAMPLE LECTURE

Today our topic is the nature of problems. We all know about them, and we all have them. We may have problems balancing our personal budgets. Those of us who have children may have problems with them. We may have health problems. We may have problems with our cars, or with our computers. Our lives are filled with problems. But what do we really know about the nature of problems? Exactly what is a problem, fundamentally?

For our purposes today, I define a *problem* as a question raised for inquiry, for solution, or for both. Let me write on the board: *Problem—a question raised for inquiry, for solution, or for both*. Let's look at that definition for a moment. First, problems are questions. Second, problems are questions that may be raised either for inquiry or for a solution. That is, we may choose to study a problem, or inquire about it, without attempting to solve it. And third, problems can be questions that are raised both for inquiry and for solution. We study the problem and we attempt to solve it as well.

Let's look at some examples. Take, for instance, the problem of our balance of trade. The United States has a trade imbalance: we buy more from other countries than other countries buy from us. Following my definition of a problem, to say simply "trade imbalance" is not to state a problem. We must turn this phrase into a question. We could ask, "Why does the United States have a trade imbalance?" Or we could ask, "Which countries contribute to our trade imbalance?" We could also ask, "What can we do to correct the trade imbalance?"

Here is an example at another level. You could inquire. "Why does my car get such poor gas mileage?" Just as we could study the question why the United States has a trade imbalance and learn a good deal about that problem without doing anything to solve it, you could likewise learn why your car delivers such poor gas mileage and do nothing about it.

Thus it is possible to study a problem—inquire about it—without attempting to solve it.

It is also possible to seek a solution to a problem without actually studying the problem. You could purchase a gasoline additive that is advertised as giving greater gas mileage without ever thinking about why your car is getting poor mileage.

Of course we can do both: we can study a problem and attempt to solve it.

What I have we said so far is this: Problems are questions. They may be raised either for inquiry or for solution; or they may be raised for both inquiry and solution.

Let's go on. Let's attempt to answer the question, "Are all problems solvable?" Many people would answer, "Of course all problems are solvable. It may take time and money and expert help, but eventually all problems can be solved."

My position is that not all problems can be solved, that we have both solvable and insolvable problems. Let's look at the characteristics of each. First, let's consider solvable problems.

When people begin to work on a solvable problem, take it apart, look at its pieces, and search out information about it, they find that the more they work on the problem, the more they see that the answers they are finding come together. All paths begin leading to the same destination—the solution to the problem.

Basically, we have two types of solvable problems: first, those that can be solved immediately or in the near future; and second, those that we know *can* be solved but that we may not yet have the technology or resources for solving. An example of the first type is figuring one's income tax: there are now home computers that will do this. An example of the second type—a solvable problem that is not yet solved—is space travel. Today, space travel is still a potentiality, not an actuality.

Now let's turn to insolvable problems. When we attempt to deal with an insolvable problem, we discover that the answers lead away from each other rather than toward each other. In fact, we may find two answers to the problem that both sound plausible but contradict each other. For instance, let's consider the question, "What is the nature of human nature?" When we begin examining this question, we encounter several points of view. Some people argue that human nature is largely determined by genetics. Others say that human nature is the product of culture and environment. Both answers sound plausible, but they certainly represent different perspectives. The question, then, though it is open to debate and argument, is in the end insolvable.

Thus we have solvable and insolvable problems. Next time, we'll begin discussing the relationship between these two types of problems.

When your friend has finished reading this selection, and you have taken your notes, go over them as suggested in "After the Lecture." Jot down the key words on the left side of your note page. Try to recall the lecture from the key words. Then write down your reaction to the lecture, or questions that you still have about it. The illustration on the following page shows a sample set of notes for this lecture. Turn to it and examine it when you've finished your own notes. No two sets of notes will be alike, of course, but your notes should contain the main points listed here.

Sept. 3	* Problems
	    Personal budget
	    Car

Definition of
"Problem"
	* Def. Problem: Question raised for inquiry,
	 for solution, or both
	    1- Problems are questions
	    2- Questions for inquiry or solution
	    3- Questions for inquiry & solution
	    EX.
	      --Trade imbalance—why? which
	           countries contribute? What to do?

Three Types of
Problems
	--Car—Poor gas mileage
	    Alternatives
	    **Study problem without solving
	    **Solve problem without study
	    **Study & solve problems

Solvable & (2 types)
Insolvable (1 type)
Problems
	All Problems solvable?
	    Many say yes
	    Prof says no
	    Solvable Problem--Answers Come Together
	    **Solve now--Ex. income tax on PC
	    **Solve soon--EX. Space Travel
	    Insolvable Problems--Answers more apart
	      EX. Nature of human nature
	        --Genetic influence
	        --Culture & environment
	             influence
	    Next Time --Relationship: solvable
	 and insolvable problems

Must problems always be posed as questions?
What about environmental problems? Must
questions be posed before these problems really
become problems?

EXAMPLE OF LECTURE NOTES

SUMMARY

- Problems with listening to lectures include: (1) inability to hear the lecturer, (2) lack of interest, (3) being distracted by the lecturer's mannerisms, (4) giving excessive attention to certain points, (5) concentrating on facts rather than ideas, (6) taking too many notes, (7) having a poor self-concept about one's listening skills, (8) inability to maintain concentration, (9) focusing on the irrelevant, (10) tuning out difficult material, and (11) fatigue.
- To improve your listening, take notes, listen for ideas, listen for signals from the lecturer, resist distractions, keep an open mind, use thought time, read before the lecture, and understand the organization of lectures.
- One useful system for note-taking is to use paper marked with spaces for recording notes, key words, and personal reflections and conclusions. The key words and personal reflections are written after the lecture.

6

TAKING EXAMINATIONS

Nearly every student fears examinations. For students returning to school after some time away, taking exams is a particularly trying experience.

In one of my research projects, where I interviewed older students about problems they faced upon returning to school, one student wrote:

> I am very uptight about exams. I hate multiple-choice tests because they are usually tricky. They don't test anything more than the professor's ability to write tricky exams. I feel insulted taking such tests. I am more comfortable with short-answer or essay questions that are pertinent to the scope of the course. True-false questions are OK if one has the opportunity to justify the answer. I prefer writing a term paper or talking with the professor in an informal way in lieu of taking exams.

This sort of statement is common among returning students, whose test anxiety results from not having taken examinations for several years. But most younger students also find taking exams an uncomfortable experience. It's understandable. Tests largely determine grades. And grades affect scholarships, financial aid, admission to graduate school, and often career opportunities.

Many students—particularly older, returning students—argue that higher education puts too much emphasis on formal examinations. Even though examinations may be overemphasized in some instances, however, they are still a useful way for you to evaluate the progress you are making in your learning, as well as a way for the instructor to measure how well you are meeting course requirements.

THINKING ABOUT EXAMINATIONS

Building Your Confidence

Building confidence as a test-taker is partly a matter of understanding what examinations are like and partly a matter of developing test-taking skills—knowing how to prepare for exams, how to take them, and how to assess your performance afterwards. This chapter will take up all these aspects of test-taking. But confidence also depends on your attitude, which we'll consider first.

Think of it this way: Taking tests goes well beyond formal education; it is part of the fabric of everyday life. To obtain a driver's license, you must take a test. To apply for a civil service job, you must take a test. When you interview for a job, you are taking an oral examination. You could even say that when you fill out your income tax form, you are taking a test.

All of us are faced with tests nearly every day. But we may not think of them as tests. They are often subtle and not labeled *test*. When your boss calls you in for a discussion of your job performance, that is a kind of test. Planning an extended canoe trip in wilderness country is another kind of test. Accepting tests as a part of life helps us to see course examinations in a new light. Next week's sociology exam is important, but it doesn't hold a candle to the tests that a single parent faces every day—and you can probably think of many similar examples. If you reflect on how you have handled everyday test situations—usually quite successfully, I would guess—you can face a course examination with more confidence.

Another thought is this: Some very useful things come from tests. All of us want to know how we are doing in a course. This is particularly true for returning students, who are justifiably concerned about whether their study skills and abilities are up to par. Tests can help provide early feedback.

Understanding Types of Tests

In a broad sense, there are two types of tests: achievement and aptitude. Achievement tests measure what you have learned; aptitude tests measure your potential.

Although our focus will be only on achievement tests, a few words about aptitude tests are in order here. If you are taking an aptitude test, be sure to study suggestions for taking such tests. For almost all aptitude tests you are likely to encounter in your college experience—such as the Graduate Record Examination (GRE), the Miller Analogies, and the Scholastic Aptitude Test (SAT)—you can find guidebooks with tips for preparation and sample questions. It is possible to increase your score on an aptitude test considerably by preparing for it, particularly if the format is unfamiliar to you.

The two basic types of achievement tests are (1) essay and (2) objective. Essay tests include items requiring short answers and items asking for extended discussions. Objective tests include true-false, multiple-choice, fill-in-the-blanks, and matching items. None of these elements is new to you; in fact, you've probably encountered all of them again and again throughout your school years. If you are a returning student, though, it may have been several years since you've faced a test with these items.

Achievement tests take various forms. You are all familiar with the written examination taken in the classroom. Other forms are the open-book examination and the oral examination. In an oral exam, the student meets face to face with one or more instructors to answer questions orally. An open-book examination may be administered in class, or it may be a take-home exam. Proponents of the take-home open-book examination argue that it is the most realistic form of testing, since in life, when you have to write a paper or give a speech, you will have a variety of resources available. But some instructors fear that students will ask their friends to help them with a take-home exam, and thus that the exam is not a true test of a student's own ability.

PREPARING FOR EXAMINATIONS

How to prepare for examinations is a controversial topic. Some people advocate intensive, systematic cramming the day and night before an exam. Others argue that this approach is futile and recommend regular study throughout the semester. For the majority of test-takers, a combination of both approaches may be most useful. But people vary considerably: some will do best with cramming, others with long-term study.

Here are some tips that may help you prepare for exams.

Read and Review

Get into the habit of continuous reading and review. If you keep up with the reading assignments, take good notes, review your notes occasionally, and spend time reflecting on the meaning of what you are studying, you are preparing well for examinations. As part of the reflection process, you should focus on the course as a whole. What is the big picture? How do the parts of that picture—the topics within the course—relate to each other and to the total picture?

If you wait until the last day or two before an examination to catch up with the readings, you are courting disaster. You may have a headful of factual information (and some of it may be useful on certain types of exams), but you will not have given yourself sufficient time to make sense out of the course content.

Study Previous Tests

Look at old exams. Many instructors distribute copies of old exams, and student groups occasionally keep copies on file. These are excellent guides for studying. They not only provide you with prompts for practicing (whether or not you actually answer the questions) but also give you an excellent idea of the types of examination questions your instructor writes. For example, how many of the questions require straight memorization of factual material? Was the exam graded automatically (as many objective tests are) or by the instructor (as tests with essay items are)? To what extent was the instructor looking for general principles in the responses, rather than specific information?

When studying old examinations, though, you should not assume that you will see the same questions or exactly the same format. Instructors almost never reuse the same questions they have given previously. And questions that are being reused will be changed slightly; thus students must read each question carefully.

Cram Systematically

Cram systematically for an examination, starting about 2 days beforehand. Systematic cramming is not the same as trying to force the content into your head in an all-night session just before the exam.

To cram systematically, you go over your lecture notes, and your notes from the readings, and jot down the big ideas that seem to form the structure of the course. Then you fill in the factual material that illustrates and amplifies the big ideas. To identify the big ideas, use the chapter headings in your textbook or the instructor's course outline. Prepare a set of summary notes that lists the big ideas from your textbook and your lecture notes. One way to do this is in outline form, with each big idea followed by a listing of related subtopics.

Use Group Study

Use group study effectively. Often, group study degenerates into a bull session that covers everything except the examination material, but if this can be avoided, group study is very useful. It is an excellent way to clear up topics about which you are unsure, try out your own conclusions, and ask and answer typical exam questions.

To be effective, group study sessions must be organized. One method of organization is to divide the study material into topics, assigning one topic to each student in the group (Four students is a good number for a study group; larger groups are more difficult to manage and tend more to drift away from the topic at hand.) Then each student asks questions about his or her topic for the others to answer. Even if the examination is to be multiple-choice, these questions should be in an essay format. One student might be designated to give an initial answer, to which the rest will add information. This method can give useful feedback on the accuracy of answers you have worked out by yourself. Occasionally, you will misinterpret what you have read or heard in class, and the group members can help by giving their interpretations.

Do not, however, rely on group study as the only form of preparation for an examination. You must spend some study time alone, figuring out the meaning of the material you are studying, in your own way and at your own speed.

Use Memorization Techniques

Use memorization techniques (see Chapter 12) to fix factual information in your mind, particularly if you know that your instructor gives exams requiring recall of such information.

Attend Class

In general, of course, you should attend classes throughout the semester. In particular, don't miss the class session immediately before an examination. The instructor will often say something about the structure of the examination and occasionally will even outline the major topics it will cover.

Maintain Your Usual Schedule

If you maintain your regular schedule of eating, sleeping, recreation, and so on, you will find yourself more relaxed at exam time and more mentally alert. For most students, a good night's sleep before an exam is far more important than a night-long marathon of last-minute cramming.

Relax

As noted above, maintaining your usual schedule will help you relax at exam time. Specific techniques for mental and physical relaxation are also helpful; some of these are described in Chapter 18.

TAKING EXAMINATIONS
General Guidelines

Below are general suggestions that students have found helpful for taking all types of examinations. Next, I'll share specific suggestions for answering objective and essay questions and taking different kinds of exams.

Arrive Early   Arrive at the examination room ahead of time so that you can find a comfortable seat and relax. To avoid distractions, find a seat away from the door or the windows. Don't sit at the end of a row of fixed seats, where students who leave early will disturb you.

Avoid conversations with other students about specific topics in the course. Such conversations, coming just before the exam, often confuse more than help.

Note Instructions Carefully   Listen carefully to any spoken instructions about the examination, and read the written directions carefully. If any direction is unclear, ask for clarification. Many students skip over the instructions quickly in their haste to begin, and often miss critical information.

Instructions will generally tell you the point value of the questions, whether you must answer all the questions or have a choice, what form the answers must take (in a mathematics test, for instance, you may be required to show your calculations as well as the results), and whether or not you must follow a particular order in answering the questions.

How well do you follow directions? Below is a test to help you find out.[1]

CAN YOU FOLLOW DIRECTIONS?

Read these directions carefully. You have 3 minutes to complete the exercise. Ask a friend to time you. Be sure to write legibly. When you have finished, check your answers against the directions. Read all the following directions carefully before beginning.

1 On a sheet of 8½- by 11-inch paper, print your name in the upper right-hand corner, last name first.
2 Make ten X's in the upper left-hand corner of the paper. Begin with a capital X, and alternate lowercase and capital X's.
3 Write the numerals 10 to 0 backwards down the right-hand side of the page, beginning just under your last name.
4 Draw a big heart at the bottom left-hand corner of your paper. Shade it in heavily with your pencil.
5 Draw a tic-tac-toe board in the lower right-hand corner of your paper.
6 Add 42 and 56. Divide that sum by 49. Draw that many triangles in the center of the page.
7 Now that you have read all the directions, simply do number 1 and turn over your paper.

Budget Your Time   Plan your time by looking over the entire test and establishing a time budget. Allot the most time for the questions that

[1] Adapted from "Test," used by Counseling Services, University of Wisconsin-Madison.

will give you the most points. If you have a choice of, say, answering five of seven questions, choose five to answer, and answer them. Don't do anything with the two you didn't choose. If you answer all seven, your instructor will probably read only the answers to the first five, and you will have gained nothing by answering the other two. (In fact, you may lose something, if the last two answers were your strongest.)

Deal with Questions Systematically   Be methodical in answering the test questions. For example:

1   First answer the questions for which you are sure of the answers; then go back and work on other questions.
2   Read every word in each question.
3   Try to answer all the questions, even if you are not absolutely certain of the answers. You will seldom be penalized for guessing; and even if you are, guessing is better than leaving a blank space.
4   Check your answers for obvious errors before turning in your examination paper.

Answering Essay Questions

An essay examination tests your ability to answer the questions, but it also tests your ability to organize your ideas and present them clearly. Here are some suggestions for taking essay exams that many students have found helpful.

1   *Budget your time* carefully, saving time at the end of the exam period for editing.
2   *Read all the essay questions* before beginning to answer any of them. Occasionally, questions are related to each other; and certain questions will earn you more points than others.
3   *Make preliminary notes.* As you read the questions, jot down alongside each of them a word or two that comes to mind for answering it. This will alleviate any fears you may have about forgetting important points.
4   *Read and underline the key words* in each question so that you can be sure you know exactly what you are required to do. Some important key words and their meanings are shown in the box on the opposite page.
5   *Develop a brief outline for your answers* before beginning to write. This will help you to be concise without omitting any important information.
6   *Begin by writing the answers you are surest of.*

KEY WORDS IN ESSAY QUESTIONS

Define: Write a concise, clear, authoritative meaning. Indicate what clearly differentiates what you are defining from everything else.

Compare: Examine qualities or characteristics to show resemblances. Emphasize similarities between things you are asked to compare.

Contrast: Stress differences or dissimilarities between things you are asked to contrast.

Outline: Develop an organized description. Give main points and essential supplementary material.

List: Provide an itemized series or a tabulation.

Analyze: Show the nature of the parts and the relationship of the parts to each other and to the whole. You may also want to state the assumptions that undergird statements.

Explain: State how and why. Reconcile any differences in opinion or experimental results. Where possible, state causes.

---

7   *Write legibly.* Remember that the person who is grading your examination—whether that is your instructor or a graduate assistant—will be reading a large number of examinations. After reading several, particularly if the handwriting is difficult, the grader will appreciate answers that are easily read. If you take time to be neat, leaving margins and being sure that your handwriting is clear, you'll immediately create a good impression. Some students find that printing their answers is a good way to ensure legibility. Avoid crossing out, drawing arrows to connect sections of your answers, and any other techniques that will produce a generally messy appearance.

8   *Be concise.* Answer the question directly; then support your answer. Avoid bringing in information that is only remotely related to the question. Feel free to quote authorities to support your answer, but *not* as a substitute for your own answer.

9   *Use complete sentences, in paragraph form,* unless asked to do something different, such as develop a list or an outline.

10   *Leave some space after each answer* for additional information that may come to mind later.

11   *After completing the examination, read through your answers.* Correct obvious errors in spelling and punctuation. Make sure that each answer says what you intended to say. Also, read each question once more to make sure that your response answers it. One of the most common errors in essay exams is not answering the question.

12   *If you run out of time, outline the answers to remaining questions* rather than leaving them blank or partially answered in discursive

form. Showing that you knew an answer, even though you did not have time to develop it fully, will often earn you points.

Answering Objective Questions

Whereas essay questions measure your ability to organize and present ideas clearly, objective questions focus primarily on your ability to recall specific information. Here are suggestions for improving your performance on objective tests.

1 *Read the directions and then survey the entire examination* to note the number of questions and their point values in relation to the time you have for the examination.

2 *Check questions against the answer sheet.* If the answers are marked on a separate answer sheet, check occasionally, while you are taking the examination, to be sure that the answer numbers correspond with the question numbers.

3 *Go through the questions quickly, answering those that you are sure about.* Then work through again, spending more time, if necessary, on the difficult questions.

4 *Answer every question,* even those you are not absolutely sure about.

5 *Pay attention to key words in the questions.* For example, in true-false items, statements containing the words *all, always,* or *never* tend to be false. Statements containing the words *usually, most, some,* or *may* tend to be true.

6 *Use logical reasoning* in attempting to answer questions. For instance, if the correct answer to a multiple-choice question is unclear to you, use a process of elimination, crossing off the choices that you know are incorrect. You may end up with one choice, which must be the correct answer; or you may have two possible choices from which you must select—an easier task than selecting from four or five.

7 *Be careful with true-false questions.* Remember: If a statement includes anything that is false, it must be marked "false," even though it may also contain something that is true.

8 *Don't look for patterns in answers.* Do not be disturbed if you mark several T's ("true") on several F's ("false") in succession in a true-false test. Don't be influenced if you think you see a pattern in the answers to multiple-choice questions. Deal with each question on its own, without thinking about how your instructor might have tried to randomize the correct answers. It's very possible that your instructor did not even consider such patterns.

9 *Use the information that is to be found within questions.* Look for information in some test questions that may help you answer other questions.

10 *Read back through your exam when it is completed,* to catch any obvious errors you may have made. But be careful about changing your answers to the questions you weren't sure about; often, your first response is the best response. Also, make sure that you understood each question. You may interpret some questions quite differently on a second reading, and then decide that it is indeed appropriate to change your answers.

Taking Open-Book Examinations

Many instructors recognize that real-life situations often require us to use available resources in attempting to solve a problem or answer a question. Accordingly, they sometimes give open-book exams. Some open-book exams are written in class; others are take-home exams, with deadlines of 1 week or more for completion.

An open-book examination, like an essay examination, measures the student's ability to organize and present ideas. It also measures the student's ability to find and organize the information necessary to answer the questions. The following tips for taking open-book examinations are generally helpful.

1 *Preparation is extremely important.* Do not procrastinate; don't let the fact that you will be able to use resources give you a false sense of security. You will not have time to do the necessary reading while you are actually taking the exam; this reading must be done ahead of time. Preparing for an open-book examination is thus no different from preparing for closed-book exam: you must review your lecture notes and your reading notes beforehand, and you must do considerable thinking about the meaning of what you have been studying and about how all the pieces fit together.

2 *Gather your resource materials.* Find the books, articles, and notes that you expect to use in the examination.

3 *Organize the material you are studying into broad topics.* These are usually stated in the course outline or syllabus. Then, indicate pages from your readings which apply to each of the topics. Key your lecture notes to the main topics in the same way.

4 *Anticipate the questions that may be asked, and outline your answers.* Refer to readings and lecture notes as necessary.

5 *At the beginning of the exam, take some time to organize.* When you first receive the examination, start by organizing your answers and noting readings where you may find assistance. Don't be in a hurry to begin writing. If you have 5 days for the exam, 2 days of thinking about the questions and organizing the answers is not too long.

6 *Make your answers concise and to the point.* For example, do not string together a series of quotations from various sources on the assumption that this will constitute an appropriate answer. Write answers in your own words, using only an occasional quotation or reference to resource materials as support.

7 *Type your answers.* For open-book take-home examinations, type your answers if at all possible. Usually you can plan your time so that you will be able to read through and edit your answers and also type them. Most instructors appreciate typewritten copy, which is easier to read than handwriting.

Taking Oral Examinations

Some instructors give oral examinations, but such exams are more common at the graduate level than at the undergraduate level. An oral examination measures your ability to analyze and integrate material and to organize it quickly as a spoken response to a question. Students have found the following tips helpful when taking oral examinations.

1 *Determine the scope of the examination.* Before the exam, find out what the scope will be. Will the entire course be covered, or only part of it?

2 *Rehearse the exam.* Anticipate questions that may be asked, and practice answering them. This procedure works best when done with another student who is taking the same exam.

3 *Listen carefully to the questions as they are asked.* If you don't understand a question completely, ask the instructor for clarification.

4 *Don't bluff.* If you don't know an answer, say so. But don't hesitate to attempt an answer when you are not sure; you may know more than you think.

5 *After you are asked a question, take time to think through and organize your response.* You may want to jot down key words on a pad, as a reminder of details of the question.

6 *Get and use feedback.* Usually, you receive immediate feedback on an oral examination. At this point, ask for clarification in areas where you weren't sure. Often, when you have finished your answer to a question, the instructor will comment at once on what you've said,

ask you a related question, or share with you the answer he or she had in mind.

Taking Specialized Tests

You may encounter other types of tests in the program in which you are enrolled. For instance, if you are taking a course in small engines, you may be given an examination that emphasizes practical problem solving or troubleshooting (for example, diagnosing the fault when an engine will not start). A course in computer science may include a test in which you must demonstrate what you have learned by building a model computer, using a computer to illustrate your work. For an engineering course, an examination may include actually constructing something.

Preparation for these types of examinations generally follows the same principles outlined above.

EVALUATING YOUR PERFORMANCE

Whatever form they take, examinations can be useful learning experiences. When you receive a corrected written examination—and you should insist on seeing it—study it to see where you made mistakes. This should give you clues about what you need to reread or where you need to do additional work.

Many instructors will spend time in class reviewing an examination and explaining the answers. This of course can be extremely useful.

SUMMARY

- Examinations are a fact of life for college students. Many students fear them, particularly older students who have been out of school for some time and are returning to the classroom.
- You can build your confidence as a test-taker by realizing that exams are part of the fabric everyday life. A driving test, a job interview, and even an income tax form are all, in a sense, examinations.
- In college, students face two basic types of tests: achievement and aptitude. Achievement tests measure what you have learned; aptitude tests measure your potential.
- The two major types of achievement tests are essay and objective examinations. Essay exams require short or long discussions, depending on the question. Objective exams include true-false, multiple-choice, fill-in-the-blanks, and matching items.

- Preparing for tests can take the form of constant long-term study or systematic cramming a few days beforehand—or both. Developing a set of summary notes is a good way to prepare for an examination because it requires you to think about the main ideas of the course.
- Successful test-taking involves following both general guidelines and specific tips. These include reading questions carefully, planning your answers, writing answers to questions for which you know the answers first, attempting to answer all the questions, and rereading your answers to catch errors.
- Much can be learned from an examination, if you are willing to check wrong answers against your textbook and lecture notes and rethink your responses.

7

IMPROVING YOUR READING ABILITY

Improving your reading (like becoming a successful test-taker) is partly a matter of developing certain skills and partly a matter of attitude. Let's start with your attitude—how you think about reading. Then, we can consider some principles that will help you become a better reader.

THINKING ABOUT READING

Common Misconceptions about Reading

There are several myths about reading, which—unfortunately—many people believe.

Myth Number 1 *With today's electronic technology—such as computers, video- and audiotapes, electronic teleconferencing, and satellite communication—reading is no longer important.* There is an increasing use of electronic storage, retrieval, and communication of information in our society generally, as well as in educational settings. But reading is still crucial. Even in the few college degree programs that are taught primarily by satellite, or with computers, reading continues to be an extremely significant dimension: students have textbooks and other reading materials. And in at least one computer-based degree program, although reference material is made available on an on-line database, the material is written and of course must be read. It is difficult to imagine that reading will ever become insignificant in our culture; it will remain important for gaining information, for understanding ideas in depth, and for sheer enjoyment.

Myth Number 2   *When I read something, such as an assignment for a course, I must read every word.* It is surprising how many students still believe this. One older returning student told me that she had a problem finding enough time to read all her textbooks from cover to cover; for the past several years, her reading had been primarily novels, which are often read word for word. But in the college setting, few reading assignments are read that way. In many subject areas, you can learn to find the material most related to your purpose and focus your attention on that material, disregarding the rest.

There are some exceptions, however. For highly technical material in disciplines like chemistry and physics, reading every word may be necessary for understanding the concepts; and in literature courses, it may be necessary to read word for word because not only meaning but use of language is analyzed.

Myth Number 3   *It is extremely difficult to improve reading skills; if I am an average or below-average reader, I will probably stay that way.* This is simply not true. By following the suggestions in this chapter, you will be able to improve your reading skills considerably. It will take some work and some practice, but it's not that tough to do.

Myth Number 4   *Everything that is read should be read in the same way.* This relates to myth 2, and it is equally misleading. Actually, you will accomplish much more if you adjust your way of reading both to different types of material (such as novels, popular magazines, research journals, and textbooks) and to your own purpose (see Chapter 8, Reading for Different Purposes).

Reading Self-Assessment

When you are trying to improve your reading ability, it's a good idea to start with a self-assessment. Read the following descriptions of common reading problems, and circle the number of each one that applies to you.

1   *I often have trouble grasping the main idea of what I am reading.* This is a common difficulty, particularly if you are reading subject matter that is new to you. Using the skills of active reading described below can help you overcome this problem.
2   *When I finish reading something, I remember little of it.* This, too, is a common problem, particularly for the passive reader. Becoming an

active reader—learning how to mark your reading material, for instance, and how to take notes—will help you remember. See the section below on active reading.

3 *I have difficulty keeping my mind focused on what I am reading.* Since passive readers have difficulty concentrating, the section below on how to become an active reader will help with this problem. In addition, Chapter 18 describes specific concentration techniques.

4 *I have difficulty reading clusters of words; I tend to read one word at a time.* One way to overcome this difficulty is to hold the page you are reading some distance from your eyes, so that you can see an entire line at a time. Then slowly return the page to your normal reading distance, trying to maintain the broader view. What you are doing here is training yourself to use more of your peripheral vision. Your goal is to see groups of words rather than single words. By training your eyes to see groups of words, you will discover that you are reading ideas instead of words.

5 *I say each word to myself when I read.* You may be doing this without knowing it: even though you do not move your lips, you may still "subvocalize" the words. To test yourself, put your fingertips on your throat as you read; do you feel the throat muscles move? Teaching yourself to read clusters of words, with attention to ideas, and pushing yourself to read faster, will make subvocalizing disappear.

6 *When I am reading, I find many words that I do not know.* Like problem 1, this is not unusual, particularly with material in an unfamiliar subject area. See the section below on how to handle difficult words.

GENERAL PRINCIPLES FOR IMPROVING YOUR READING

Previewing Reading Materials

When you go on a trip, you could just follow road signs, perhaps asking someone for directions now and then, and probably reach your destination eventually. But spending a few minutes with a road map, looking at the cities and states you will pass through and the highways you will take, would give you an overview of your trip that would very likely save you valuable time. Making a preview of a reading assignment has a similar purpose—to give you an overview of what lies ahead.

How to Preview a Book When they are assigned an entire book, many students simply begin reading it at the first page. This is a mistake; previewing the book first is a much better strategy.

Following are useful steps for previewing nonfiction books, including textbooks.[1]

1 *Turn to the title page.* Note the complete title, including the subtitle, if any. Often, a book will have a subtitle that tells you more about the book's content than the title does. You will also see the author's name and the book's publisher on the title page.

2 *Look at the copyright page.* The copyright date is usually printed on the page immediately following the title page. This page, in recent years, often includes Library of Congress Cataloging Data. In brief form, this information categorizes the book into a topic area. For example, *Developing Critical Thinkers,* by Stephen D. Brookfield, has this Library of Congress Data printed on the copyright page: "Bibliography; Includes Index. 1. Critical thinking. 2. Critical thinking—Study and teaching. 3. Psychology, Applied."[2]

3 *Read the author's preface or introduction.* You will usually learn why the author wrote the book, how the book is organized, and what important topics are covered.

4 *Examine the table of contents.* This will list parts, chapters, and often the main topics within chapters. Thus it will show you the structure of the book.

5 *Look through the index.* Note what terms the author uses and which ones are unfamiliar to you. Some books also have a separate index of authors whose works are cited in the book.

6 *Check the bibliography* (if the book has one). Here you can see the references the author has used. You may recognize some of them, if you have read previously in this field. And if you are planning to do more work in this subject area, the bibliography can point you toward additional materials.

7 *Read the publisher's statement on the back cover or jacket* (if the book has one). Though such a statement is obviously written as an advertisement, or to capture the attention of someone browsing in a bookstore, it is often a good summary of the book.

8 *Read "about the author."* This can appear on the dust jacket or the back cover, with the material at the front of the book, or at the end. Here you can learn about the author's background and experiences that relate to the topic of the book.

9 *Select one or two chapters that seem central to the main topic.* Read the first paragraph or two of each of these chapters, and then read the

---

[1] In general, this technique is *not* appropriate for fiction, drama, and poetry, although some of the individual steps can be useful for works of this nature.

[2] Stephen D. Brookfield, *Developing Critical Thinkers,* Jossey-Bass, San Francisco, Calif., 1987.

last paragraphs. Note the subheads that appear within each of these chapters, to see what topics are covered and how the chapters are organized. Inspect any illustrative material, such as photographs, graphs, charts, and maps. What do they tell you?

A preview of a book, following these steps, should take no more than 15 or 20 minutes.

Once you've done the preview, reflect on the book in terms of your purpose for reading it. If the book is assigned reading, you have no choice but to read it. But if you are writing a paper and searching for appropriate reference material, you may decide, after the preview, to spend no more time with the book. Or—and this is more often the case— you may discover that material in, say, Chapters 4 and 6 applies to your task, and the other chapters are irrelevant.

You may want to make notes about books you have previewed, since this information can be useful for future projects. The box on page 74 shows a form for keeping a record of a book you have previewed.

How to Preview an Article or a Chapter   When previewing a book chapter or an article, first determine its relationship to other chapters or articles in the work as a whole. What kind of book, journal, or magazine does the article or chapter appear in? A periodical, for instance, might be a popular magazine for the general public or a scholarly journal. A book might be a nonfiction book for the general public—perhaps a best-seller—or a textbook.

Determine the structure of the article or chapter. Read the headings, which are signposts the author uses to show the reader how the material is organized. Determine relationships among the ideas by noting levels of headings. Which are the main ideas, and which are the secondary ideas?

Look for introductions and summaries. Research articles, for example, often have a summary paragraph at the beginning (an abstract), that says what the article is about, usually in 50 words or less.

Becoming an Active Reader

Unfortunately, many people read passively, believing that one goes along and somehow soaks up information from the pages. This is a primary reason why many people have difficulty reading.

Students often mention inability to concentrate as a major problem, particularly with long reading assignments. Becoming an active reader is one way to solve this problem: you are not likely to lose concentration when you are actively involved in what you are doing.

FORM FOR RECORDING INFORMATION ABOUT A PREVIEWED BOOK

Title:

Subtitle (if any):

Author(s) or editor(s):

Library call number:

Copyright date (record the most recent date if several dates are given):

Preface (record the author's reasons for writing the book, if given):

Table of contents:

How many parts?

How many chapters?

Major sections within chapters

Index (note unfamiliar terms):

Is there a bibliography?

Are there appendixes? What topics do they take up?

Publisher's statement (record what such a statement—if there is one—says about the contents):

"About the author" (how is the author's experience related to the subject of the book?):

Sample chapters (examine one or two chapters and note the following):

Are there chapter introductions?

Are subheadings used for emphasis?

Is there illustrative material (diagrams, charts, graphs, maps, photographs, etc.)?

Is the writing style easy to read, or are there many long sentences and technical terms?

Are there end-of-chapter summaries?

Four Basic Questions to Ask as You Read   No matter what type of material you are reading, it is possible to read actively. To become an active reader, you should ask questions while you read, and try to answer them as you go along. Here are four basic questions to ask while reading:[3]

Question 1: What is the material about?   In a sentence or two, state the main theme of the work you are reading.

Question 2: What does the material say?   That is, what are the main ideas, and how are they developed?

Question 3: Is the material true?   Is the content of this article, chapter, or book actually true? Of course, you cannot make up your mind about this until you have answered questions 1 and 2—and even then you may have difficulty if the material is in an area new to you. Nevertheless, you should attempt to answer this question.

Question 4: Of what value is the material?   This question boils down to "So what?" What is the significance of the writing? Why does the author think the material is important? Do you think the material is important? Why or why not?

Techniques for Active Reading   If you own the book, magazine, or journal you are reading, you should do the following. If you do *not* own it, and it is relatively short, you may want to photocopy it so that you can use these techniques.

Underline key terms   Underline or use a transparent marking pen to indicate key words or phrases. Usually it is better to do this after you have read through the material once, so that you can put what you are reading into perspective and can identify the important and less important points. Some people err by underlining or marking nearly all the material. The key is to be selective, marking only important words or phrases. Passages to mark include definitions, items in lists, and main ideas within a paragraph.

Often, you will want to mark the topic sentence in a paragraph. The topic sentence is usually the first sentence of the paragraph. It tells what the paragraph is about and is followed by sentences that amplify and further explain it. Occasionally, the topic sentence is last in a paragraph, serving as a summary of material that precedes it. Some paragraphs have both a topic sentence at the beginning and a summary sentence at the end, which in effect restates the topic sentence.

Make marginal notations to indicate key passages   In the margins, draw a vertical line adjacent to an important paragraph. Place an asterisk in the margin adjacent to an important sentence; you might use two asterisks to

---

[3] Mortimer J. Adler and Charles Van Doren, *How to Read a Book,* Simon and Schuster, New York, 1972, pp. 137–167.

mark key sentences. If the author is developing several points, number them in the margin. Write key words from the text in the margins.

These techniques may sound like gimmicks, but they will help you to become an active reader. Furthermore, if you are reading material that you know you will want to review again—for an examination or for a paper you are writing—the clues in the margins can speed up your reviewing process.

Write marginal questions and comments Carry on a conversation with the author. If you don't understand something you're reading, make a comment to that effect in the margin. If you read something that explains what was hazy on a previous page, note that. If you've read something in another book or journal that contradicts what you are reading now, note the other source and the difference of opinion. Think while you read, and note some of your thoughts in the margins.

Take notes You may have learned the rudiments of outlining in elementary school, or later. If you are comfortable with formal outlining— the type taught in many schools—use it. The formal outline is most easily developed by using roman numerals for the author's first-order headings (I, II, III, etc.), capital letters for the second-order headings (A, B, C, etc.), arabic numerals for the third-order headings (1, 2, 3, etc.), and lowercase letters for the fourth-order headings (a, b, c, etc.). Rewrite the author's headings as statements that give the main idea of the subsumed material. (Sometimes it makes sense to rephrase headings in the form of questions.) After listing the main ideas in this way, you will often want to include important details such as definitions of terms and supporting data.

If you are not comfortable with a formal outline, you may find it useful to develop another way of listing the main ideas and the supporting details. For instance, you could draw a circle, placing the main idea inside it, and then drawing connecting lines to other circles where related material is noted. Or you could draw a sort of a wagon wheel, with the main idea as the hub and the related ideas becoming spokes.

Relate what you are reading to your own experience Returning students particularly have an advantage here, because they have a great deal of experience. But all students have some experience, and often a subject being studied is related to that experience.

Reflect on your experiences while you read. Constantly ask yourself whether what you are reading is related to something you remember from your work, your family, your social life, your travels, and so on. You can often make a reading understandable by using your own experiences as examples of what the author is saying. And often a reading can help you make sense out of experiences you have found hard to understand. This is particularly so if what you are reading is quite theoretical. One of the purposes of a theory is to help us make sense out of our experience, so that further experiences can be planned with some confidence about the outcome. Practical examples—where a theory fits and how it may be applied—make theories come alive.

Summarize When you've finished a reading, write a paragraph or two stating what it was about. You can summarize what a book was about on the blank pages at the front or the back, assuming that you own the book. Doing this forces you to reflect on the content and the meaning of what you've just read. It also provides you with an excellent summary when you come back to the book at some later date, if the book has become part of your personal working library.

Exercises for Active Reading *Exercise 1* Reread the preceding section, "Techniques for Active Reading," and mark it according to the suggestions given. When you have finished, compare your work with the marked copy in the illustration on pages 78–80. But don't be concerned if your marking is not the same as what you see in the illustration—there is no single "correct" way to mark reading material.

Exercise 2 Once again, reread "Techniques for Active Reading." This time, take notes on the material and record them in the box on page 81. When you've finished, turn the page upside down to read the sample notes at the bottom of the box. You'll find it interesting to compare your notes with the example; but remember that there are many ways to take notes while reading, and no one way is "right." Use whatever style is comfortable for you and involves you in the material.

Controlling Your Reading Speed

We're often urged to "increase our reading speed." It can sometimes be useful simply to read faster, but a more generally helpful approach is the concept of *controlling* our reading speed. Controlling your reading rate means adjusting your pace according to what you're reading and why you're reading it. First, though, it's important to know how to determine your present reading rate.

How to Determine Your Reading Rate Following is a method for finding out how fast you read. (It is summarized in the box on page 82.)

1 Select a chapter in a book or an article in a journal or magazine.
2 Count the number of words in the chapter or article. (Count the number of words in ten lines. Divide by 10 to determine the average number of words per line. Count the number of lines in the chapter or article and multiply by number of words per line.)
3 Read the chapter or article. Note your starting time and ending time in minutes and seconds.
4 Divide the total number of words by time in minutes to determine words per minute.

Techniques for Active Reading If you own the book, magazine, or journal you are reading, you should do the following. If you do *not* own it, and it is relatively short, you may want to photocopy it so that you can use these techniques.

Underline key terms Underline or use a transparent marking pen to indicate key words or phrases. Usually it is better to do this after you have read through the material once, so that you can put what you are reading into perspective and can identify the important and less important points. Some people err by underlining or marking nearly all the material. The key is to be selective, marking only important words or phrases. Passages to mark include definitions, items in lists, and main ideas within a paragraph.

Often, you will want to mark the topic sentence in a paragraph. The topic sentence is usually the first sentence of the paragraph. It tells what the paragraph is about and is followed by sentences that amplify and further explain it. Occasionally, the topic sentence is last in a paragraph, serving as a summary of material that precedes it. Some paragraphs have both a topic sentence at the beginning and a summary sentence at the end, which in effect restates the topic sentence.

Make marginal notations to indicate key passages In the margins, draw a vertical line adjacent to an important paragraph. Place an asterisk in the margin adjacent to an important sentence; you might use two asterisks to mark key sentences. If the author is developing several points, number them in the margin. Write key words from the text in the margins.

① Mark during second reading

② Clues for review

These techniques may sound like gimmicks, but they will help you to become an active reader. Furthermore, if you are reading material that you know you will want to review again—for an examination or for a paper you are writing—the clues in the margins can speed up your reviewing process.

Write marginal questions and comments Carry on a conversation with the author. If you don't understand something you're reading, make a comment to that effect in the margin. If you read something that explains what was hazy on a previous page, note that. If you've read something in another book or journal that contradicts what you are reading now, note the other source and the difference of opinion. Think while you read, and note some of your thoughts in the margins.

Take notes You may have learned the rudiments of outlining in elementary school, or later. If you are comfortable with formal outlining— the type taught in many schools—use it. The formal outline is most easily developed by using roman numerals for the author's first-order headings (I, II, III, etc.), capitals letter for the second-order headings (A, B, C, etc.), arabic numerals for the third-order headings (1, 2, 3, etc.), and lowercase letters for the fourth-order headings (a, b, c, etc.). Rewrite the author's headings as statements that give the main idea of the subsumed material. (Sometimes it makes sense to rephrase headings in the form of questions.) After listing the main ideas in this way, you will often want to include important details such as definitions of terms and supporting data.

③ "Talk" with the author

④ Outlining

79

If you are not comfortable with a formal outline, you may find it useful to develop another way of listing the main ideas and the supporting details. For instance, you could draw a circle, placing the main idea inside it and then drawing connecting lines to other circles where related material is noted. Or you could draw a sort of a wagon wheel, with the main idea as the hub and the related ideas becoming spokes.

Relate what you are reading to your own experience Returning students particularly have an advantage here, because they have a great deal of experience. But all students have some experience, and often a subject being studied is related to that experience.

Reflect on your experiences while you read. Constantly ask yourself whether what you are reading is related to something you remember from your work, your family, your social life, your travels, and so on. You can often make reading understandable by using your own experiences as examples of what the author is saying. And often a reading can help you make sense out of experiences you have found hard to understand. This is particularly so if what you are reading is quite theoretical. One of the purposes of a theory is to help us make sense out of our experience, so that further experiences can be planned with some confidence about the outcome. Practical examples—where a theory fits and how it may be applied—make theories come alive.

Summarize When you've finished a reading, write a paragraph or two stating what is was about. You can summarize a book on the blank pages at the front or the back, assuming that you own the book. Doing this forces you to reflect on the content and the meaning of what you've just read. It also provides you with an excellent summary when you come back to the book at some later date, if the book has become part of your personal working library.

⑤ Our experiences

⑥ Content and meaning

80

NOTE-TAKING

Example notes

Techniques for the active reader

1 Underline key words and phrases:
   Underline during second reading
   Be selective

2 Mark what is important:
   Vertical lines by important paragraphs
   Asterisks by important sentences
   Numbers by sequence of points

3 Write questions or comments in margins:
   Conversation with author
   Note thoughts about material

4 When finished reading, write statement of what book is about.

DETERMINING YOUR READING RATE

Complete this form

1 Material read: _____

2 Number of words in ten lines: _____

3 Words per line $= \dfrac{\text{Words in ten lines}}{10} =$ _____

4 Number of lines in chapter or article: _____

5 Number of words = words per line × number of lines = _____

6 Beginning reading time: _____

7 Ending reading time: _____

8 Total reading time: _____

9 Reading speed per minute $= \dfrac{\text{Total words (line 5)}}{\text{Total reading time}} =$ words per minute

Example

1 Material read: _____ Introduction chapter, Sociology _____

2 Number of words in ten lines: ___104___

3 Words per line $= \dfrac{\text{Words in ten lines (104)}}{10} =$ ___10.4___

4 Number of lines in chapter or article: ___250___

5 Number of words = words per line (10.4) × number of lines (250) = ___2600___

6 Beginning reading time: ___8:00 P.M.___

7 Ending reading time: ___8:20 P.M.___

8 Total reading time: ___20 minutes___

9 Reading speed per minute $= \dfrac{\text{Total words (2600)}}{\text{Total reading time (20 min)}} =$ ___130___ words per minute

When to Adjust Your Reading Rate Speed-reading courses have been and continue to be popular. Some of them advertise that participants can increase their reading rates well beyond 1000 words a minute, with a high degree of comprehension. Most of us can, and probably should, learn to read more quickly. But not all material should be read quickly.

To attempt to study and understand a statistics text by speed reading would be absurd, for example, and the same is true for almost any science or mathematics book—or for a research report, a philosophical argument, or even a good novel. Some materials, on the other hand, can be read rapidly and then read more carefully later, once the overall ideas have been determined. Depending on the purpose, some materials can be read rapidly to provide you with information you are seeking; there is no reason to read them slowly and carefully.

Thus an appropriate reading rate depends on the type of material you are reading and the purpose for which you are reading it. Since many people are not aware of the rates that are considered "good" or appropriate in various circumstances, Raygor and Schick suggest the following four guidelines:

1   When reading recreationally—a light novel, a short story, an article in a popular magazine like *Reader's Digest*—your reading rate should be 500 words per minute and up.
2   When reading fiction with some focus on the characterization, and when reading nonfiction to find the main ideas, an adequate reading rate is 350 to 500 words per minute.
3   When reading complex fiction with the intent of analyzing the plot or determining more subtle elements of characterization, or when reading nonfiction to note details or to determine relationships among ideas, a reading rate of 250 to 350 words per minute is suggested.
4   When reading highly technical material, when attempting to criticize the merit of what you are reading, or when reading to solve a problem or follow directions, a reading rate as slow as 100 to 250 words per minute is appropriate.[4]

You'll find it helpful to consider your reading rate in terms of these guidelines. On the form you completed earlier, note what kind of reading you selected and what your purpose was in reading it; then compare your calculated rate with the rate suggested for that type of reading and that purpose.

To sum up: Most of us can read faster than we do. But the key is not reading faster but learning when to read fast and when to read more slowly and deliberately. When we are reading material that does not de-

---

[4] Alton L. Raygor and George B. Schick, *Reading at Efficient Rates*, McGraw-Hill, New York, 1970, pp. 68–69.

mand complete and careful attention, we should push ourselves to move through it quickly. But when we are reading critically—for example, when we are writing a book review—we should read much more slowly and deliberately.

Mastering Difficult Words

You may be surprised at how many words you do not know, particularly when you are reading in an area that is relatively new to you. Several techniques can help you deal with unfamiliar words.

First, try to figure out words from their context. For example, consider the sentence, "Jimmy Wilson hoped to emulate his father's success at Elm Manufacturing by working as hard as his father." If you don't know the meaning of *emulate,* you should be able to figure out that it means "try to equal."

Referring to a dictionary is of course a good way to find the meaning of an unfamiliar word. But it's still important to know the context in which the word is used. For example, suppose that you see the word *prolific* in the following sentence: "Isaac Asimov is a prolific writer." The dictionary will tell you that *prolific* means "producing many offspring" or "creating many products of the mind." When there are alternative definitions, context generally tells you which one is correct. (By the way, Isaac Asimov has written several hundred books and many articles.)

Each time you encounter a word you don't know, write it on one side of a 3- by 5-inch card. Write the definition on the other side of the card. Carry the cards with you so that whenever you have a spare moment (waiting for a bus, for instance), you can take them out and review them.

Finding Signal Words

Authors use signal words to help readers follow what they are saying. Suppose you are driving one car and following a friend who is driving another; you would watch the car's brake and signal lights as clues to when your friend is slowing down, turning, or stopping. Likewise, you should look for word signals an author uses. Knowing signal words can help you follow an author's presentation, line of reasoning, and development of ideas. Here are some examples.

"Keep Going" Words   The road is clear; your friend is driving at a constant speed in one direction and wants you to follow. An author who wants you to continue along the same "mental road" uses "keep going" words such as *also, and, another, in addition, next,* and *another reason.*

Emphasis Words   Your friend in the car ahead sees something important—a landmark or a historical site, for instance—and wants you to notice it. Accordingly, he or she points out the window. An author "points" to important ideas and concepts by using emphasis words: *remember that, above all, key factor, essential feature, primary concern,* and *important to remember.*

"Change Direction" Words   Your friend's turn signal is on, and the car is slowing down. This prepares you to turn in that direction. An author prepares you to turn in a new direction by using "change direction" words such as *but, however, instead, in contrast, conversely,* and *on the other hand.*

Conclusion Words   Your friend wants you to know that you've reached the destination and accordingly slows down and perhaps activates the brake lights once or twice. An author who is preparing to stop will use conclusion words such as: *therefore, finally, in conclusion, in summary,* and *as a result.*

Learning about Authors

Try to learn something about an author's age and education, the kinds of jobs he or she has held, and the kind of writing he or she has done. This will often allow you to form expectations about the author's perspective and bias. For example, if you know that an author is a student of Marxism and has written several works on it, you may have some idea of what to expect in the material you are about to read. If you know that the author of a reading on human learning was a student of B.F. Skinner and subscribes to Skinner's theories, you may have a fair idea of what to expect.

However, although knowing something about an author's background and experience can give you some perspective, it is also important to read with an open mind. An author's ideas may have changed considerably since publication of a book 10 years ago, for instance.

Bear in mind that articles and textbooks, poems and plays, and all other writings are the creations of human beings. Some readers appear to lose sight of this fact. Everyone has emotions and goals and needs to earn a living. Knowing something about authors whose works you are reading gives you a perspective on them as human beings.

Reading Broadly

I often ask my students what they are reading, other than assignments associated with their courses. The answers I receive from most of them are disappointing.

For one thing, many students tell me that they just don't have time to read anything except assignments. In fact, several students have said that they don't even have time to read a newspaper. Many of these students are older, have families, and are working full time or part time—they obviously have a heavy load of responsibilities in addition to their studies. But I hear the same thing from many younger full-time students.

If I ask my students what novels they are reading, a number of them tell me that they can see no good reason for reading fiction. After all, fiction is a lie, isn't it? These are often students in the social sciences who believe that they ought to concentrate on social science readings, particularly in their major or a special area of interest.

A small number of students are reading broadly, however—novels, poetry, and nonfiction outside their area of specialization. These students all report that their outside reading has helped them. They argue—and I agree with them—that reading broadly gives them a wider perspective and allows them to see where their own area of specialization fits in. These students do not argue against specialization, but they do argue for specialization with perspective.

Just as you set aside time each day for study and reading of materials related to your courses, you should set aside time for recreational reading. You might do outside reading before you go to sleep at night, first thing in the morning, or after you've finished lunch—it doesn't matter when. But it is important to set aside a specific time within your daily schedule. Waiting to do recreational reading during a vacation, though a good idea, is not the answer. Reading for even half an hour a day every day will give far better results.

SUMMARY

- Myths about reading often keep students from improving their reading ability. It is *not* true that electronic communication will replace reading, or that you must always read every word, or that reading skills are extremely difficult to improve, or that everything should be read in the same way.
- To begin improving your reading skills, start with a self-assessment, and then concentrate on areas of difficulty.
- Principles for improving reading include: (1) previewing reading materials, (2) becoming an active reader, (3) adjusting your reading speed according to your purpose for reading and the type of material, (4) developing a strategy for mastering difficult words, (5) looking for authors' signal words, (6) learning about authors, and (7) reading broadly.

8

READING FOR
DIFFERENT PURPOSES

Knowing the purpose of reading determines how fast you should read and in large part sets the stage for becoming an active reader. The focus of this chapter is on nonfiction—articles, books, chapters in books, and research reports—since most of the reading you will do in college is nonfiction. I'll suggest guidelines for four purposes: reading for specific answers, reading for directions, reading for understanding, and reading critically.

READING TO FIND SPECIFIC ANSWERS

Scanning

The term *scanning* is often used for reading to find specific answers. Suppose that you want to know the date on which Lincoln delivered the Gettysburg Address. If you use an encyclopedia, you won't read every word in the article about the Gettysburg Address. Instead, you would scan through the article for the date. In a minute or two, you should be able to find it. You may already be a competent scanner. When you are checking spelling in a dictionary, you scan quickly until you find the word you need. When you look for a telephone number, you scan the directory until you find the name you want.

Techniques for Scanning

When scanning, you should know what you are looking for and look for it as rapidly as you can. Don't worry about all the "good information" you are passing over and disregarding on the way.

One practical technique to follow in scanning is to fix your question in mind and then run your eyes as fast as possible down the pages or columns of print until you find the answer. The key to this technique is keeping the question fixed in your mind. Don't be enticed away from it if your eyes spot a topic that looks interesting. Sometimes it helps to write your question on a card and to keep the card in front of you during your search. If the reading columns are narrow—say, of newspaper width—practice running your eyes down the center of the column. Make use of headings, indentations, and italicized words. These will often give you clues about where the information you are seeking is located.

If you catch yourself falling into the trap of reading every word, stop and start over again, giving yourself a new "fix" on the question you want answered.

READING FOR DIRECTIONS

Sometimes you read because you want to learn how to do something: write a research report, perform a laboratory experiment, and so on. Here scanning doesn't help. When reading directions on how to do something, you must usually read every word. Sometimes you must read every word several times, particularly if the directions are not clear.

A strategy that works for many people is first to read quickly through all the directions, and then go back and read thoroughly the directions that apply most to what you are trying to do. Let's assume that you have purchased new software for your computer. The book of directions will contain far more instructions than you may immediately need to know. You need to find those directions that will help you install the software on your computer and get it up and running. You will return to the complete directions when you want to perform additional functions.

READING FOR UNDERSTANDING

What Is Reading for Understanding?

Several terms are used to describe reading for understanding; they include *thorough reading, reading completely, mastering the material,* and *studying.* The most common term is *studying,* although studying can and should involve more than reading.

Many people—not only students—ask, "How can I assimilate more of what I read?" But for students the translation usually is, "How can I glean enough from my reading to pass the examinations?" One way is simply to try to memorize what you are reading. But without a systematic approach to reading, without some planning, and without active involvement with the reading material, it is difficult to know whether you are memorizing what is important. The question then becomes, "How can I recognize what is important, so that I can proceed to memorize it?" Since recognizing what is important involves understanding, we must set aside memorization, for the time being at least.

Memorizing and understanding differ considerably from each other. We can memorize material—long lists of definitions and pages of formulas, for example—without understanding it. As an undergraduate, I memorized all the veins in a frog, though I never really understood the context of what I was memorizing. (I passed the exam, but just barely, because several of questions required an understanding I didn't have.) And we can read—and read well—without memorizing. If you are able to read for understanding, you don't have to worry about memorizing. When you understand the material you are reading, you are well past the memorization stage. You know the material far better than you would if you had only memorized it.

Reading for understanding means reading so that you truly *know* what you are reading, and reading so that the material becomes a part of you. When you read for understanding, you can reformulate the material in your own words with confidence that you are not distorting the author's meaning.

How to Read for Understanding: Eight Questions

How do you read for understanding? What procedures should you follow? The method suggested here, a series of eight questions, applies to any nonfiction writing, whether it is an article in a research journal, a chapter in a book, or an entire book.

Question 1: What Is the Writing About?   What, in overview, is the writing about? You'll find it helpful to refer back to Chapter 7, which describes the process of previewing reading material.

Question 2: What Is the Author Attempting to Answer?   What question or questions is the author trying to answer? Complete this step of the process by turning each heading within the reading into a question. By paying attention to the levels of headings, you can determine what major questions and secondary questions the author is dealing with.

Question 3: What Important Terms Are Used?   What important terms does the author use? These terms may appear in the headings. In the running text, they may be in **boldface type** or *italicized*. Sometimes they appear in the opening sentences of paragraphs.

Question 4: How Are Key Terms Defined?   How does the author define key terms? For example, you may be reading an article criticizing education in the United States. *Education* is obviously a key word, but how does the author define it? There is no general agreement on the meaning of this term: some people use it to describe something a person attains; others define it as the process of learning; still others define it as both an attainment and a process. To understand what the author of this particular article is talking about and the questions that will be raised, you must know how he or she is defining *education*. Of course, the author may write, explicitly, "I define education as..." But you may find that the definition is implicit, so that you must infer it from the context—from how the word is used and what examples are given.

Question 5: What Answers Does the Author Give?   What answers does the author give to the questions raised? At this point, understanding the structure of nonfiction can be helpful.

Paragraphs are the building blocks of nonfiction. Within a paragraph, there are usually three kinds of statements: (1) a topic sentence, which is the main idea of the paragraph; (2) supporting material, statements that restate the topic sentence, illustrate it, or amplify it some way; (3) a summary sentence that briefly restates what was said in the paragraph.

Not all paragraphs are written in exactly this way. As I mentioned in Chapter 7, sometimes the topic sentence serves also as the summary sentence and appears at the end of the paragraph. Sometimes there is no actual topic sentence; instead, phrases in several sentences contribute to the topic or main idea of the paragraph. Sometimes a topic is so broad that the author writes several paragraphs about it, with subtopics in each paragraph.

Knowing the structure of writing gives you clues about how a writer goes about answering the questions that are raised. Also, if you know the kind of structure used by most good writers, you will be able to distinguish what is central and important from details, illustrations, and support.

Question 6: What Questions Are Unanswered?   What questions does the author raise but answer incompletely, or perhaps not at all?

Question 7: What Is the Author's Point of View?   What point of view is the author taking? All writers have a point of view, even if they claim to be completely objective and unbiased.

Sometimes writers will openly state the assumptions that guide their work. If so, you will know at least their intended point of view; but you must be alert in your reading to see if what the authors actually say is consistent with their stated assumptions. Reading the preface or introduction of a book can also give you valuable information about the writer's point of view, as can information that may be included concerning the author. (Introductory material like this should be examined as part of your reading preview; see Chapter 7.)

Another way to determine an author's point of view is to read material on the same topic by another author. Often instructors will assign readings that appear to duplicate one another. What they are usually doing is providing you with an opportunity to read several points of view on the same topic, recognizing that authors do have biases.

Question 8: How Does the Writing Relate to Your Experience?   How does what the author says relate to your own experience, and to your other reading? From what you know about the subject—what you have learned from other reading in the general area and (equally important) what you have experienced in life—how does what the author is saying fit in? Do the author's statements make sense on the basis of your experience?

Sometimes this kind of comparison is difficult: you may be reading in an area where you have had no experience and have done no other reading. But complete lack of experience is rare; almost everything you read, if you think about it for a moment, will have a relationship to something you have experienced. And with experience—even if it is somewhat remote from the material—you can often bring a reading into focus. You can better understand something new if you can relate it to something specific you have experienced.

Attempting to relate your reading to previous reading and experience is an active process, and so question 8 is another way to move from being a passive, nonparticipating reader to becoming an active, involved reader. It is a way of carrying on a conversation with the author. What you are doing, in effect, is saying to the author, "I did something like that a few years ago, and what you are writing here is related." Or, "I read something about this last year. You're using different words, but you're talking about the same thing."

READING CRITICALLY

What Is Reading Critically?

What does it mean to read critically? First, reading critically *doesn't* mean trying only to find fault with what you are reading. When you read critically, you are also interested in discovering good points. Second, as you read critically, you are examining the writing at its most fundamental level. You search for flaws in the arguments, and evaluate the evidence used to support positions the author is taking. Your examination will give you information and insight for making judgments about the author's writing.

What to Do before Reading Critically

Before you can read something critically, you must understand it. You must know what the author is talking about, and it must make sense to you. Thus a requisite for reading critically is reading for understanding, coming to grips with the author so that you can say, "Yes, I know what he or she is talking about."

Many people don't hesitate to criticize material before they have understood it, and sometimes even before they have read it. Too often, people are willing to criticize writing on the basis of what someone else has said about it. Some people will comment on a book after seeing only a review of it—they themselves have never even opened the cover. (This is about on a level with criticizing a neighbor's wallpaper on the basis of a friend's judgment, though you yourself haven't seen it.)

Many people say that they have read something and disagree with it; but when asked why, they reply, "I didn't understand it." This is a subtler problem. If you have read something carefully and made every effort to understand it, then you may reasonably comment that it is difficult to understand. But that is hardly a reason for disagreeing with it. A more appropriate reaction would be to withhold judgment because you could not understand the material.

It is sometimes suggested that all disagreement is, at bottom, due to lack of understanding: get two people to understand something, and they will no longer disagree about it. Certainly, some apparent disagreements occur because people do not understand something in the same way; it would be better, though, to refer to these as *misunderstandings* or *lack of understanding* rather than *disagreements*.

For a true disagreement to occur, both parties must first understand each other. Each must know as fully as possible what the other is saying. In our case, the reader must know as fully as possible what the author is saying. Until this level of understanding is achieved, it is not possible for a true disagreement to take place. But once understanding is attained, there is certainly room for disagreement. A variety of thoughtful perspectives on a topic, sometimes opposed to each other, can enrich our understanding.

An important related point is that it is also impossible to agree with an author until you understand as fully as possible what he or she has written. Agreement is unfounded if, when asked why you agree with a writer, you say only, "It sounds right to me." That's not a good enough reason. Why does it sound right? What specifically do you agree with, and why? Feelings are a valid part of your response: that is, you may say that you "feel good" about the material. But you must go beyond the level of feelings. What, specifically, about the writing causes you to feel good about it?

Often, material you read will be new or relatively new to you. This may present a problem if you want to read critically: you must, through careful reading and deliberation, bring yourself up to a level of understanding that allows you to make in-depth comments.

When to Read Critically

When do you read critically? A quick answer is that you should read critically all the time, but this is impractical. You should read critically the materials that are most important to a course you are taking, to a writing assignment you are working on, or to a research project you may be doing.

Reading critically is an extremely active process. To do an adequate job of reading material critically, you may need to read it several times. By attempting to make a judgment about it, you will find that your understanding deepens. Although, as I said above, understanding is a prerequisite for critical reading, critical reading also contributes to understanding.

If your assignment is to write a book review or comment on a research report, you must of course read critically. Too often, students write a book report, not a review; they describe what is in the book but don't make judgments about it, or about the author's approach. And many students will simply describe a research project rather than preparing a critical review.

A Process for Reading Critically

Here is a four-step process for critical reading.

Step 1: Read for Understanding   Read the piece as you would to understand it, becoming fully acquainted with the topic.

Step 2: Determine What Evidence Is Advanced   What evidence does the author use to support the positions taken? An author may support a position through logical argument. Or an author who has actually experienced a situation may be sharing that experience. An author may also rely on other researchers and writers to support his or her arguments. Many authors use a combination of evidence and argument.

Step 3: Determine the Author's Assumptions   What assumptions is the author making? Often, the preface or introduction—and sometimes the publisher's comments about the author—will contain information about what the author assumes.

For example, one author who is writing about an economic problem may assume that economic growth is fundamental to any economic system; another author, writing on the same topic, may assume a no-growth status for a future economic system. The two pieces of writing will obviously be quite different from each other, basically because they start with very different assumptions.

Often, as a critical reader, you will need to derive an author's assumptions from the material because the author does not state them explicitly. Figuring out an author's assumptions is crucial to critical reading; without a good concept of the assumptions, you will have difficulty making judgments about the writing.

Step 4: Determine Your Own Opinion   Do you agree or disagree with the writing, or must you withhold judgment?

If you *disagree* with part or much of the writing, carefully consider your reasons. Four basic reasons for disagreement are: (1) the writer is uninformed, (2) the writer is misinformed, (3) the writer has not argued logically, and (4) the writer's analysis is incomplete. Let's look at each of these.

If you believe that a writer is *uninformed,* then you must be able to show specifically what information is missing and why the missing information is important to the position the author is taking. For example, you may have recently read an article about research that relates directly to what the author is saying, but the author hasn't mentioned it. If you have reason to believe that this research puts an entirely different slant on what the author is saying, then you are in a position to say that the author is, at least in this area, uninformed. But you must be specific; you must be able to cite specific information to support your point.

Arguing that a writer is *misinformed* is a more difficult: you are obligated to show where the author's information is inaccurate. For example, suppose that the author is using a research report to support a position taken, but the report is grossly inaccurate. If you know this, and if you have adequate evidence, you can legitimately point it out and conclude that the author is misinformed.

Showing that an author has *argued illogically* also takes careful work. Basically, an author can be illogical in two ways: by drawing conclusions that do not follow from the statements offered, and by taking inconsistent or contradictory positions.

Let's consider the first, drawing conclusions that do not follow from the statements offered. Such conclusions are often referred to as *non sequiturs,* and the initial statements as the *premises.* Suppose that an author makes the following points: (1) The supply of natural gas in the United States is decreasing. (2) The supply of coal would seem to be sufficient to last for at least 200 years, and perhaps more. (3) The oil supply, like that of natural gas, is also limited. The author then concludes, "Given this information about our supplies of coal, natural gas, and oil, we should each try to grow more of our own food." This conclusion cannot be drawn from the premises. A critical reader is alert for non sequiturs; but remember that if you think you have found one, you must show *how* the conclusion does not derive from the premises.

As for contradictions and inconsistencies, these are sometimes easy to identify, but often they are hidden and take considerable digging to ferret out. For example, on page 23 an author may write, "Most people, in order to succeed, need considerable imposed motivators such as salary incentives." Later, on page 53, the same author writes: "One assumption we can make about human nature is that people have an inward drive which is stronger than any outside influence." The critical reader must ask, "Which is it? Are people influenced mostly by inward forces or by so-called imposed motivators?" As a critical reader, you would point out this contradiction in your analysis of the writing.

It sometimes happens that after careful reading, you cannot show that an author is uninformed, misinformed, or illogical, yet you still disagree with what he or she has said. On the basis of the same evidence as the author's, you may simply reach different conclusions. Honest disagreements can develop in this way; but it is also possible that at this point you may consider and comment on the what the author has not done. That is, you may want to argue that the author's presentation is *incomplete.* If you do this, you must be able to show specifically how the author has not covered the topic or analyzed the problem completely (for example, you may be able to show that the author has not used some of the available evidence). You must also be able to show how a more complete analysis of the material might have taken the author further. Almost any piece of writing could be taken further. As a critical reader, you should use your judgment to show how a writing would have been more complete, and probably more important, if the author had done certain specific things to deepen or broaden the analysis further.

As I noted above, disagreeing with an author is one possibility when you are determining your own opinion of a work. Two other possibilities are agreeing with the author and withholding judgment.

If you decide that you *agree* with an author, you must consider your reasons just as carefully as if you were disagreeing. The basic reasons for agreeing are counterparts of the reasons for disagreeing, but they are of course positive rather than negative. You are likely to agree with an author if you conclude that he or she is well-informed, has argued logically, and has been sufficiently complete. This conclusion, like any other, must be supported by specific evidence.

When can you reasonably decide to *withhold judgment?* I mentioned earlier that one good reason for withholding judgment about a piece of writing is simply being unable to understand it. Another reason is lack of experience with a subject: you may want to postpone judgment on one writing until you have examined others on the same topic. An important thing to bear in mind about withholding judgment is that you should be able to state legitimate reasons for doing so; this is not a way to avoid thinking critically about a reading or to get around the problem of deciding whether you agree or disagree with a writer.

SUMMARY

- Different purposes for reading suggest different approaches. Four purposes of reading are: (1) reading to find specific answers, (2) reading for directions, (3) reading for understanding, and (4) reading critically.
- Reading to find specific answers is often called *scanning*. It involves keeping your question firmly in mind and looking very quickly to find the answer, ignoring anything that is not the answer.
- Reading for directions is reading to learn how to do something. It usually involves reading every word, though you may read first only what you need first and wait until later to cover the rest.
- Reading for understanding is sometimes called *studying*. It is not memorizing; it goes far beyond memorizing and involves making the material genuinely your own.
- One method of reading for understanding is to ask eight questions as you read: (1) What is the writing about? (2) What is the author trying to answer? (3) What important terms are used? (4) How are key terms defined? (5) What answers are given? (6) What remains unanswered? (7) What is the author's viewpoint? (8) How does the writing relate to your own experience?
- Reading critically is an active process which requires understanding the material; material that is important for courses you are taking or projects you are working on should be read critically.
- One good procedure for reading critically involves four steps: (1) read for understanding; (2) identify the evidence advanced; (3) identify the author's assumptions; (4) form your own opinion.

9

BECOMING
A BETTER WRITER

Writing will demand much of your time as a student; in terms of time, it will probably be second only to reading.

A WRITING PROCESS

Below I describe a writing process that I follow myself and have taught to hundreds of students over the years. The process does not fit all types of writing, of course, but it does fit any nonfiction writing which involves research. It is particularly appropriate for term papers, various kinds of reports, and theses and dissertations. It can also be used by students who might, in the future, write nonfiction books. The process has seven steps.

Step 1: Decide on a Topic

Your instructor may assign a topic, but generally you will have some choice regarding the topic of a paper that you write for a course or a research project that you pursue and report on. At the beginning of the writing process, you may not be able to state your topic exactly. If so, don't be alarmed. The process is designed to help you refine your general topic into a specific, manageable assignment.

Step 2: Translate the Topic into Questions

Ask questions that you will attempt to answer. At this early point in the planning stage, it may be difficult to formulate specific questions, but try nevertheless. As you move into the project and begin your research, you will sharpen, or perhaps expand, these early questions.

Questions give you a solid starting point for planning your writing. For instance, if you are writing a paper on the changing climate of the earth, you might ask: "To what extent has the climate changed in the past 100 years?" "Has it changed more in the northern hemisphere than in the southern hemisphere?" "What are the reasons for the changes?" "Are the changes part of a natural cycle, or are they caused by air pollution, the destruction of the ozone layer in the atmosphere, and the clearing of tropical rain forests?" These are broad questions which need refinement, but they—and questions like them—will give you a place to begin.

Step 3: Establish a Timetable for the Project

Before you launch a writing project, decide how you will use the time available to complete it. A rule of thumb I have followed for many years is to plan to spend about one-third of the time doing research, one-third of the time writing the first draft, and one-third of the time revising the draft.

Here is an example of how this formula would be applied in practice. Work backwards. Let's say that your term paper is due on December 15, and that it is now October 1. Let's also assume that the completed paper must be between 20 and 25 pages (in other words, it is not a short piece that you might be able to complete in a day or two). And finally, let's assume that you have other assignments and can't begin working on this project until November 1. This means that you are giving yourself 6 weeks to write the paper. Using the formula, write the following on a card and pin it above your desk:

Term paper for course X due: December 15.
Begin project: November 1.
Research completed: November 15.
First draft completed: December 1.
Final draft completed: December 12.

Notice that the date for completing the final draft (December 12) is 3 days earlier than the actual due date for the paper (December 15). This is to allow some time for correcting previously overlooked errors, doing the final typing or printing, and dealing with the unexpected.

If you have more than one writing project during a semester, you will want to incorporate these individual projects into your semester planning schedule.

Step 4: Research the Topic

Using your broad questions as guides, begin an information search (see Chapter 15 for details on how to conduct a formal search). First consult the computerized card catalog in the library; then, perhaps, the traditional card catalog, if you want earlier material. Depending on your topic, you may want to do a database search: a CD-ROM search or an on-line search or both. Your reference librarian can help you with this.

For each source you select for further reading, prepare a 5- by 7-inch note card. On the card, write the date of the source, its library call number (or some other identification), and complete bibliographic information—author, title, publisher, etc. Write a sentence or two (from the abstract, if any) about what is included in the source.

Once you have identified several references that seem to relate to your writing project, find the materials and begin examining them, one at a time. As you find passages that appear relevant to your project, make notes or—even better—photocopy the material. Photocopying, although it usually entails some cost, will save you time because you will have the material exactly as it is written and need not worry about having made errors in copying. It is also much faster to photocopy material you think you may need than to copy it laboriously by hand. In any case, be sure to record the title and copyright information for future reference.

On the note card for each of your sources, write a number, starting with 1. Then write the same number on each page of your notes or your photocopied material for that source. This will allow you to file your notes and photocopied material in numerical order, and use the cards as keys to find any piece of research quickly. Thus you have two sets of materials—the note cards, which contain brief information; and your full notes and photocopied material. These two sets are cross-referenced to each other.

Step 5: Develop an Outline

Outlines have little appeal for most people, but some kind of outline is necessary for good writing. An outline can serve as a road map. It will guide you generally; make you aware of any detours you may be taking (often in writing, as in traveling, we follow an attractive side road for a while); and, when you begin revising, let you check on whether you have actually done what you planned to do. However, sometimes in the midst of writing, you will strike on a totally new approach that is much better than your original idea; in that case, you may decide to abandon part of your outline or even all of it.

Some students outline by listing ideas and then rearranging the items to identify major ideas and related subideas. Others are comfortable with a more formal approach; they start with main ideas and then develop subideas within each major idea. An approach to outlining that I started using a few years ago is extremely informal but surprisingly effective— and also fun to do. I call it *freewheeling*. Let's look at it in some detail.

Freewheeling (the term, as you'll soon see, is a pun) is based on the image of a wheel, which has a hub in the center and spokes radiating out from it. It works as follows. First, write in the center of a piece of paper the working title for your writing project, and draw a circle around it. Then draw a line from this center circle and at the end of the line write an idea that relates to the title. Draw another circle around this related idea. Next, draw lines out from that new circle, leading to ideas (also circled) that contribute to it. Soon you will have wheels connected to wheels, all around the page. This is the "free" part of the method; at this point, you allow yourself to write every idea that comes to mind, without trying to order anything.

Your next step is to begin relating ideas to each other. Sometimes, as you freely write ideas, you discover that an idea relating to one wheel also relates to another. Whenever this happens, you draw a connecting line. Soon your page will be filled with circles and lines, but you will find it relatively easy to sort them out and organize your paper.

The freewheeling approach, sometimes called *branching,* has much going for it. For one thing, you need not start at the beginning, as you must with a linear outline. Freewheeling starts from a center and radiates outward. As you develop a freewheeling outline, you can add new ideas anywhere at all, as they pop into your mind.

Second, freewheeling is a whole-brain process (see Chapter 2): it draws on both the left side of the brain (the highly organized side), and the right side of the brain (the artistic, intuitive, creative side). As you work through a freewheeling process, you will often discover that many new ideas appear on the page. Freewheeling allows you to express them without restriction.

Third, freewheeling allows you to see the totality of what you are planning and the relationship of the various parts to each other. In fact, this is one of its most important features. Generally, your logic will be sounder when you use this approach, for the relationships of ideas to each other are before you on the paper.

Fourth, freewheeling is compact. You can fit a complete outline for a 25-page project onto a single sheet of paper. A linear outline, on the other hand, would probably take 3 or 4 pages, or even more. As a result, with a linear outline you can't see the relationships among ideas so easily; you would have to flip through several pages of outline.

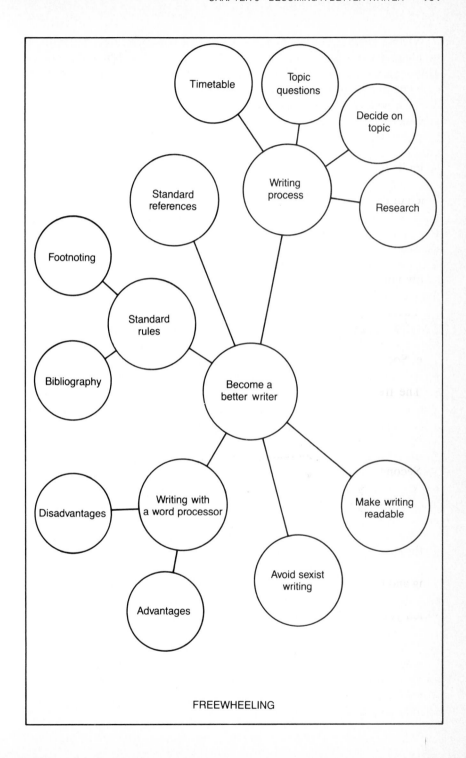

FREEWHEELING

When I have completed a freewheeling outline, I write the identification numbers of my research material next to the appropriate circles. This step saves me much time when I am actually writing, because I don't have to wade through my research notes searching for something I remember only vaguely. Also, it ensures that I won't leave out any supporting material simply because I forgot about it.

The illustration on the preceding page shows part of the freewheeling outline I used in writing this chapter.

Step 6: Begin Writing

Up to this point, you have been planning. Now it is time to sit down with your typewriter, your word processor, or your blank paper and begin writing.

A term paper, a research report, or any other nonfiction work has a beginning, a middle, and an end. The beginning states what you are planning to say; the middle says it; the end summarizes it.

Opening   How should you begin writing? You should simply do it. Often, the first page or two of whatever you are writing seems most difficult. You want the beginning—the *introduction*—to set the tone of the piece and to be at the same time provocative and informative. And so you write a paragraph. You read it, decide that you don't like it, and start again. You write another paragraph or two, and you toss them away. This goes on until you become so frustrated that you quit.

The way to handle this problem is to keep writing. Don't look back. Don't read the first paragraph after you've written it; instead, keep on going. Write a third and fourth paragraph, and then a second page, and so on. Discipline yourself to keep writing, to keep stringing words together. Then you will have something to work on later. You can't revise and rewrite if you have nothing to work with. Write complete sentences (not merely phrases and words), and write in a form that you yourself can understand and make sense of later. But don't go back to correct misspelled words, poor syntax, or other such problems.

When, eventually, you have written enough to work on, it will be time to go back to the introduction and refine it. What should you include in your introduction? The purpose of the introduction (professional writers call it the *lead*) is threefold: (1) to capture the reader's attention, (2) to state the central idea, and (3) to lead the reader into the paper.

Sometimes raising a question or several questions is a good way to introduce your topic. Sometimes you can use an anecdote that clearly illustrates the main idea. Sometimes a quotation will succinctly illustrate what is to follow.

Avoid lengthy introductions. Readers want to get on with it. Once you have aroused their interest and they have some idea of what to expect, they want to find out what you have to say.

Body The middle, or *body,* of your paper should be relatively easy to write if you've been careful and thoughtful in developing an outline.

Headings and subheadings The major headings in your outline become heads in your paper; the secondary headings in the outline become subheads; and so on. Be sure to use heads and subheads; they serve as visual guides for the reader who is trying to follow the logic of your presentation and also as clues for readers who are scanning to determine the main ideas and perhaps to decide if they should read the paper in its entirety.

What should your heads look like? One traditional system is used in this book. First-level (or rank 1) heads are capitalized and positioned as a separate line, starting at the left. Second-level (rank 2) heads are also separate lines, flush left, but they are in capital-and-lowercase style. Third-level (rank 3) heads are capital-and-lowercase style, flush left, but the text runs in on the same line. Thus:

THIS IS A FIRST-LEVEL HEAD

This Is a Second-Level Head

This Is a Third-Level Head Notice that the text starts on the same line.

Usually, you would leave a line or two of space above a head. But you could also indent the rank 3 head and leave no extra space above it.[1]

Paragraphs Use paragraphs as building blocks for your paper. A classical way of writing a paragraph is to state a point and then illustrate or support it. To illustrate or support your point, you can use examples, quotations from authorities, anecdotes, dialogue, statistics, and research data.

In a paper about solar energy, for example, you might write a paragraph such as this:

> No matter where you live in the northern climates, solar energy can provide a substantial amount of heat for your home. Hans Anderson, of Eli, Minnesota says, "When I put solar panels on my roof, my neighbors thought I was crazy. Even my wife said I was throwing away money. But in two years I've saved nearly half of what I usually pay in heating bills." Professor John

---

[1]You'll notice, of course, that this book also has a fourth-level (rank 4) head, which is italicized and in which only the first word starts with a capital letter. But a student paper is not likely to require a rank 4 head.

> Wilson, a solar energy researcher, says, "You can save money with solar heat. Some people living in the upper midwest have paid for their solar equipment with fuel savings in only 5 years."

You have first made the point about solar energy as a heat source and then backed it up with first-hand evidence and a researcher's statement.

This is but one approach. You could write your entire paper this way, but it would soon become extremely boring. You may want to begin some paragraphs with an anecdote or a quotation and end them with the topic sentence (the main point). And you should write some longer paragraphs—up to one-fourth of a page in length—though some of your paragraphs may consist of only two short sentences. Paragraphs of different lengths provide variety for the reader, as does changing the order of ideas.

Transitions   If paragraphs are the building blocks of writing, then transitions are the mortar. Transitions hold the writing together and help move the reader from paragraph to paragraph.

Transitions take several forms. Transition words such as *also, along with, furthermore,* and *especially* may be used to suggest that something is being added. Transitions may also summarize, using such words as *so, finally, therefore,* and *consequently.* You may use transition words to establish time: *now, then, afterwards, later, meanwhile, soon, frequently, never, always, occasionally.* Transition words may indicate cause and effect: *because, therefore.* They may suggest that alternatives should be considered: *yet, however, but, still, nevertheless, though, whereas.* Without transitions, writing becomes choppy and difficult to read. But when transitions are used properly, they are unobtrusive: the reader benefits from them but may not even be conscious that they are present.

Conclusion   The ending—the *conclusion*—ties your writing together. You should not stop writing as you might turn off a faucet; you owe it to your readers to provide a conclusion. The ending usually relates to the introduction. You reemphasize the important points you have made or perhaps rephrase any important position you have arrived at. You summarize for your readers what you have told them.

Title   Before you write the title of your paper, you should have written the first draft. Why is this? The reason is that you now know what the paper is about.

Titles should be written with three criteria in mind:

1   *Accuracy*—the title must accurately communicate what the paper is about.
2   *Attractiveness*—the words should catch the reader's eye.
3   *Conciseness*—the title should consist of a few carefully selected words.

Titles of academic papers often violate criterion 3—conciseness—because they are attempts to tell the reader everything that is in the paper. As a result, they become unnecessarily long, clumsy, and dense. Here are two examples:

An Analysis of Selected Background Factors as Possible Predictors and Correlates of General Life Satisfaction among Young Adults from Ten Rural Wisconsin Communities

Motivational Orientations of Adult Educational Participants: A Factor-Analytic Exploration of Houle's Typology.

Step 7: Revise and Rewrite

Write your paper from beginning to end before you consider revising and rewriting it. Nothing hinders creative writing more than constantly stopping, going back, and revising. Finish your piece, no matter how long it is, before you start a revision.

When you have finished the first draft, set your writing aside and allow it to rest for a minimum of 2 or 3 days or—better—a week. Time, more than anything else, has a way of making you objective. And you want to be as objective and as rigorous as possible, when you put on your editor's hat and begin reworking your paper, article, report, or thesis.

You should make at least two revisions. The first revision will focus on content. The second revision will focus on technical matters such as spelling, punctuation, and usage.

To begin the revision process, read your work from start to finish. Make no marks on it; correct no misspelled words; read only for meaning. Then, put your work aside and go for a walk. Ask yourself this fundamental question while you are strolling: What is this piece of writing about, in 10 words or less? When you return from your walk, write on a note card your 10-word (or shorter) statement of what your piece is about.

Several years ago, when I first began to write books, I went to New York City to meet an editor and discuss a book I was working on. The editor had a copy of my manuscript. When I arrived at the publisher's Manhattan offices, the editor, a bearded man in his sixties, looked me in the eye and said, "What is your book about, in a sentence?" I began to tell him what the book was about, but it took me several minutes. He said again, "Tell me in one sentence." "But I have to use several sentences," I replied. He stroked his beard and once again looked me straight in the eye: "If you can't tell someone what your book is about in a sentence or less, you don't know what it's about. Go home and decide what your book is about; then we'll talk again."

I have never forgotten that lesson. Do not begin revising anything you are writing until you have written a very brief, clear statement of what it is about. Place that statement where you can see it, and then begin revising. Remove everything you find that does not relate to your statement. If you have trouble tossing away pages of your hard work, set them aside. Establish a file for future reference; some day you may use the discarded material.

This first revision usually means cutting, cutting, and more cutting. Sometimes, you will find passages that are obviously incomplete; in these instances, you will need to go back to your research material and add. But if you are like most writers, you will cut far more often.

In the first revision, you should also examine the logic of the material. For example, would some of your topics work more logically if they came ahead of others? You may decide that entire sections of the work should be rearranged.

You are very likely to find that your first few pages are most heavily revised; in fact, generally, you will cut the first page or so. As difficult as it may have been to write those first few pages, often the real beginning of your paper appears later—sometimes you will even find the beginning at the end. If so, bring it forward. Remember that at the start, you were warming up to the project—finding your voice and becoming comfortable with the topic. All of us who write go through this. Seldom do we find our voice immediately. It often takes several paragraphs, and sometimes several pages.

After you have worked through the first revision (the revision for content), you are ready to go on to the second revision—the technical revision. At this stage, correct misspelled words, punctuation errors, and other problems that interfere with good writing. (The next section of this chapter discusses ways to improve your writing.) Bear in mind that good writing never calls attention to itself. It simply communicates, clearly and concisely, what you have to say.

Finally, set your revised paper aside for a day or so, and then read it once more, for both logic and technical errors. Almost always, on this final reading you will catch a few errors that had escaped your attention. One way to make sure that you will catch such errors is to read the piece aloud and listen to yourself. Your ears may hear what you eyes haven't seen.

IMPROVING YOUR WRITING

In this section, I give you a number of guidelines for improving your writing style. These will help you not only to avoid some errors of usage but also to write more clearly and gracefully.

Eliminate Unnecessary Words

Most writers use too many words. A carpenter doesn't use more boards than necessary to build a house; an artist doesn't use more brush strokes than necessary to paint a picture; an engineer doesn't use more beams than necessary to build a bridge. Likewise, a writer shouldn't use more words than necessary to communicate a message. This doesn't mean that writers should always use exceedingly short sentences or a stilted, choppy style. But a writer should make every word count.

Often, you can cross off many words in a sentence and not change the meaning. For example, in the following list the words in parentheses can be eliminated without affecting the meaning:

(absolutely) complete
are (as follows)
(at a) later (date)
big (in size)
blue (in color)
he (is a man who)
(do a) study (of) the outcomes
(it is) John (who) said
(the field of) psychology
(the process of) chemical analysis
(in order) to
join (together)
later (on)
repeat (again)
by (means of)
continue (on)
during (the course of)
(every) now and then
for (a period of) 2 weeks
(general) rule
(there are) many people (who)
(two equal) halves
was (completely) filled
(qualified) expert

You can often eliminate unnecessary words by choosing a single word that has the same meaning as several words. For example, consider the following list of phrases and the single words that can replace them:

Phrase	*Word*
on behalf of	for
along the lines of	like
as a result of	because
did not remember	forgot
at the present time	now
meets with my approval	I approve
on the subject of	about
prior to	before
in the amount of	for

Avoid Pseudo-Technical Words and Vogue Words

It's best to avoid pseudo-technical terms, which sound pretentious and are often graceless; and vogue words, which tend to be overused and are likely to go out of date quickly.

A *pseudo-technical word* often ends with the suffix *-al, -ize, -ive, -ion, -ate,* or *-ance.* In the literature on education, for instance, you can find *randomize, motivational, instrumental, dialectical,* and so on. Such words sound heavy and stuffy.

Another category of pseudo-technical words results from making a verb into a noun by adding *-ance* or *-ion.* For instance, *realize* becomes *realization, implement* becomes *implementation, negotiate* becomes *negotiation.* When you turn a verb into a noun, you must include another verb in the sentence, and that makes the sentence longer. For example, compare these two sentences; in the first, a verb has been turned into a noun, but in the second, it remains a verb: (1) "It was the realization of the committee that the stock should be sold." (2) "The committee realized that the stock should be sold." The first sentence has 13 words; the second has 9.

Vogue words are the popular jargon of the day. Some vogue words today are *impact* as a verb, *bottom line* (ultimate benefit), *interface* as a verb (it means connecting one or more elements, including bringing people together), and *having a dialogue* (this means only that people are talking to each other). Many vogue words are rather silly to begin with, and most are eventually worked to death.

Be Precise

Writing precisely involves both *choice of words* and *ordering of words.*

Look for the right word, not the "almost right" word. To find the right word, you must of course know exactly what you want to say. For instance, if you write, "Amy went home for the holidays," you are being imprecise. Did she drive home, fly home, take the train, or what?

Keep the order of words in mind. Keep related elements of a sentence together and place modifiers as close as possible to the words they are intended to modify. Consider the following sentence:

> Flying at half-mast, my heart grew sad when I saw the flag.

Surely this person's heart was not flying at half-mast. The sentence should read:

> My heart grew sad when I saw the flag flying at half-mast.

Here is another example:

> While climbing the stairs, a new idea popped into John's head.

Did you ever see an idea climb stairs? This sentence should read:

> While John was climbing the stairs, a new idea popped into his head.

Emphasize Nouns and Verbs

Nouns and verbs are the basis of good writing. Nouns provide things; verbs show activity. The more concrete nouns are and the more active verbs are, the more concise and powerful writing will be. Adjectives and adverbs are often necessary to make the meaning exact, but they should be used sparingly.

Verbs should picture or imply action. Overworked verbs with little sense of action include *is, are, was, were, have, has, had, want, seem,* and *get.*

The following sentences use "weak" verbs; note the suggestions for improvement:

> Students who study generally get better grades.

Here, substituting *earn* for *get* would make the sentence sharper:

> Students who study generally earn better grades.

Consider another example:

> Many urban areas have air pollution.

A better version would be:

> Many urban areas suffer from air pollution.

Suffer is a "stronger" verb than *have.*

Emphasize the Active Voice

Which of the following sounds better and is easier to understand, (1) "A cold was caught by Mary" or (2) "Mary caught a cold"? Version 1 is in the passive voice, version 2 in the active voice.

The answer should be obvious: version 1, the active voice, is better. But many writers tend to use the passive voice, particularly in academic writing. A good rule to follow is that you should use the active voice unless there is some specific reason for using the passive voice.

Use the passive voice when the person or thing doing the acting is unknown or when the person or thing being acted upon is more important than the actor. For instance, the actor is unknown in the following sentence: "Ten years ago the goals of American automobile manufacturers were clearly stated." In the following sentence, the person who is acted on is more important than the actor: "The mayor was hit by the noon train."

You may also want to use the passive voice to vary sentence structure within a paragraph; but in that case, be sure the sentences you choose are appropriate for the passive voice.

Keep the Average Length of Sentences Short

Short sentences are easier to understand than long sentences. What is a good length for a sentence? Eighteen to 20 words per sentence is a reasonable goal. But you should write some sentences that are longer than this and some that are shorter. Use variety.

When writing begins to average 30 words or more per sentence, it becomes increasingly difficult to read and understand. And longer sentences are also more difficult to write: you will often tangle ideas, misplace modifiers, and become confused about what you are trying to say.

Pay Attention to Tone and Rhythm

You can follow all the suggestions in this chapter for improving your writing and still sound lifeless and dull. Attention to tone and rhythm brings writing to life.

Tone evokes feeling. How you use words, develop paragraphs, and organize your thoughts creates a tone which in turn will create feelings in your readers. The attitude you take toward your readers also establishes tone. Whether your readers will continue reading often depends on the tone you develop; for example, if you talk down to readers, they will quickly note it and often resent it.

Rhythm helps make your writing more interesting. You can generate rhythm by varying sentence length and sentence construction. For example, as I noted above, occasionally you can use the passive voice for the sake of variety. You can also generate rhythm by using parallelism—which means using the same form for words, phrases, clauses, or sentences within a series. Sometimes you can create rhythm simply by omitting words. For instance, compare the following sentences:

On my farm I see deer, bear, muskrats, and sandhill cranes.

On my farm I see deer; big black shaggy bears; cute little brown and sometimes elusive muskrats; and the ever-popular, difficult to see, but often heard sandhill cranes.

The second sentence, although providing more information, lacks rhythm.

Another way to create rhythm is to arrange elements in pairs and series from simple to complicated. For instance, count the syllables in pairs or series of words, and arrange them so that those with fewer syllables appear before those with more syllables. If the number of syllables is the same, you may need to count the letters to place shorter words before longer ones. For example, write, "ferns, trees, and mountains," rather than "mountains, trees, and ferns"; or, "Akron, Chicago, and New York City," rather than "New York City, Akron, and Chicago."

Check tone and rhythm by reading your material aloud. Some words and phrases will strike your ear like fingernails on a chalkboard. The reason is very likely a problem with rhythm.

Use "I"

Don't be afraid to write "I." Too often, students write, "This researcher found...." Why not write, "I found..." if that is the case?

As a rule, don't use "we" when you mean "I." This is an artificial device, and there is always a danger that readers will take it literally. A reader who envisions some mysterious person or persons working with you will want to know who they are.

Avoid Sexism

The two sexes must be treated equally in writing, even though the English language, particularly in the use of pronouns, sometimes makes this a challenge. Here are some guidelines for avoiding sexism.[2]

Beware of Masculine Pronouns Do not use a masculine pronoun when you are referring to both males and females. It is inappropriate to write, "Everyone opened his book" or "A poet writes best when he..."

---

[2]These are based on McGraw-Hill's *Guidelines for Bias-Free Publishing*.

To avoid constructions like these, you can do the following:

1 Reword to eliminate gender-specific pronouns. Instead of writing, "The average American drinks his coffee black," write, "The average American drinks coffee black (*or,* drinks black coffee)."

2 Rewrite using the plural: "Most Americans drink their coffee black."

3 Rewrite using *you:* "If you are an average American, you drink your coffee black."

4 Use *he or she:* "The average American drinks his or her coffee black." This method can be useful, but remember that *he or she* should be used sparingly.

5 Use *one.* Instead of, "A person is greatly influenced by his parents," you can write, "One is greatly influenced by one's parents." Like *he or she, one* should be used sparingly.

6 Alternate male and female examples. "John, for instance, may...; but Mary may..." "Mr. A. is...; Ms. B. is..."

Some writers resort to devices which are better avoided. Don't use *he/she* or (even worse) *s/he;* these are awkward and obtrusive. And, on the whole, it is better not to alternate *he* and *she* when referring to hypothetical persons whose gender is not specified; that is, don't say "A lawyer is most effective when he..." and then, "But a doctor is most effective when she..." The devices suggested above are better for this kind of situation.

Avoid Stereotyping of Occupations   When using examples in writing, avoid stereotyping jobs. Women as well as men work as lawyers, doctors, truck drivers, professors, judges, bank presidents, members of Congress, accountants, engineers, pilots, plumbers, etc. Men as well as women are secretaries, nurses, teachers, etc.

Avoid Stereotyped Descriptions   When describing men or women, be careful to avoid stereotypes. Do not describe women in terms of physical attributes while describing men in terms of mental attributes or occupation. For example, it is improper to write, "Henry Harris is a shrewd lawyer, and his wife Ann is a striking brunette." More appropriately, you might write, "The Harrises are highly respected in their fields. Ann is an accomplished musician, and Henry is a shrewd lawyer." Or, "The Harrises are an interesting couple. Henry is a shrewd lawyer and Ann is very active in community affairs." Or, "The Harrises are a good-looking couple."

Don't Use Sexist Terms   When describing women, avoid sexist terms such as:

the fair sex
girls or *ladies* (when adult females are meant)
lady used as a modifier, as in *lady lawyer*
the little woman
sweet young thing
coed (as a noun)—write *student*

Treat Females as Participants   Write about women and girls as participants in actions, trends, and so on. For example, women should not be spoken about as possessions or adjuncts of men. Do not write, "Pioneers moved west, taking their wives and children with them." Rather, write, "Pioneer families moved west." Or "Pioneer men and women (*or* pioneer couples) moved west, taking their children with them."

Avoid Using *Man* for *Humanity*   The English language has a long history of using the word *man* to refer both to the male of the species and to humanity generally. You should probably avoid using *man* for *humanity*, though, because to many people, *man* connotes maleness. Some possible substitutes for *man* words are:

humanity, human beings, human race, people (not *man*)
primitive people or *peoples, primitive human beings, primitive men and women* (not *primitive man*)
human achievements (not *man's* achievements)
the best person for the job (not *the best man...*)
artificial, synthetic (not *man-made*)

Use Gender-Neutral Terms for Occupations   When referring to occupations, whenever possible use terms that can refer to both men and women. Here are some examples:

business executive, business manager (not *businessman*)
business people (not *businessmen*)
fire fighter (not *fireman*)
mail carrier, letter carrier (not *mailman*)
sales representative, salesperson, sales clerk (not *salesman*)

MECHANICS OF WRITING

In this section, we'll consider three important aspects of the mechanics of writing: use of word processors, manuscript preparation, and use of standard reference works.

Using a Word Processor

Many students today write all their assignments on a word processor; many others are considering switching from typewriters to word processors. What is involved in using a word processor?

A word processor is nothing more than a microcomputer (a computer with a keyboard, a screen, and disks—either floppy disks or a hard disk), and an appropriate program that tells the computer to work as a word processor. Several excellent word-processing programs are available, and they are constantly updated and improved. Consult the computer center of your college or university for information about using computers for word processing, as well as for recommended word-processing programs. Many computer centers also offer non-credit workshops on using microcomputers, word-processing software, and other software.

Advantages of Word Processors   I have yet to meet a student or any other writer who, once acquainted with a computer and a word-processing program, would go back to a typewriter. The advantages of a word processor for the writer are numerous.

Writing is physically easier with a word processor. You never have to stop in mid-thought to insert a new piece of paper. You don't need to throw a carriage, listen to the hum of an electric typewriter's motor, or hear the pounding of the keys of a manual typewriter. The only sound you hear is a faint click as you keyboard words.

Writing with a word processor is also faster. If you are able to type at, say, 40 words a minutes, I would predict that once you are comfortable with a word processor, your typing speed will accelerate to 50, 60, or even more words per minute.

But the greatest benefits of using a word processor come when you are revising. Never again will you need shears and tape—the time-honored way of moving material from place to place in a typewritten manuscript. Now you can move words, sentences, paragraphs, and entire pages from place to place with a few keystrokes. You can revise endlessly without ever having to retype the manuscript. You will probably print it only once—when you are satisfied that you have refined the writing as far as possible.

Word-processing programs also offer some special features. Most programs include dictionaries which allow you to search for misspelled words electronically. But a caution is in order here: No computer speller can tell when you should use *to*, *too*, or *two*; or when you should use *their* and *there*. You still must read your manuscript carefully. The computer speller, however, will quickly spot obvious typos, saving you both time and embarrassment. Many word-processing programs also include a thesaurus, so that you can look for "just the right word" with a few keystrokes.

Storage of material is very easy with a word processor. You can store your writing conveniently on disks for future use. If you eliminate a section from one of your papers, you might want to keep the material on disk. Later, you can easily work the discarded material into a new writing project, without retyping.

With the addition of a telephone modem, a device that allows your computer to "talk" with other computers, you can consult national computer databases (you should expect to pay for doing this). And on some campuses, your computer and modem will give access to your library's electronic card catalog, a great saving in time and energy.

Finally, some people, once they have learned how to write on a keyboard, find that the computer is a motivator. They like pushing buttons and watching words appear on a screen, and so they are eager to write.

Disadvantages of Word Processors   Despite their many advantages, word processors do have some drawbacks.

If you can't type, a word processor will be of little use to you. You may want to take typing lessons; in fact, some computer programs will teach you how to type while you are learning how to operate a computer.

Although the price of word processors has come down dramatically in the past decade, they still cost several times more than good typewriters.

Also, whereas a typewriter takes up only a small part of your desktop, a computer may take up the entire desk after you have arranged the keyboard, the box containing the microprocessor and disk drives, the screen, the printer, and the special paper for the printer. (However, there are lap-top computers—portable machines—which combine everything except the printer into one compact unit.)

A serious problem is incompatibility. Today, most computer equipment still works only with other equipment of the same brand. Printers are an exception; most of them are designed to operate with an array of computers. But even printers may require special ribbons (generally unique to a particular printer) and special continuous fanfold paper with holes in each side.

Some people say that word processors have another disadvantage: using them is so easy that writers tend to generate too much low-quality material. Learning how to revise and cut should solve this problem, though.

It is possible to lose material on a word processor by striking the wrong keys or mishandling your disks, or if there is a power failure or surge. Everyone will lose material a few times before learning how to take the necessary precautions. But thereafter, losing material for these reasons is rare—although computer "gremlins" sometimes strike, stealing valuable material.

Finally, some people have the odd idea that working with a word processor will lower the quality of their writing because it reduces suffering—the physical fatigue associated with writing in longhand, typing on a manual machine, and then cutting and pasting paragraphs together by hand. They think that quality emerges from suffering. This is nonsense. Physical suffering does not produce quality, and using a word processor does not reduce quality. A word processor simply makes it easier to capture, modify, and arrange ideas.

Of course, it's important to point out that using a word processor will not ensure quality either. All it does—to repeat—is make the *act* of writing easier. The quality of the writing still depends on the writer.

Preparing Manuscripts

Format   A manuscript should be typed or printed double-spaced, on only one side of the paper, with a 1½-inch margin at the left and a 1-inch margin at the right and on the top and bottom of the paper.

Use 8½- by 11-inch white paper, of good quality. If you are typing, don't use "erasable" paper; though it is handy to use, it smudges easily.

Make sure that your typewriter or printer has a fresh ribbon.

Footnotes   Various disciplines, departments, and publishers have different requirements for footnotes. When you are preparing a paper, you should always be clear about such requirements, and adhere to them. The following general comments should also be useful.

Two important aspects of footnoting are *placement* of footnotes and *style* of footnotes.

For displaying footnotes—placement—four systems are commonly used:

1 *At the bottom of the page, numbered,* with the corresponding number appearing in the body of the manuscript.
2 *At the end each chapter or section, numbered.* Numbers in the body of the manuscript refer to numbered notes at the end of the chapter or section.
3 *At the end of the work* (arranged by chapters or sections if the work has them), *numbered.* Numbers in the body of the manuscript refer to section-by-section numbered notes at the end of the work. For each chapter or section, footnote numbering starts with 1.

4 *At the end of the work, arranged alphabetically by author or source.* In the body of the manuscript are parenthetical citations consisting of author's name, date, and page reference.

For writers using a word processor, systems 1 and 2 are nearly automatic—the computer even keeps track of the numbers.

Footnote *styles* vary widely, but one standard form for books is:

1. J.R. Kidd, *How Adults Learn,* Association Press, New York, 1973, pp. 3–8.

A standard footnote style for an article is:

1. Shelia Tobias, "Math Anxiety," *M.S.,* Vol. V., No. 1, Sept. 1976, pp. 56–59.

Bibliographies As with footnotes, the style for bibliography entries varies greatly in different fields, different college and university departments, and different publications. Always check, and follow, any rules that may apply to you when you are preparing a paper, a report, etc.

Here is one widely used style for a book:

Lauffer, Armand: *The Practice of Continuing Education in the Human Services,* McGraw-Hill, New York, 1977.

Here is a common style for an article:

Gillespie, Gilbert W., Jr.: "Using Word Processor Macros for Computer-Assisted Qualitative Analysis," *Qualitative Sociology,* Vol. 9, No. 3, Fall 1986, pp. 283–292.

Using Standard References

The following are standard general references for writers.

College desk dictionary, such as *Webster's New Collegiate Dictionary.*

Thesaurus, such as *Webster's Collegiate Thesaurus.*

Apps, Jerold W: *Improving Your Writing Skills,* Follett, Chicago, Ill., 1982. This is a guidebook designed for systematically improving your writing skills.

Atchity, Kenneth: *A Writer's Time,* Norton, New York, 1986. This is an excellent guide for planning a major writing project. It includes ideas on how to do library research and how to keep records.

Strunk, William, Jr., and E.B. White: *The Elements of Style,* 3d ed., Macmillan, New York, 1979. This should be on every writer's shelf. It includes rules of usage, elementary principles of composition, and words and expressions commonly misused.

Following are some references on grammar and style:

Fowler, H.W.: *A Dictionary of Modern English Usage,* 2d ed., rev. by Sir Ernest Gowers, Oxford University Press, New York, 1965. This is the most authoritative source for questions of usage and style.

A Manual of Style, 13th ed., University of Chicago Press, Chicago, Ill., 1982. If your instructor asks you to follow the "Chicago Manual," this is the book he or she means.

Publication Manual of the American Psychological Association, 3d. ed., American Psychological Association (APA), Washington, D.C., 1988. A style often required for psychological papers is the APA style; this book presents it.

Turabian, Kate: *A Manual for Writers of Term Papers, Theses, and Dissertation,* 4th ed., University of Chicago Press, Chicago, Ill., 1973.

Turabian, Kate: *Student's Guide for Writing College Papers,* University of Chicago Press, Chicago, Ill., 1976. Both of Turabian's books are excellent guides for students. They give particular attention to headings, footnotes, and bibliographies. They also include information on choosing a topic, collecting material, and planning and writing papers.

SUMMARY

- One good process for writing term papers, reports, theses, and dissertations, has seven steps: (1) deciding on a topic, (2) translating the topic into questions, (3) establishing a timetable, (4) researching the topic, (5) developing an outline, (6) beginning to write, and (7) revising and rewriting.
- To make your writing more readable, eliminate unnecessary words, avoid pseudo-technical and vogue words, be precise, emphasize nouns and verbs, emphasize the active voice, keep the average length of sentences short, pay attention to tone and rhythm, use "I," and avoid sexism.
- Many students use word processors—computers with word-processing programs. Word-processing equipment makes many writing procedures easier, particularly revising. But word processors also have some disadvantages.
- In preparing a manuscript, use the format, footnote style, and bibliographic style of the appropriate discipline, department, or publication—or the general guidelines and styles described in this chapter.
- Several standard references for writers are helpful; these include general references and works on grammar and style.

10

SHARPENING YOUR SPEAKING SKILLS

Of all the fears people have—disease, financial disaster, heights, and so on—speaking to a group ranks near the top. Yet nearly everyone, from time to time, will be asked to make a speech.

Students often have this opportunity. You may be asked to report to your class on a project. You may be asked to speak to a large group as a representative of an organization to which you belong. You may have to give an oral seminar report. You will probably be a part of many groups in which you are expected to contribute actively to discussions. And you may be called on to give impromptu presentations when you do not have time to prepare a formal speech. All these are examples of public speaking, although they differ considerably from one another.

THE FORMAL SPEECH

In some ways, preparing a formal speech is like preparing a written paper, but there are also major differences. For one thing, if readers don't understand some point you've tried to make in a paper, they can reread the section; people listening to a speech can't do this, and so as a speaker you must be absolutely clear. Also, a speaker—even more than a writer—must keep people interested; this means developing not only interesting content but an interesting style of presentation.

Planning a Speech

In planning a speech, you should be concerned with three things: (1) the situation, (2) the audience, and (3) the actual content of the speech.

Situation When you agree to give a speech to a group, you should find out several things (probably from the person who has invited you):

What is the purpose of the meeting?
Where and when are you expected to speak?
How long a speech is expected?
What else is on the program, preceding you and following you?
What specific points is your speech expected to cover?

Audience You should also find out certain things about your audience:

How large is the group expected to be?
What is the age range and the proportion of men and women?
What is the audience's knowledge of your topic?

Learning about your audience—like learning about the situation—is an important preliminary step in preparing your speech: the context of your speech is a vital consideration. Yet many speakers arrive late, give unexpectedly long or short speeches, and talk down to the audience or talk over its head. Only *after* you have the necessary preliminary information should you start planning the content of your speech.

Content Before rushing off to the library and doing a computer data search on the topic of your speech, sit down and consider what you already know about it. You may surprise yourself; in fact, a few minutes of self-reflection may provide you with the main topics or ideas you want to cover in your speech.

Once you've noted what you know about the topic, you are ready to search for additional material. Generally, this will take the form of support for the major topics you have outlined: it can include quotations, examples, definitions, and statistics (but use numbers sparingly; they tend to put listeners to sleep).

Stories from your own experience can also provide support. And such anecdotes will add more dimensions to your speech: they personalize your comments, they can often give emotional depth, and they are usually interesting to audiences—people will listen to a story above all else. Weaving in an appropriate story from your personal experience (it must be germane to the topic) will often help you to capture even the poorest listeners.

Preparing the Speech

A speech has three parts: (1) introduction, (2) body, and (3) conclusion. You should usually allot your speaking time as follows:

Introduction—10 percent

Body—80 percent

Conclusion—10 percent

Introduction   The introduction should capture the audience's attention, and prepare your listeners for what you have to say. It also gives the audience a chance to get used to your voice and speaking style before you begin the major part of your presentation. This is important, since an audience has to work hard to hear and understand what you are trying to communicate.

Include an attention-getter in your introduction. This can be a startling quotation related to your topic, a provocative question, a relevant story from your own experience, or impressive or startling statistics.

The introduction may also include a brief outline of what is to come. For instance, after the attention-getter you might note the major topics you plan to cover in your speech. The best advice I know for a speaker is this: Tell people what you're going to say; then tell them; and finally tell them what you've said.

There are some things to avoid in an introduction. For instance, many speakers start off weakly: "Tonight I'm going to talk to you about the subject of adult illiteracy in this country." But then they go on to a strong remark: "Did you know that 28 million adults can't read the label on a bottle of poison?" How much better this introduction would have if the speaker had started with the second sentence!

Avoid telling a joke or a humorous anecdote that has no real relevance to your topic. Many speakers do this, confusing or even alienating the audience rather than preparing their hearers for what is to come.

Above all, never begin a speech with an apology. Don't say that you really aren't very knowledgeable about the topic, that you didn't have enough time to prepare your speech, on the like. The audience isn't interested in excuses. Your listeners want to hear what you have to say.

Body   Arrange your topics in logical order, and for each topic develop the supporting information you plan to use.

Think carefully about organization, remembering that there are some considerations other than strict logic. For instance, if two of your points are quite complicated to explain, don't present them one after the other. Also, if you have an excellent personal story that could logically appear at more than one point, present it toward the middle of your speech, where it will refresh your audience.

You may want to write your speech out, word for word. Sometimes, in fact, you will have to do this, as when you are asked to provide a written copy to be included in proceedings of a meeting. But writing your speech does *not* mean that you will read it to the audience—as you will see below.

If you do not actually write your full speech, in most instances you will still want to make extensive notes for each of the main topics. You might write approximately 60 percent of your speech in the form of notes, which will provide you with cues while you are delivering it. Of course, quotations should be written verbatim, and their sources should be noted.

Conclusion   At the end of your speech, do not merely say "Thank you" and sit down. You will have not *concluded* your speech but simply stopped it.

To create a true conclusion, summarize the main points of the speech. Then, end with a quotation, an anecdote, a question, or a call for action.

Visuals   As you plan your speech, plan for whatever visuals you will use. For example, if you are talking to a large group and an overhead projector is available, you have a very useful way of reinforcing your speech with visuals.

I use overhead projectors extensively when I speak. With a computer, it is easy to make overhead visuals that will project well to audiences of up to 200 or 300 people. (One caution is in order here: Make sure that the letters or numbers on each visual are large enough to be seen by every-one, even people in the back row. Typewritten copy is not large enough, but many speakers make visuals using it. These speakers would be more effective without any visuals; most of the audience are straining so hard to see the visual that they can't follow the speech.) For a 40-minute speech, I use no more than five or six visuals. The first visual lists the major topics I will cover. Succeeding visuals show words that reinforce each major point. Finally, the last visual, presented at the end, lists the major points I have covered. Often, I "mask" all of a visual except the part I am talking about, using a blank sheet of paper that I pull down as I move to the next point. I arrange for the overhead projector to be placed next to the microphone so that I can change the visuals easily as I talk.

Slides are also useful and appealing as visuals. But if your speech can be illustrated with slides—say, if you are talking about historical build-ings in your state—be careful not to spend valuable time describing what a slide has already illustrated.

Practicing the Speech

Practice your speech standing up, and go through it just as you plan to give it. Make sure to practice with your visuals so that you become com-fortable using them.

Go through your speech once; then, go through it a second time, timing it and tape-recording it. Listening to the tape will help you identify rough transitions, weak arguments, and vague explanations.

Do not memorize your speech. And don't be concerned if your speech doesn't come out exactly the same each time you practice it: that is to be expected when you're talking from notes.

Do practice to make sure that you are covering all the points you intend to cover and including all the evidence you plan to include.

Practicing helps you remember the ideas in your speech and gives you confidence. It also helps you figure out the mechanics of dealing with visuals.

Delivering the Speech

Arrive at the auditorium at least 20 minutes early so that whoever is running the event will know that you have indeed arrived, and to check on the arrangements (overhead projector and screen in place, microphone in place and working, etc.). These minutes before the speech are valuable, but they become sheer agony for many speakers: this is the time when stage fright hits.

Controlling Stage Fright   The symptoms of stage fright are well known: your mouth is dry; the palms of your hands sweat; your heart pounds; your knees may shake. No matter how many speeches you give, some of these symptoms will probably always appear.

Stage fright is not necessarily completely bad. The tenseness you feel as you walk to the podium gives you an edge—a little extra that will serve you well as you speak. Famous speakers say that if they do not feel butterflies in the stomach as they stand up, they become concerned about the quality of the speech.

But to be effective, stage fright must be managed. First, you should not let it get out of hand. Remember that you are not the first person, nor will you be the last, to have the jitters before a speech; thousands feel as you do. Remember also that to your audience you will appear far more confident than you feel. (If you don't believe this, watch yourself give a speech on videotape.) It also helps to bear in mind that your audience wants you to succeed—and that the more you speak, the easier it will become (the jitters don't disappear, but you deal with them better).

Second, you should follow some practical tips for managing stage fright. Breathe deeply before you walk to the stage, and try to relax completely, not thinking about your speech. (You might think about your summer vacation, or some other pleasant experience.) When you begin talking, focus on what you are saying. As you talk and hear your voice, your stage fright will slowly disappear.

Third, the most important way to control stage fright is to prepare your speech so well that you feel confident about its content and your ability to deliver it.

Tips for Speakers   Following are some useful tips for delivering a speech.

Tip 1: Get set to speak   Get set before starting to speak. Place your notes on the lectern, look out over the audience, make sure that the microphone is adjusted correctly, and make sure that your visuals are in order.

Tip 2: Establish eye contact   Begin talking without referring to your notes, establishing eye contact with your audience. Look at one person for, say, 2 to 3 seconds; then look at another. Move your gaze around the room to give the impression that you are talking to each individual person. Continue making this kind of eye contact as you go on talking.

Tip 3: Don't fidget   If you usually tug on an ear, rub your head, stand on one foot, or run your fingers up and down the edges of the lectern, work at changing your behavior. Watching yourself speak on videotape is an excellent way of spotting these bad habits, which detract from your message.

Tip 4: Speak clearly   Speak slowly and distinctly, in a voice slightly louder than normal. If you are speaking to a group of about 50 and do not have a microphone, you may have to project your voice to be heard. Always make sure that everyone can hear you. If you have any doubt, ask as a part of your introductory comments.

Tip 5: Vary pitch and speed   Vary the pitch of your voice and the speed at which you speak. If you speak each sentence in exactly the same way, you will soon lull your audience to sleep.

Tip 6: Use gestures naturally   To learn about your use of gestures, again, watch yourself speak on a video. Are you a talking post who never lifts an arm, or are you a windmill, flailing your arms in all directions? Use of gestures should obviously be somewhere between these two extremes. As you become more relaxed as a speaker, you'll discover that your gesturing becomes more relaxed.

Don't write in your notes, ''Move arm here'' or the like. A gesture produced in this way will appear as artificial to the audience as it looks on paper.

Tip 7: Speak in phrases   Practice speaking in phrases rather than single words. Phrases are clusters of words that communicate the ideas you want to communicate. Concentrating on phrases also helps your audience grasp what you are saying.

Let's say that your speech includes the following sentence:

From national statistics we can see that adult illiteracy continues to increase in this country, and at a phenomenal rate.

Here is one way to divide this sentence into phrases; the slash marks (/) indicate divisions:

From national statistics / we can see that adult illiteracy continues to increase in this country / and at a phenomenal rate.

Obviously, you have considerable choice in how you divide passages into phrases, depending on what you want to emphasize. A rule to follow is: The larger the audience, the more phrases. (The more phrases you have, the more pauses there will be in your presentation, and thus the more time the audience has to think about what you are saying.)

Tip 8: Avoid "fillers" Avoid saying "ah" or making other sounds during pauses. Speakers who do this often don't know they are doing it, and you may not know it either unless it is called to your attention.

Tip 9: Don't read your speech Do not read your speech unless it is a prepared statement that must be spoken exactly as you have it on paper. Few people can read well enough to keep an audience's attention. And further, it is extremely difficult to maintain eye contact and manipulate visuals while you are reading.

Tip 10: When you've finished... When you've finished your conclusion, don't add an apology such as, "I've gone over my time, and I'll sit down before I keep on going." Even worse is completing your conclusion and then remembering some related topic and launching into it. Once you have prepared your audience for the end of your speech, they will hear little if anything you say about an additional topic—and with every additional sentence you speak, your risk of alienating them increases.

For a formal presentation, when you have finished your concluding remarks, remain standing at the lectern or table, say nothing, and do nothing. Wait for applause. Acknowledge it. Then sit down.

Tip 11: If there are questions... If you are expected to respond to questions from the audience, keep your place at the table or lectern, or resume it. Generally, the chairperson of the meeting will decide how much time to allot for questions and answers.

OTHER SPEAKING SITUATIONS
Group Discussions

In nearly all your courses you will have opportunities to speak in a group. Even large lecture classes usually have discussion sections, and some courses, particularly at the graduate level, are entirely in group-discussion format.

Problems with Group Discussions Some students have problems in group discussions. Students occasionally say to me, "I want to participate, but by the time I've thought through what I want to say, the discussion has moved to another topic." Or, "I'm just not comfortable speaking in a group. I don't want to sound stupid."

Of course, some students have the opposite problem: they want to take over the discussion and go on talking, whether or not they are saying anything relevant. Sometimes I describe these students as people who continue talking in the hope that they will think of something to say.

Tips for Speaking in a Group Following are some tips that should help you if you have difficulty speaking in groups.

Tip 1: Be open Be open to what is being discussed. Remember:

There is nothing so depressing as a group of people sitting like zombies while another is speaking. Response and reaction are essential to cooperative thinking and good interpersonal relations. When you agree, show it with a nod or verbal assent. When you disagree, show it. When you have a question, ask it. When you have a feeling of warmth for others, communicate it with a word, smile or gesture.[1]

A topic may not interest you at first, but as you become involved—if you allow yourself to become involved—you will often be surprised at how interested you become.

Tip 2: Listen Listen to what is going on. A common error is to spend so much time thinking about your own contribution that you forget to follow the discussion.

Tip 3: Accept some responsibility for the outcome Accept your share of responsibility for the success of a discussion group. The discussion leader is not solely responsible. You can help the group succeed by raising procedural questions from time to time, such as, "It seems to me we are discussing X. Do others have this impression?" Or you could ask a question about someone else's comments. Sometimes a question about how various ideas relate to each other can help a group move ahead.

Tip 4: Stick to one point When you contribute, make one point rather than several. You are not participating in a group discussion if you give a speech ranging over several topics. Keep your comments brief and concise.

Tip 5: Relate your point to the context When you contribute, relate your comment to what preceded it. State your point, and state how it relates to the discussion so far.

---

[1]John K. Brilhart, *Effective Group Discussion,* 2d. ed., Brown, Dubuque, Iowa, 1974, p. 57.

Tip 6: Don't try to impress   Avoid trying to impress people. Particularly, don't flaunt your vocabulary. You will only slow down, and perhaps confuse, the discussion. Remember that the purpose of a group discussion is for everyone in the group to learn and to teach. The purpose is not for you to show off how well you understand the lesson or how well you are able to express yourself. A little humility often helps to move a discussion along.

Impromptu Speeches

You arrive at a meeting prepared to sit and listen. But the chairperson of the meeting greets you with, "Jane, I'd like you to share what you've found about X when we get to that place in the program."

Your immediate response is likely to be panic, because you will have only a few minutes to prepare. But rather than worry about how poorly you may do, use the time wisely. Decide on the main points you want to cover, support those points with whatever specific information you remember, and include an anecdote if you can think of an appropriate one. Remember that everyone knows you haven't had time to prepare and that everyone is on your side.

When it's time to speak, take your time. Present your points and your support calmly. Don't ramble, and don't apologize for your presentation. You will probably be surprised at how well you do. And the next time you are asked to speak in a situation like this, you will be more confident.

If you are asked to speak without any preparation time at all, the task is more difficult. But try to focus on two or three major points, and jot them down if necessary.

Seminar Reports

Many of you will enroll in seminars—courses in which each student is responsible for preparing certain material to present to the group.

Often, students in seminars are required both to prepare a written report and to make an oral presentation to the group. The content of the written report and the oral report will be the same. But the presentation should vary considerably. Some students simply read segments of the written report to the group—an unfortunate approach, for even the most interesting topic suffers from being read. A better strategy is to develop an oral presentation from the written report, following the procedures suggested above for giving a formal speech. Don't overlook the possibility of using visuals in a seminar report, even if your visual is nothing more than an outline on a chalkboard of the major points.

Class Projects

In many courses the instructor will divide the class into small groups of two or three people and each group will be required to report to the entire class on a class project. Class projects like this may seem easier than giving a speech on your own, since you will be supported by one or two others. But in fact a group presentation is generally more difficult than an individual speech.

For one thing, you have a double challenge. As always, you need to prepare what you want to say and how you want to say it; but you must also mesh your material with what your partners are planning to say and do.

Second, a common problem is finding out-of-class time for the group to meet—and such meetings are essential both to plan who will have responsibility for what and, later, to practice the actual presentation.

However, although they are challenging, group presentations can be exciting ways of communicating ideas. Each person can of course simply give a speech, following the usual procedures and making sure that the speeches relate to each other. But it is also possible to use other techniques, such as panel discussions, dialogues, and role-playing. If your class is not too large, it may also be possible to involve other class members in the presentation through a group discussion or some other activity. Remember that having three members in your group does not mean that you have to give three separate speeches. Try something more creative.

SUMMARY

- All students will from time to time give speeches. Some speeches will be formal, prepared talks; some will be in group discussions; some will be impromptu; some will be seminar reports or class projects.
- Preparing a formal speech involves planning—learning about the situation and the audience, developing the content of the speech (developing an introduction, body, and conclusion), and planning for visuals.
- Tips for delivering a speech include managing stage fright, speaking slowly and distinctly, avoiding disruptive mannerisms, varying the pitch of your voice and your speed of speaking, gesturing naturally, speaking in phrases, avoiding saying "ah" during pauses, and concluding properly.
- Speaking in a group discussion requires being open, listening, sharing responsibility, making one point at a time, relating what you say to the context, and not trying to impress.

11

THINKING:
THOUGHTS ABOUT THOUGHT

At this point in your schooling, you have learned many techniques for accumulating information—and for successfully repeating it back on examinations. But if you are typical, you have spent far too much time learning how to memorize and far too little time learning how to think. You have spent more time accumulating information than learning how to use it. And much of the information you have accumulated will probably soon be obsolete—perhaps only a few years after you've earned your degree. Inventors, scientists, and researchers will continue to make old facts obsolete, at ever-increasing rates. You may soon find that it is hard to keep up with information about your own work, and all but impossible to keep up with information in other fields.

Learning how to think is very different from learning how to acquire information. Learning how to think includes learning how to solve problems, create new ideas, and examine things critically. It is a lifelong skill that will never go out of date. Once you have learned how to think, you will always be able to deal with new information—even to manage the onslaught of information in today's world.

This chapter is about improving your thinking. I will explore the nature of thought, describe several categories of thinking, examine some blocks to effective thinking, and then discuss three specific approaches to effective thinking: problem solving, critical thinking, and creative thinking.

THE NATURE OF THINKING

Although no one really knows what happens in the brain when thinking is going on, most people agree that thinking is a natural process like eating, breathing, or observing—and that it is possible to improve your thinking skills.

What is thinking? According to Rudolf Flesch, it is the manipulation of memories.[1] We could also say that thinking is the process of using our experiences and information.

We think with words, which are symbols for our ideas. One thing we do when we think, according to Flesch, is to "detach ideas from one set of words and attach them to another."[2] In this way, our thinking focuses on ideas and doesn't become bound up with words. Some of us also think with pictures, shapes, and textures and may or may not translate these into words.

CATEGORIES OF THINKING

One way to consider thinking is to focus on the various kinds of thinking each of us does.

Daydreaming

When we allow our thoughts to drift and ramble, we are daydreaming. Some people refer to this process as *free association of ideas*. Generally, daydreaming is centered on yourself—what you plan to do on vacation, how well you have handled some situation, what you will do when you complete your degree, etc. Daydreaming is usually considered pleasurable; it is something one does while waiting for a bus or attending a boring meeting.

Defensive Thinking

Defensive thinking is sometimes called *rationalizing*—that is, finding "good" reasons for some action or decision. When we think defensively (and all of us do it at times), we seek explanations for our own doings. We may buy cars loaded with gadgets that reduce gas mileage and add to the purchase price; then we think about ways to "defend our decision" when talking with friends. I might say I've always wanted a car with adjustable seats and a sun roof. You might say that all your friends have cars like this, and it just seemed time for you to have one.

---

[1]Rudolf Flesch, *The Art of Clear Thinking*, Harper and Row, New York, 1951, p. 8.
[2]Ibid., p. 49.

We can think defensively not only about our actions but also about what we believe, and indeed about everything that has value because of its relationship to us. We tend to think defensively about decisions we've made, beliefs we hold, and possessions we have that may be criticized by others.

Snap Judgments

From time to time, you need to make decisions quickly. Can you cross the street before an oncoming car arrives? Do you accept an invitation for a party on a night when you planned to study? In many situations like these, you must make up your mind immediately.

Daily life requires thousands of snap judgments. Whether they are trivial or important, each of us must make them, and quickly. Sometimes, as we gather additional information, we may discover that a snap judgment was wrong. If the decision is one we can change, we do so. If it is not, we go on, realizing that life requires us to keep making decisions, whether we are prepared or not.

Problem Solving

Problem solving is sometimes called *rational thinking*. It is coupled with observation and experimentation and is basic to scientific method. Later in this chapter, I will describe in some depth how to do problem solving.

Creative Thinking

Creative thinking is sometimes referred to as *intuitive thinking, lateral thinking,* or simply *creativity.* I'll also discuss creative thinking later in this chapter.

Critical Thinking

Critical thinking involves becoming aware of contexts; of values; of beliefs and assumptions, such as those of writers; of human actions; and of operations of agencies and institutions. As with problem solving and creative thinking, I devote a section to critical thinking later in the chapter.

BLOCKS TO EFFECTIVE THINKING

Problem solving, creative thinking, and critical thinking are the most effective forms of thought, but they are not used as often as they could be or should be. What prevents people from thinking effectively?

Lack of Time

You've probably heard people say, "I don't have time to think." This is not necessarily just an idle comment. Some people have become so busy living, and making a living, that they scarcely have a spare moment to breathe deeply, let alone think deeply.

Thinking does require time. Although it is possible to think and do other things at the same time, usually such thinking takes the form of daydreaming—or defensive thinking, particularly if we are worried about some action we've recently taken.

Groupthink

If you have children, you've no doubt heard them say again and again, "Buy this for me because everyone else has one." The herd influence, sometimes known as *groupthink,* is at work here.

As adults, we are also susceptible to the herd instinct, perhaps even more so than children. Being different from the rest of the crowd is not well accepted in our society. We have a long history of intolerance toward people who are even slightly different—people who dress differently, people whose lifestyles are unusual, and so on. We have developed a culture based to a great extent on "group thought"; what interests or pleases the majority of people is considered "right." By and large, television programming follows this philosophy, as do mass-circulation magazines, clothing designers, and fast-food establishments.

Effective thinking can be blocked when an individual fears or hesitates to consider something that he or she believes will run counter to group norms. In extreme cases, a person will not do *anything* that seems opposed to group thought.

Multipurposeness

We live in a "multipurpose" age. Adjustable wrenches allow us to tighten several sizes of nuts; adjustable caps fit all heads; stretch socks fit all feet. And we've carried the idea of "multipurposeness" into the world of thoughts and ideas.

Do you have a problem? Here is an assortment of possible solutions. Find one that comes close to solving your problem, and use it. Or keep a variety of solutions stored in a computer. When you have a problem, punch it into the computer and wait for an answer to clatter out. It's simple, and you don't have to do any thinking. But when you become a searcher and a selector, you may actually forget how to think.

Reliance on Authorities

Many people, including many students, have the notion that to answer a question you need only examine information from some authority who has already dealt with the topic, find the answer, and copy it.

It is tempting for a student to copy fifty paragraphs from fifty "authorities," and easier than thinking up an original answer to a problem or a question. What sometimes happens in this case is that the student's paper is little more than one huge footnote, with a few *ands* and *buts* thrown in. Students aren't entirely to blame for this unthinking approach to writing papers. Many instructors are more interested in how many authorities their students can cite than in whether the students are able to do any original thinking. It is also true that some students do have original ideas but lack the confidence to share them and so hide behind the cloak of an authority. Thus as a result of mental laziness, pressure, or timidity, many students go through school searching for authorities to quote in their papers and speeches and never once generate an idea or thought they can claim as their own.

The writings of authorities are of course important, but what students do with these writings is even more important.

Fear of Solitude

Most of us think best when we are alone, but our society frowns on being alone. We glorify groups. If you prefer to spend time by yourself, you are considered "different." In your free moments, you are expected to do things with others—to interact and interrelate. As a result, many people have developed a fear of solitude.

If it looks as though you might be alone next weekend, for instance, you will probably plan your time to make sure that others are around—or your friends will plan to spend time with you because they feel sorry that you will be alone. You are thus prevented from experiencing even a few hours of solitude—though thinking is generally most active and productive then.

Lack of Openness

"Don't bother me with the facts; my mind's made up" may be a cliché, but it is a good description of lack of openness. A thoughtful person—an effective thinker—is open to new ideas, new problems, and new situations and doesn't always insist that a preconceived answer is right.

We all have opinions and biases. Being open requires us to put these opinions and biases on hold and try to take perspectives that may be different from our own. If we can't be open, our personal views can confine our thinking to a sort of "tunnel vision." Such thinking seldom moves us beyond where we are now.

Problems with Vocabulary

An insufficient vocabulary can sometimes block our thinking—as can a vocabulary that is overly reliant on essentially useless words. Jargon, catchphrases, and impressive-sounding but imprecise words are blocks to clear thinking.

Some perfectly good words, such as *relevance* and *impact,* have become jargon and have lost their original meaning and usefulness. Some words become divorced from the ideas they originally represented, assuming new meanings. For example, most people will say that they know what *democracy* means. But then if you ask three people to define it, there is a high probability that you'll get three very different answers.

To think effectively, we must overcome our tendency to use words for which we don't have precise definitions. Using words imprecisely leads to fuzzy thinking, and fuzzy thinking results in foggy speaking and vague writing.

Rote Learning

You've probably learned to memorize quite well as part of your formal education. But memorizing is not thinking. Thinking is what you do with information once you have it in your head.

THREE APPROACHES TO EFFECTIVE THINKING

In this section I discuss, in some depth, three approaches to effective thinking: problem solving, critical thinking, and creative thinking.

Problem Solving

How Does Problem Solving Work?   According to John Dewey,[3] problem solving consists of four steps:

1 Stating a problem (in question form)
2 Analyzing the problem situation
3 Generating possible solutions
4 Testing and verifying the solution or solutions

Below are introductions to each of these steps, followed by a problem exercise for you to work through.

[3]John Dewey, *How We Think,* Heath, Boston, Mass., 1933.

A Process for Problem Solving Let's go through the problem-solving process, step by step.

Step 1: State the problem What are you trying to find out? What do you want to know? What is wrong and needs correcting? For some people, stating the problem is the most difficult part of the entire process of problem solving. In facing a situation, they sense that something is wrong, but they are unable to ask a precise question—and until they can ask a question precisely, they don't know what answer to seek.

Two rather simple considerations can often help us in stating a problem, however. First, the words *why*, *what*, and *how come* are very useful. Second, it is important to be as concise and specific as possible in formulating questions. Both of these strategies are ways of sharpening our focus.

For instance, consider the following situation. You are a corporate executive and are reviewing your firm's gross revenues for a 5-year period: $45 million in 1985, $68 million in 1986, $106 million in 1987, $156 million in 1988, and $160 million in 1989. What questions might you ask after reviewing these figures? You might conclude that no questions need to be asked, that no problem exists: the company has grown steadily, even impressively, over these 5 years. But notice that each year the gross revenue has been about 50 percent more than that of the previous year, except for 1989, when it was nearly the same as in 1988. You would probably decide, after noting this, that a problem does exist—a question does need to be asked. You might ask, "*What* are we seeing here? Is this the beginning of a downward trend?"

Step 2: Analyze the situation Once you've stated a question or questions, the next step in problem solving is to find out as much as you can about the situation. In our example, what are the facts? What was the nature of the economy in 1989? What changes did your competitors experience? Has your firm grown too rapidly, so that it must now go through a period of reappraisal? Questions to ask during the analysis phase include *what*, *where*, and *to what extent?*

Analyzing the situation also includes identifying sources of information. Some questions to ask about sources of information are: "Who can help me with answers?" "What databases might include facts I need?" "How much of the information I need may be at my fingertips but may have been overlooked simply because it is so readily available?"

As you search for specific information, you must throttle your impulse to jump at a solution, using the first information you've found. Force yourself to obtain as much information as you possibly can about the problem, and withhold judgment until you are satisfied that you've analyzed the situation carefully and precisely.

Step 3: Generate possible solutions Once you've stated questions and analyzed a situation, you are ready to look for possible solutions to the problem. This step in the process can be quite creative. Force yourself to identify possible solutions beyond those that "look right" at first glance. And be careful about accepting ready-made answers out of hand. If someone else has worked on a similar problem, and the answers to the problem sound as if they would work in your situation, determine how similar the situation really is to yours. Ready-made solutions must be tested in your situation—which leads us to the next step.

Step 4: Test and verify solutions After possible solutions to your problem have been generated, test and verify them to find out if they work— that is, if they answer the questions you raised in step 1.

Let's go back to our example. You might suggest that the growth in profits fell off during 1989 because of a sluggish economy. But to check the accuracy of that answer, you would have to examine the gross profit figures for similar businesses, the stock market history during the year, and so on.

It should be pointed out that in this example no one answer is likely to be the solution. With problems of this nature, multiple answers must be considered. Nevertheless, no matter how many answers seem appropriate, they must all be checked and verified. Such information would support or cast doubt on the answer.

An Example of Problem Solving Here is a practical example that requires problem solving.[4]

RATIONAL THINKING

A fire had swept through a vast section of forest, and a ranger had rapidly assembled twenty-seven volunteer firefighters. He divided them into groups and, working quickly, gave each group a two-way radio.

"A helicopter will patrol the area," he announced. "If you get in trouble, radio the 'copter and it will pick you up." Then each team was instructed in the use of the radio.

Later, when the fire was extinguished, one of the groups (consisting of three men) was missing. After a 2-day search, their charred bodies were found in a valley.

1 *Statement of the problem (in question form):* Write a question (or questions) that will focus on the problem in this situation.

_____

_____

_____

---

[4]Adapted from Richard W. Samson, *Problem Solving Improvement*, McGraw-Hill, New York, 1970, pp. 26–41. Used with permission of McGraw-Hill Publishing Company.

Answer: Examples of questions you might have written are, "Why weren't the men rescued?" and "What killed these men?" It is premature to ask, "How can these deaths be prevented in the future?" What must be established first is the problem—the question that must be answered.

2 *Analyze the situation:* Go back and read the incident again. In step 1, the problem was pinpointed with the question, "Why weren't the men rescued?" Now the ranger must analyze the situation. Write at least four questions the ranger might ask to learn more about this situation.

———————————————

———————————————

———————————————

———————————————

Answer: Good questions to ask are the following:

Where, when, and by whom were the men last seen?

Did the helicopter crew receive a call from the men?

Was this the only failure of the rescue plan, or were there other, more minor failures?

Where and in what condition were the remains of the men (and of the radio) when found?

Have there been similar failures of the rescue plan in the past?

The following are *not* appropriate questions to ask at this time because they attempt to get at the cause of the problem. They should be reserved for step 3:

Did the radio fail to work properly?

Did the men panic and forget how to operate the radio?

Did the heat from the fire damage the radio?

3 *Generate possible solutions:* Once you have identified the problem and have gathered all the pertinent facts about the case (analyzed the situation), you are ready to look for possible reasons for why the men weren't rescued. Before the ranger can learn how to prevent future accidents of this type, he must search out the cause. When the ranger analyzed the situation, he learned the following:

The helicopter crew said that they had not received a call from the three men.

The men had last been seen walking over the crest of a hill, into the valley in which their bodies were later found.

The metallic parts of the radio were found next to men's bodies.

Another group of firefighters, trapped on a knoll by encircling flames, had radioed the helicopter and were rescued.

None of the other firefighters needed rescuing.

During another fire, 9 months earlier, a team of firefighters had died in the flames; the helicopter had reported receiving no call for help; the bodies were found in a dry streambed between two hills.

Write at least two possible causes for the failure of the rescue plan.

———————————————

———————————————

———————————————

Answer: Here are examples of five possible reasons why the men weren't rescued:

The men did not know how to operate the radio properly. (a)

The members of the helicopter crew *did* receive a call for help, but they said they didn't in order to hide their failure to rescue the men. (b)

The radio signal was cut off by the crest of the hill and was never picked up by the helicopter's receiver. (c)

The radio was defective, possibly affected by the heat. (d)

The men panicked and were unable to radio for help. (e)

4 *Test and verify:* Now you must determine which of the possible solutions is most likely to be the right one.

First compare each suggested solution with the facts generated during step 2, analysis. Which of the five suggested solutions listed above is the most likely to be correct? Circle its number below.

(a)   (b)   (c)   (d)   (e)

Also, in a sentence or two, suggest a method that may be used to verify the solution you suggested, to determine if it is the correct one.

_____

_____

_____

Answer: The most likely solution is (c): "The radio signal was cut off by the crest of the hill and was never picked up by the helicopter's receiver." It fits all the facts: that no call for help was received; that the radio was found near the bodies; and that in the other incident, 9 months ago, the men perished in a similar location—between two hills. The other four suggested solutions are not as likely, for the following reasons:

"The men did not know how to operate the radio properly." Although solution (a) cannot be ruled out entirely, it does seem unlikely. The men were instructed in the use of the radio.

"The members of the helicopter crew *did* receive a call for help, but they said they didn't in order to hide their failure to rescue the men." No evidence for solution (b) has been presented.

"The radio was defective, possibly affected by the heat." Although possible, solution (d) is unlikely. How does it explain the fact that the two failures occurred in similar physical environments?

"The men panicked and were unable to radio for help." Solution (e) is mere speculation. The facts do not point to it as a likely cause. It could be true, but many assumptions are required.

The most distinctive fact is that the two tragedies occurred in similar terrain, in a valley or depression. The only suggested solution that grows out of this distinction is 3. Of course it may not be correct. How do you find out? You attempt to verify it, to check it out in the field.

Here are two procedures that the ranger might follow to verify, to determine if his suggested solution is the correct one:

Station a person with a radio in the location where the three men died, have a helicopter patrol overhead, and see if and where the signal is cut off.

Establish the location of the helicopter at the time the men would have tried to radio it. Do this by autopsy (establishing probable time of death), by finding out the time at which the men were last seen, etc., and by questioning the crew and fire fighters as to the location of the helicopter at that time. In other words, find out if the helicopter was in a position where a signal from the men would have been cut off by the crest of the hill.

In summary, rational thinking is a systematic way of answering questions and dealing with problems. The process involves a careful attention to each of the four steps (1) statement of the problem (in question form), (2) analysis of the situation, (3) generation of possible solutions, and (4) testing and verification. You do not move on to another step until the step you are presently dealing with is properly carried out.

A difficulty faced by many people is to hurriedly jump to step 3, searching for solutions and answers, before carefully defining the problem and learning all the facts about it.

Critical Thinking

How Does Critical Thinking Work?   Critical thinking resembles problem solving in that it begins with a situation about which you are concerned. For example, you may be reading a history of the Civil War and become uneasy about how the writer describes the role of African Americans. The more you read, the more concerned you become, yet you don't know how to deal with your unease. Or suppose that you have decided on a major in your college program and have completed a year's worth of courses. Your grades are satisfactory, but something is wrong. Somehow, you don't feel right about the major you've selected. Still, you continue on, because you don't know what to do about your discomfort. The process of critical thinking would be appropriate in both these situations.

Critical thinking goes beyond problem solving, however. Stephen Brookfield says,

> Being a critical thinker involves more than cognitive activities such as logical reasoning or scrutinizing arguments for assertions unsupported by empirical evidence. Thinking critically involves our recognizing the assumptions underlying our beliefs and behaviors. It means we can give justifications for our ideas and actions. Most important, perhaps, it means we try to judge the rationality of these justifications.[5]

Critical thinking fits well in two broad contexts. First, it is appropriate for examining what other people say—textbook authors, lecturers, etc.— and for examining the activities and policies of organizations, agencies, and institutions. Second, it is appropriate for examining personal con-

[5]Stephen D. Brookfield, *Developing Critical Thinkers,* Jossey-Bass, San Francisco, Calif., 1987, p. 13.

cerns—career choices, relationships with others, and fundamental beliefs and assumptions about religion, politics, and so on.

A Process for Critical Thinking   Critical thinking has five steps:

1   Becoming aware
2   In-depth examination
3   Searching for alternatives
4   Transition
5   Integration

Following is a description of each step in critical thinking.

Step 1: Becoming aware   When you become aware, you realize that something is wrong. This is the first step in critical thinking. You feel uncomfortable, although sometimes without knowing why. Before you can think critically, you must identify the nature of your discomfort.

You could become aware if an instructor's lectures paint a picture of society that flies in the face of everything you have been taught at home and have learned from growing up in your community. Traveling to another country can also make you aware. Getting fired from a job can make you aware (it can remind you painfully that something was wrong with your performance or with how you related to others, although a host of other factors could have been involved).

At another level, you can become aware when you read the works of two authors who consider essentially the same evidence but reach entirely different conclusions and make entirely different recommendations.

Once you are aware something is wrong, you are ready for step 2, examination. But bear in mind that the process of critical thinking, although it involves steps, doesn't always move neatly from one phase to the next in a linear way. As you wrestle with step 2, you will become much more aware of the nature of your discomfort than when you began the process with step 1.

Step 2: In-depth examination   In step 2 of critical thinking, the focus of your examination is to discover assumptions.

For example, let's say you are writing a paper about how to teach adults, and two books you've found offer quite different perspectives on this topic. You begin your analysis by examining the assumptions each of these authors holds about the nature of adults as learners. Different sets of assumptions will probably account for their different perspectives.

Or let's say you are reading an article in a sociology journal about the role of women in a modern-day church, and you cannot readily accept the conclusions. The place to start figuring out why is examining what assumptions the author holds about women in this church.

On a personal level, let's say you and two of your friends have heated arguments about recreational drugs. You are opposed to them; your friends favor them. One way to begin understanding each other's perspectives is to begin thinking about assumptions and making them explicit—assumptions about effects of long-term drug use, legal situations, personal rights, appropriate recreational activities, and so on.

Step 3: Searching for alternatives   In step 3 of critical thinking, you begin looking for alternatives to what you are reading or hearing. You search for new ways of doing things, new ideas, new ways of organizing your thinking.

During this step, you may decide to leave an old idea behind and accept a new one in its place or to modify an idea you presently hold—or you may consciously decide not to make any changes. If you decide to make a change, that will lead you to the next step, transition.

Step 4: Transition   Of all the steps in critical thinking, transition is often the most difficult, because it is during this phase that you leave behind old ideas, old assumptions, or old ways of thinking about something and accept something new.

It is easier to continue thinking as you have done in the past than to adopt a new set of ideas. Similarly, it is usually easier to accept what an author has written, commit it to memory, and repeat it back on an exam than to examine it critically.

Step 5: Integration   During the integration step of critical thinking, you become comfortable with and begin acting on your new ideas and assumptions. Sometimes you may not know when integration has taken place, since all these steps can from time to time overlap. A good way to recognize that integration has occurred is feeling at ease with yourself about a new position you have taken, a criticism you have expressed about an author, the workings of a club you've joined, or a new set of beliefs you've formulated.

For many of you, critical thinking will be the most difficult, and the most wrenching, of your experiences in college. But learning how to think critically can also be one of the most important skills you learn, because it can be applied throughout life. In fact, it is difficult to imagine a situation where critical thinking is *not* appropriate.

Creative Thinking

How Does Creative Thinking Work?   Creative thinking brings something new into being. Like problem solving and critical thinking, creative thinking takes place in steps, although in creative thinking these are probably better described as *phases*. As with critical thinking, these steps or phases often overlap.

Literature and scholarly writings offer many and varied descriptions of creative thought. One of the early writers in the field, Graham Wallas, suggested the following phases for creative thinking, which he referred to as "stages of thought":

1 Preparation
2 Incubation
3 Illumination
4 Verification[6]

A Process for Creative Thinking   Let's examine each of Wallas's phases of creative thinking in turn.

Phase 1: Preparation   In phase 1, formulate as clearly as possible a question you want answered, or describe a situation you want changed. If you are not aware of any question to be answered or any situation to be changed, little creative thought may take place. In that case, Roger von Oech says, you may need some external stimulus:

> We all need an occasional whack on the side of the head to shake us out of routine patterns, to force us to re-think our problems, and to stimulate us to ask new questions that may lead to other right answers.[7]

Preparation means total involvement with a question or situation. You learn all the facts of the situation; you force yourself to put off searching for easy answers to the question. But, more than that, you become emotionally involved. You search for the essence of the question or situation. You look at it from every possible angle. You look behind it; you look at it from the side, from the top, from the bottom, and from several feet away. You concentrate intensely, spending considerable time and energy.

As you search for information about the question or situation, you accept whatever you find, even if at the moment it seems to bear no relationship to the subject. You write it all down, but you don't worry about organizing or categorizing it; you simply record it. You also talk to others, gathering their information and opinions, and you record this information as well—again, not worrying about whether it fits or where it fits. In short, you read, listen, and record.

During the preparation phase of the creative thinking, you may find it necessary to reword your question or your description, perhaps several times. But at all times during this phase, a carefully worded question or description is your guide to collecting information.

---

[6]Graham Wallas, *The Art of Thought*, Harcourt, New York, 1926, pp. 80–81.
[7]Roger von Oech, *A Whack on the Side of the Head*, Warner, New York, 1983, p. 12.

Phase 2: Incubation In the second phase of creative thinking, you leave your question or situation. Take a walk. Sit on the back porch. Go to a movie. Read a story to your child. Do not think about the subject you've just spent so much time with.

During the incubation phase, try to do something entirely different from what you have been doing. While you are not consciously working on your problem, your unconscious will probably work overtime. The *unconscious* is not something mystical or supernatural, but simply a part of our psychological makeup. (Dreams are one product of the unconscious.) The unconscious can help you sort out and make sense of the mass of information you've collected during the preparation phase. As described in Chapter 2, you are allowing the right side of your brain—the creative, intuitive part—to function uninhibited.

We never know what to expect from our unconscious, from right-brain activity. Sometimes it offers brilliant solutions to problems, but sometimes it gives us nothing. We can't force it to operate; we can't make it come up with creative thoughts. The best we can do is give it the opportunity—the space—to work. This is what the incubation period is all about; it gives the creative portion of our brain space to work.

The unconscious may give us answers when we least expect them. For some people, creative ideas pop into their heads just before they go to sleep. For others, creative thoughts come when they are walking or jogging. Be ready. You may want to keep a note pad at your bedstead or carry one while you're walking or jogging, to record sudden thoughts.

Phase 3: Illumination When an "insight"—the product of incubation—pops into your head, you have reached the illumination phase of creative thinking.

When an insight breaks through into our consciousness, we almost always recognize it as the "right" answer to a question or the "right" way to change a situation. We are often impressed with the simplicity of the insight—in fact, we are likely to say, "Why didn't I think of that before?" However, although we know that the idea is "right," we have no way of proving it. Nor do we know the source of the idea, other than that it somehow came from the mass of information we collected, which interacted with the years of experience we've gained through living.

Usually, the moment when an insight strikes is joyous. We are struck with wonder and astonishment that, after all the work we've put into a question, the answer should be so simple and straightforward.

Phase 4: Verification In phase 4 of creative thinking, we try out an insight to see if it does indeed answer our question or change our situation. We test it to make sure that it works as well as we think it will, or that it fits the situation we have been working on.

Barriers to Creative Thinking   The most pervasive barrier to creative thinking has to do with our inability to state exactly how we arrived at an insight: many people will not accept ideas they consider "nonrational," and insights are nonrational by definition. Our culture values rational thought and often discounts or mistrusts insights. There is a tendency to believe that the only legitimate ideas are those developed logically and rationally; people who believe this often fail to realize that the contributions of poets, novelists, painters, musicians, dancers, and other artists result from creative thought.

Another barrier to creative thought is an unfortunate tendency in our society to separate the artist from the scientist, and thus to separate creative thought from problem solving and critical thought.

Still another barrier to creative thought is fear:

Fear of being different—If you come up with a new idea, you will of course to that extent be different from other people.

Fear of being thought a fool—People with new ideas have often been thought fools. The Wright brothers, Einstein, Edison, and Ford at one time or another were all considered foolish.

Fear of making a mistake—If you believe you must always be right, you will find it difficult or impossible to do creative thinking.

When Is Creative Thinking Most Useful?   In general, creative thinking is most useful in two kinds of contexts:

1 *Creative thinking is useful for generating new ideas.* If you are interested in finding new ways of organizing things, new approaches or viewpoints, or new ways of communicating ideas to others— fresh ways that haven't been considered before—try creative thinking.

2 *Creative thinking is useful for solving certain types of problems.* Edward de Bona says that there are three types of problems: first, problems that require new information or improved techniques for handling information; second, problems that require no new information but do require new ways of rearranging existing information; and third, problems that are not initially seen as problems. (This third type describes situations in which one is satisfied with a state of affairs to the point of not being able to see any problem in it; the problem, therefore, is realizing that a problem exists. See the discussion above about the preparation phase of creative thinking.) Problems of

the first type may often be solved by conventional approaches, but the second and third types require creative thinking.[8]

SUMMARY

- Thinking is a natural process for all of us, and thinking skills—like other skills—can be improved. Formal education tends to emphasize accumulating information rather than developing thinking skills; but information becomes obsolete so quickly that all of us should develop thinking skills which will help us gain new information, and use it effectively, throughout life.
- Categories of thinking include daydreaming, defensive thinking, snap judgments, and the three most effective forms of thought: problem solving, critical thinking, and creative thinking.
- Blocks to effective thinking include lack of time, groupthink, multipurposeness, reliance on authorities, fear of solitude, lack of openness, problems with vocabulary, and dependence on rote learning.
- A process for problem solving consists of four steps: (1) stating the problem, (2) analyzing the problem, (3) generating possible solutions, and (4) testing and verifying the solutions.
- A process for critical thinking has five steps: (1) becoming aware, (2) examining in depth, (3) searching for alternatives, (4) transition, and (5) integration.
- A process for creative thinking has four phases: (1) preparation, (2) incubation, (3) illumination, and (4) verification.
- Creative thinking is often inhibited because we cannot state the source of insights or describe the process we used in reaching them; as a result, many people do not give credence to insight. Creative thinking may also be inhibited by fear: fear of being different, fear of being thought a fool, and fear of making a mistake.
- Creative thinking is most useful when we want to create new ideas or solve problems for which the traditional problem-solving process is not appropriate.

[8]Edward de Bono, *Lateral Thinking: Creativity Step by Step,* Harper and Row, New York, 1973, p. 58.

12

STRENGTHENING
YOUR MEMORY

Your ability to remember obviously influences your learning. Understanding how you remember can help you improve this fundamental skill.

THE PROCESS OF REMEMBERING

Remembering involves three processes: (1) registration, (2) retention, and (3) recall. *Registration* means coming into contact with information, acquiring it, and then recording it in the brain. *Retention* means keeping that information in the brain. *Recall* includes the search and retrieval used for recovering (that is, actually remembering) the information.

Does the process of remembering change as we get older? There do seem to be some differences between younger and older students. First, as we grow older, registration becomes more of a problem. As Knox points out,

> The recall or retrieval of information is greatest when the material is meaningful and when the recall conditions are very similar to those under which the original registration occurred. This is especially so for older adults. When individuals try to respond to and store new information at the same time that they are trying to recall stored information, there is a memory deficit for older adults. This occurs, for example, when someone's comment triggers a flood of old memories and the next few sentences are missed.[1]

---

[1] Alan B. Knox, *Adult Development and Learning,* Jossey-Bass, San Francisco, Calif. 1977, p. 435.

Thus if you are an older returning student you may confront registration problems more often than younger students who have not had as many years of experience. The words a lecturer says, or the image a visual projects, will often elicit memories of related experiences; and as the recall of these memories is taking place, you may miss new information.

Second, as we grow older, we may also experience problems with recall, that is, with remembering itself. Researchers believe that this is due to interference from information previously stored. But how we store information in the first place also makes a difference when we are trying to recall it, and this may be more significant than effects of age. You can recall information stored in categories and groups more easily than information stored haphazardly. Knox says,

> Although there is some decline in registration with age, it appears that the decline in memory with age mainly reflected a decreased ability to recall or retrieve information mainly because of inadequate organization at the time of input.[2]

Forgetting also seems to be somewhat different in older and younger students. Those of you who are older, returning students will probably have noticed that as you get older, your ability to remember material from your past, sometimes in great detail, is much greater than your ability to remember what you studied yesterday.

Despite these differences, however, all of us—regardless of age—can take certain steps to improve our memory. In the remainder of this chapter, I'll describe some useful approaches.

IMPROVING YOUR MEMORY

Tips for Improving Short-Term Memory

Short-term memory is often called on as we prepare for examinations; and some older students may find that they have to work on their short-term memory more than younger students do. Here are some tips for improving short-term memory.

Practice   As you read material you are trying to learn, use a variety of approaches that will help you register it in your memory. For example, outline it, think about it, and talk about it with others.

Organize   Develop ways of organizing material you are learning. Develop outlines, categories, structures, and models—whatever will help you see how information forms large patterns.

[2]Ibid., p.436.

Use Reinforcement   Seek reinforcement for your learning. Use the feedback your instructor provides on examinations, papers, and other assignments. Successful completion of learning projects helps provide the motivation needed to ensure that material is adequately registered.

Use Your Experience   Remember that your previous learning and your life experience (particularly if you are a returning student) may enhance new learning. But you should also be aware that previous learning and experience can also interfere with new learning or may sometimes have no effect at all. As a learner, you need to recognize the effects of previous learning and experience on what you are trying to learn now.

Pace Your Learning   How you pace learning sessions can improve short-term memory. You can improve registration if you work intensively and often, but for relatively short periods of time—an hour or two, or even less.

Each student's learning pattern is individual, of course; but returning students tend to slow down and give more attention to accuracy than to speed. You need to decide what is your most comfortable learning speed.

Be Interested   The more interesting a topic is for you, the more you will attend to it in learning sessions—and the more of it you will remember.

Tips for Memorizing

Memorizing is a very small part of learning. As I have stressed throughout this book, learning is complex and involves many processes, of which memorizing is only one. To learn something well, you need to understand its relationship to other things; you need to be able to see large ideas and concepts and to place what you learn in new situations. Learning often involves critical analysis—searching for fundamental assumptions. Memorizing, then, is not the beginning and end of learning, although it may look that way to you after you have taken some courses where it is heavily emphasized.

If all this is so, why should you want, or need, tips on memorizing? One reason is suggested in what I've just said: memorizing is emphasized in certain courses. In some subjects, memorization is essential before you can go on to higher levels of learning; examples include foreign languages, mathematics, and many sciences.

Following are suggestions that many students have found useful in improving their memorization skills:

Use Association   Mnemonic devices are one familiar way to relate something you must memorize with something that is already familiar to you.

I imagine that almost everyone who has studied music associates the notes on the lines of the treble staff—e-g-b-d-f—with "every good boy does fine." Many of us remember the names of the Great Lakes—*H*uron, *O*ntario, *M*ichigan, *E*rie, and *S*uperior—by associating the initials with the word *homes.*

Reorganize Material   Reorganization can be very useful. For instance, if you are trying to memorize key words related to something you are studying, first memorize them in order, and then shuffle your notes so that the order changes. Often, for objective tests, you will be required to recall factual material out of context. Memorizing key words and ideas in a different order will help you recall them no matter what order you find them in later.

Use Flash Cards   Flash cards are especially useful for memorizing new vocabulary words and their meanings. Write each new word on one side of a 3- by 5-inch card and the meaning on the other side. Look at each word, try to recall its definition, and if you can't, flip the card over. Go through your cards again and again, until you have memorized all the definitions. Occasionally, change the order of the cards in the pack, so that you are not recalling on the basis of order.

Flash cards can also be useful for memorizing biological terms, mathematical formulas, words in foreign languages, etc. To make this approach even more productive, you can carry a small pack of cards with you, and when you are waiting for a class to start or waiting for a bus—whenever you have a spare moment—you can flip through your cards.

Overlearn   When you think you have memorized something—words and meanings, formulas, or whatever—go over it again and again and again. Many of us learned the multiplication tables this way and never forgot them.

Overlearning can be powerful, but it takes time, patience, and tolerance of boredom, for it is often a boring activity.

Work in Short, Intensive Sessions   Work at memorizing in several short, intensive periods of time, rather than in fewer but longer sessions. The key is intensity: you must completely attend to what you are trying to memorize. During longer sessions, you tend to become fatigued, and your attention wanes.

Be Confident   Develop confidence in your memory. Many people have difficulty recalling material they have memorized—particularly on exams—simply because they believe that they will have difficulty. First memorize, and then have faith in your memory. You'll be surprised at how well a positive attitude will assist you.

SUMMARY

- Memory involves three processes: registration, retention, and recall. These processes may work somewhat differently for older students than for younger students. For instance, registration may be influenced by our previous experience. Something an instructor says, or something we see, evokes a memory; and as we dwell on the memory, the new information being presented slips by.
- Short-time memory may be more of a problem for older students than long-term memory. Ways to improve short-term memory include (1) practicing, (2) developing ways to organize material, (3) seeking reinforcement for learning, (4) being aware of effects of previous learning and experiences, (5) pacing your learning sessions, and (6) being interested.
- All learners must sometimes memorize. To increase your ability to memorize, consider using association, reorganizing material, using flash cards, overlearning, working in short intensive sessions, and developing confidence in your memory.

13

LEARNING WITH ELECTRONIC MEDIA

The word *media* sounds very modern, but students have always learned with media. Over the years, slates, chalkboards, easels, and—later—overhead projectors, films, slides, three-dimensional replicas, and the like have been used by instructors in many disciplines.

As a college student today, you will probably be exposed to all these educational media. In addition, most of you will also encounter micro-computers, videotapes, educational television, audiotapes, and perhaps even teleconferencing. Colleges and universities use these technologies in a variety of ways, both on and off campus. At some colleges and universities, it is possible to earn a degree without ever coming onto the campus. This new form of education, called *learning at a distance,* uses educational technology in interesting ways.

PROS AND CONS OF ELECTRONIC MEDIA

Depending on your background and experience, you may or may not be comfortable using a computer, watching a lecture on videotape, or listening to an audiotape while driving to and from school or work. These newer electronic media offer some interesting advantages over the traditional approach to learning—sitting in a classroom with an instructor several times a week—but there are also some disadvantages.

Advantages

Control One significant advantage of electronic media is that you have control over your learning. If you are using a computer, an audiotape, or a videotape, you can usually choose when you will learn, how much time you will spend, and where you will learn.

For many learners, these media provide access that they ordinarily wouldn't have. Electronic technology can bring education to students, so that students do not always have to go where education is being offered.

Students also have some control over how they learn. For instance, you can work through a computer exercise and, if it is not clear, do it again and again until you figure it out. If you are watching a videotape or listening to an audiotape, you can reverse it at any time and repeat something. You can also come back to the material later and review all or part of it. Thus, educational technology lets you individualize your learning.

Versatility Educational technology is versatile; it appeals to a variety of learning styles. If you learn better by watching than by listening, a videotape may enhance your learning. If you learn best by listening, an audiotape may be best.

Actually, for most students learning is enhanced when several media can be combined. You may read about something in a textbook, listen to it on an audiotape, and perhaps watch a videotape on the same topic. Although these media—the book, the audio, and the video—cover the same subject, you may find yourself learning quite different things from each of them.

Disadvantages

Working Alone Probably the greatest disadvantage of learning with electronic media, even those designed specifically so that you can learn by yourself, is the absence of other people. Many of us enjoy the social interchange that goes along with group learning. It is possible to communicate with others when using certain media (even though your "classmates" may be scattered around the country), but that is not the same as having them physically together in the same room. A group of students, coming together face to face over a period of time, will develop a learning community. They are of course learning a subject, but they are also learning about each other—and they generally come to enjoy each other's company at a social level. This aspect is missing in electronic media; also missing are the interactions that occur during coffee breaks and gatherings of students before and after class.

Operating Equipment The necessity of operating electronic equipment is another disadvantage for some students. Many people, particularly adult learners, are put off by computers, videotape machines, and other technology. It is true that some modern computers and other devices are quite easy to operate, but some people nevertheless find it difficult to get past the hurdle of simply making them work.

Inappropriateness for Some Subjects   Certain subjects, such as those requiring laboratories (chemistry, physics, bacteriology, etc.) do not lend themselves well to electronic instruction alone. On the other hand, both computers and video can be used effectively as aids in teaching laboratory techniques, and in reinforcing principles taught in laboratories.

UNDERSTANDING ALTERNATIVE LEARNING MODES

You will learn different things from different media (such as a videotape, a live lecture, and an audiotape), even though the subject may be the same. Also, different media require different kinds of mental activity. For example, you may learn a subject differently by watching a videotape or a film as opposed to working through a simulation on a computer, listening to an audiotape, or reading a book. Students are sometimes aware that they are learning different things and learning in different ways when they use different media; but often they do not realize this. It is important to understand that *the various learning modes are not merely alternative ways of transmitting information.*

If you have a strong tendency to learn better with one mode, or medium, than another, you probably are aware of it. For instance, if you are an older, returning student, you may be most comfortable and learn best when you read a book or listen to a live lecture—particularly if you have had little or no experience with computers or with videotapes other than popular movies. On the other hand, if you have used computers throughout your formal schooling, you are likely to be quite comfortable using them as learning devices in college and may prefer them to more traditional media such as lectures and books.

As with students, some instructors are aware of differences that result from using different media, but some are not. Many instructors do not believe that various instructional media affect what is communicated. That is, they think that teaching by computer is no different from teaching by lecture. And many instructors believe that even without training, students will learn from a videotape or a computer just as easily as from a book. This is a mistake: students must learn how to use a computer, a videotape, or any other electronic learning device before they can become comfortable with it and before it will work well for them. Actually, most of us spent years learning how to read and understand textbooks, and so it is unrealistic to expect that students can master learning with a videotape machine or a computer in one or two sessions.

Gavriel Salomon has conducted research comparing different teaching approaches, which he calls *symbol systems*. He writes,

> One symbol does not communicate better than another. It calls for better-mastered skills than another. And, the better mastered the requisite skills are, the better is the acquisition of knowledge from the coded message.[1]

Salomon also recognizes the importance of individual differences and the requirements of different learning situations:

> Symbol systems differ as to their congruity with a learner's internal representations. Thus some symbol systems call for better-mastered, more automatically executed recording systems than others, given a particular task, content, and learner.[2]

With regard to learners, Salomon holds that if you are by nature a verbalizer (someone who prefers to work with printed words or a spoken lecture), certain learning modes will work better for you than if you are by nature a visualizer (someone who prefers illustrations, pictures, and visual imagery). He implies that the better you know yourself as a learner, the better you can prepare yourself for learning with different media.

Other researchers would agree with Salomon that each of us brings a personal perspective to any learning situation, and that this perspective influences our perceptions and ultimately our learning. John Fiske and John Hartley point out:

> Our perception is not so much an inherited mechanism as a learnt one—the daily manifestations of our whole personal history of socialization and interaction with the cultural environment. Hence the awareness we bring to the television screen is a precondition for making sense of what we see, but that awareness is itself produced in us by what we have experienced hitherto.[3]

Our personal histories influence what we bring not only to the television screen but to all other forms of learning as well. Our perceptions are influenced by our backgrounds. But if we can learn to be open and flexible, and can listen and look for things we are not accustomed to seeing and hearing, we will often learn new things and develop new perspectives.

---

[1] Gavriel Salomon, *Interaction of Media, Cognition, and Learning,* Jossey-Bass, San Francisco, Calif., 1981, p. 219.

[2] Ibid., p. 220.

[3] John Fiske and John Hartley, *Reading Television,* Methuen, London, 1978, p. 69.

AUDIOTAPES AND VIDEOTAPES

Below are some guidelines that students have found useful for learning from audiotapes or videotapes. These guidelines are also appropriate for films and television.

Listening and Note-Taking with Audios and Videos

Fundamentally, listening and note-taking skills are the same, no matter whether you are listening to a traditional lecture in a classroom with other students or listening at home to an instructor on an audiotape. But there are some differences.

For one thing, I don't think anyone would deny that there is a certain excitement which comes from hearing and seeing a good lecturer in person; but it takes an exceptional lecturer to convey this excitement on tape. Usually, therefore, listening to an audiotape presents students with the challenge of keeping focused on what the lecturer is saying. On the other hand, the audiotape has the advantage of allowing students to rewind it and listen to the lecture, or parts of the lecture, again. This is also, of course, an advantage of videotape.

Depending on the complexity of the topic and your own skills, you may be able to take notes while hearing an audiotape for the first time. But for some topics, particularly those that are new to you or have been difficult for you, you may want to listen to the entire lecture once without taking notes, and then take notes while you listen to it a second time. This strategy is also appropriate with videotapes. It gives you an overview of the lecture and lets you hear how ideas are developed. As a result, when you listen the second time, you should be able to write down the main points quickly and thus have more time to concentrate on hearing the supporting material.

Reading Films and Videos

You may think the idea of "reading" films somewhat odd. After all, can't anyone "read" a picture? And isn't one picture supposed to be worth a thousand words?

To be sure, almost anyone can gain something from looking at a picture. Inability to read words—illiteracy—is a fairly straightforward situation: if you are illiterate or nearly so, a page of words will have little or no meaning for you. But a picture will almost always tell you something, even if you have had no training with pictures. Problems with "reading" pictures have to do more with nuances, and you can gain much more from pictures if you understand some of these nuances.

Reading a film or a videotape is an advanced form of reading a picture.

To learn how to read a film or a video, you should know something about how the filmmaker works; this helps you to understand the product.

A film or a video has both a denotative meaning, that is, a literal meaning; and a connotative meaning, that is, a subjective, emotional dimension which goes beyond the literal meaning. When you are learning from a film or video, you must learn to capture both types of meaning. Thus in watching well-made films and videos, you are interested not only in the content (what is denoted) but in how this content is presented; subjective or connotative meaning rests in the subtleties filmmakers use. For instance, lighting is a powerful way to develop subjective meaning: when something is highlighted, the filmmaker calls attention to detail; when something is backlighted, a sense of drama is created.

According to James Monaco, a filmmaker uses five "channels of information": (1) a visual image, (2) print and other graphics, (3) speech, (4) music, and (5) noise (sound effects).[4] He also makes this point:

> We "read" images by directing our attention; we do not read sound, at least not in the same conscious way. Sound is not only omnipresent but omnidirectional. Because it is so pervasive, we tend to discount it. Images can be manipulated in many different ways and the manipulation is relatively obvious, with sound, even the limited manipulation that does occur is vague and tends to be ignored.[5]

Also, according to Monaco,

> Even before the image appears, the frame [the television or film screen] is invested with meaning. The bottom is more "important" than the top. Left comes before right, the bottom is stable, the top unstable; diagonals from bottom left to top right go "up" from stability to instability. Horizontal will also be given more weight than vertical; confronted with horizontal and vertical lines of equal length, we tend to read the horizontal as longer, a phenomenon emphasized by the dimensions of the frame.[6]

Developing Learning Strategies for Audios and Videos

To learn from audios and videos, we must develop active learning strategies. Unfortunately, for most of us television and films are primarily recreational media. When we sit down in front of a television set or go to a movie, we want to relax, tune out the world, and be entertained. Learn-

---

[4] James Monaco, *How to Read a Film,* Oxford University Press, New York, 1981, p. 179.

[5] Ibid., p. 179.

[6] Ibid., p. 156.

ing from media that resemble television and films requires a shift of attitude: we must be actively involved, not passive spectators.

Note-taking, of course, is one way to become actively involved. Another way is to look for symbols, listen for music and other background sounds, note the use of color and lighting, and reflect on how these nuances affect the factual material being presented—that is, the information you are obtaining.

COMPUTERS

So far, computers have not had a prominent role in college instruction, though many colleges and universities were early users of computers for numerical analysis. With the advent of the microcomputer, however, new vistas have opened up for computerized learning. Moreover, today many software developers are producing computer programs for subjects ranging from basic mathematics to elaborate simulations of world economic conditions.

Understanding Computer Terminology

Before continuing, it might be useful to define some of the terms that are tossed around so freely by people who work with computers. Returning students, particularly those who have never used a computer, may find these definitions especially useful.

Cursor: A small, usually flashing, image on the computer screen that tells you where you are.

Disk: Three kinds of disks are popular today—5¼-inch "floppy" disk, 3½-inch microdisks, and hard disks that are a permanent part of many microcomputers. Information is stored on disks (thousands of pages can be stored on a hard disk; a few hundred on a floppy disk or a microdisk).

Disk drive: The machinery that physically runs disks. A disk drive stores and retrieves information.

Hard copy: The paper copy produced by a computer printer.

Hardware: The physical computer equipment—a television-like screen, disk drives, a printer, a microprocessor, a keyboard, and so on.

Printer: A computer printer looks and performs like a typewriter without keys. A printer connected to a microcomputer prints the results of your keyboarding as hard copy (that is, on paper). Printers come in several varieties—dot-matrix, daisy-wheel, and laser, to mention three of them. The output of laser printers is nearly identical to professional typesetting and printing. The output of daisy-wheel printers is comparable to that of a high-quality typewriter; and the output of dot-matrix printers is not quite equal to that of a fair typewriter. Cheap dot-matrix printers produce poor-quality hard copy—some of it is all but illegible.

Software: Software is also called a *program.* It is usually on a disk, and it tells a computer what to do. Software makes a computer function as a learning machine, a word processor, a number manipulator, and so on.

Word processor: A microcomputer used for writing. A variety of word-processing software programs are available which perform everything from simple typewriter-like functions to elaborate editing functions.

Getting Started with a Computer

Before you can learn effectively and comfortably with a computer, you must become comfortable with the machine itself. If you know how to use a typewriter, you probably remember your first efforts to become familiar with the keyboard, to insert and remove the paper, to "tune out" the noise, and so on. Becoming comfortable with a computer is similar in many ways.

You may want to begin by taking a short course that will show you the basics of operating a computer and teach you how to use a word-processing program (word-processing software is helpful for creating papers and other written assignments). Or you may want to learn on your own by carefully working through the written instructions and "hands on" tutorials that come with most personal computers and software programs.

If you don't type, you may want to learn how before, or while, you learn to use a computer. It is next to impossible to do word processing without knowing how to type (a few people do become two-finger experts, but they are the exception rather than the rule); and it is difficult, though possible, to follow many computerized learning programs without typing.

Learning with Computers

At present, computers are used in several important types of learning situations. Let's look at these.

Drills   In a drill, problems of various types are given and the answers are available for checking. Drills are commonly used in such areas as mathematics and statistics. A drill is usually not much fun, but many computer programs can make drills at least somewhat interesting. Touch typing and foreign languages are other examples of drill programs.

Tutorials   In a tutorial, concepts and theories are presented with practical applications. For example, a grammar tutorial may explain the correct use of pronouns, give examples of correct use, and then offer exercises which test what you have just learned. A computer can give instant feedback on whether you have performed an exercise accurately.

Simulations   In a simulation, real-life situations are presented and you are asked to respond to them. For instance, with a videotape player and a computer, a student training to be a social worker might examine several case situations and decide how to handle them. As with a drill, the student receives instant feedback about the consequences of a particular action or decision. Medical students are now learning how to handle a variety of real-life situations through computer simulations.

Problem Solving   Problem-solving programs are designed to teach thinking and reasoning skills. A problem is presented, and the student works through a solution, following various steps and receiving feedback at each step.

Creativity Software   "Creativity programs" allow you to draw pictures on the screen, create designs, and build models. These programs are used in art, engineering, creative design, and a variety of other courses.

Productivity Software   "Productivity programs" are designed for word processing, filing, checking spelling, electronic spreadsheets, and data processing.

Communication Software   Communication programs allow you to communicate electronically with other students, with instructors, and with on-line computer databases. These programs offer almost unlimited access to information, but generally there is a cost for telephone use and for the time that you are connected to an on-line database. You also need a "modem" to connect a computer to telephone lines.

AUDIO TELECONFERENCING
What Is Teleconferencing?

If your instructor wants to present a guest lecturer who lives in another part of the country, that can be done via telephone lines: you and your fellow students would interact with the guest lecturer by telephone. You would not actually see the lecturer, but otherwise the interaction would be quite normal and would even include questions and answers. This is an example of audio teleconferencing.

   With teleconferencing it is also possible to have some students meet in a traditional classroom while others are scattered at different "listening sites.'' That is, not only instructors but also learners can be at remote locations—and all can participate at the same time, live.

Guidelines for Teleconferencing

Participating in audio teleconferencing does take some getting used to. For example, many of us depend on looking at other people in order to gauge their reactions to what we say, and that of course becomes impossible in a teleconference session. In fact, in my experience teleconferencing seems to work best when students have some face-to-face meetings during a course, so that they can put names and faces together; then, when they are on the telephone network, their exchanges are easier.

Following are some useful guidelines for learning through teleconferencing:

1 *In a teleconference question-and-answer session, do not overreact if a silence follows your question.* Someone is probably thinking of an answer and needs a moment or two to collect his or her thoughts. But if no response at all is forthcoming after a reasonable time, you may want to rephrase your question. For instance, you may want to direct the question specifically to one of your fellow students if you know them by name (this is easier if you have actually met some or all of your classmates at face-to-face sessions). When you ask or answer a question, give your own name and your location.

2 *Take notes during a teleconference lecture,* just as you would if the speaker were in the room with you. (Use the tips on note-taking in Chapter 5.)

3 *Pay attention to visuals.* In most teleconferencing sessions, some visuals will be available. Pay careful attention to them; they usually present important ideas and emphasize major points your instructor is covering.

4 *Be flexible.* Try to develop a flexible, accepting attitude toward the limitations of teleconferencing. Not being able to see your instructor or your fellow students does have drawbacks; but remember that this is the only way for some people to be involved in learning.

LEARNING AT A DISTANCE
Studying Off Campus

Correspondence study has existed for a long time; as early as the nineteenth century, correspondence courses on a variety of subjects were available in the United States. But modern electronic technology has revolutionized correspondence study, which today is called *learning at a distance*.

Print materials are still an important element of learning at a distance, but there are now many additional features, including teleconferencing, videotape, audiotape, computers, and courses broadcast on radio and television.

In fact, today it is possible to earn a degree without ever setting foot on a campus; you can study at your workplace or at home, at any convenient time. Learning at a distance is, obviously, attractive to people who are working full time, have family responsibilities, or live in areas where it is inconvenient to attend classes on a campus. All the problems of on-campus study—commuting, finding a parking place, arranging for child care, and so on—disappear.

Learning at a distance is as rigorous as learning on campus, and expectations for off-campus students are just as high. Many off-campus students receive exactly the same instruction as on-campus students except that the off-campus students see their instructor on videotape.

The National Technological University (with offices in Fort Collins, Colorado) is one example of learning at a distance. This nontraditional master's degree program for engineers is based on videotapes of instructors working with on-campus students. The classrooms are equipped with video cameras and microphones; class sessions are videotaped or transmitted by satellite, microwave, or fiber optics to off-campus students at their job sites. These part-time students can be linked to the classrooms by telephone so that—from their workplace—they can ask questions during the class session; or they can call in with questions that will be answered later. Other off-campus degree programs—many of which are designed especially for adult students—follow a variety of formats. Often, electronic media are combined with one or more face-to-face sessions during a semester, at different locations around the country.

What Off-Campus Study Means for Students

A fundamental characteristic of learning at a distance is of course the physical separation of student and instructor. The student may also, most of the time, be physically distant from other students in the same course. In fact, in many programs a student has no idea of who the other students in a course are, how many there are, or anything else about them. Obviously, this has implications for learners. Charles Wedemeyer, a longtime proponent of learning at a distance, says,

The person who learns through technology is not only physically distant from the teacher, using print, mechanical, or electronic media for communicating, he is also as a learner required to be both more responsible and more autonomous.[7]

Learning at a distance is not without problems. In a study conducted in 1981 in the United Kingdom—where the Open University has thousands of students learning at a distance—students reported the following problems (in decreasing order of frequency): (1) lack of time, (2) difficulty concentrating, (3) family commitments, (4) difficulties with organization of time and planning, (5) low levels of motivation, (6) difficulties with study skills, (7) anxiety, and (8) isolation.[8] These are problems that many on-campus students also experience; but students learning at a distance don't have the motivation provided by attending classes and meeting strict deadlines—the kind of motivation which keeps many campus students on the straight and narrow.

However, it is possible (as explained above) to design certain courses so that off-campus students can interact immediately with their instructor and with other students; this provides motivation to keep up with the work. Teleconference courses are good examples. Of course, not all programs are designed in this way; and many off-campus students prefer the flexibility of courses they can study at their own convenience and their own speed. Learning at a distance often gives this option, and indeed encourages it. Videotapes and audiotapes make it easy for students to work at their own pace.

The advantages of learning at a distance clearly outweigh its disadvantages. Most important, it offers an access to learning for people who might otherwise be cut off by constraints of time, distance, family responsibilities, and work. Learning at a distance does require considerable discipline and the skills of self-directed learning. Throughout this book, I point out how you can become self-directed and take charge of all facets of your own learning. This approach is essential for most forms of learning at a distance.

SUMMARY

- Increasingly, colleges and universities are using electronic media to supplement traditional teaching and sometimes to replace it.
- Learning with electronic media offers several advantages. Students have more control over what they learn, how much time they spend

[7]Charles A. Wedemeyer, *Learning at the Back Door,* University of Wisconsin Press, Madison, Wis., 1981, p. 111.

[8]B. Robinson, "Support for Student Learning," in A. Kaye and R. Rumble (eds.), *Distance Learning for Higher and Adult Education,* Croom-Helm, London, 1981.

learning, and where they learn. Electronic technology also appeals to a variety of learning styles.

- But there are disadvantages to electronic media. Lack of personal contact with other students and the instructor is probably the greatest disadvantage. The need to operate equipment provides a barrier for some learners; and certain subjects (such as those requiring laboratory work) do not lend themselves to computers, videos, or other electronic formats.
- To learn successfully with the audiotapes and videotapes, you must sharpen your listening and note-taking skills and learn how to "read" films and video.
- Learning with computers entails becoming familiar with computer-related terminology, learning to use the equipment, and understanding a variety of computerized learning programs.
- Teleconferencing combines audiotapes, telephones, and broadcasting; it is often used for learning at a distance.
- In learning at a distance, students and instructors are physically separated. Learning at a distance is growing in prominence, particularly now that new teaching technology is available. Some colleges and universities offer entire degree programs in this way.

14

STUDYING
THE DISCIPLINES

When I enrolled in my first college chemistry course, I had never taken high school chemistry. I remember vividly those first weeks of chemistry lectures. Surrounded by several hundred eager freshmen, all frantically taking notes while the instructor talked and demonstrated principles, I too frantically scribbled in my notebook and tried to understand what was going on. But I had no idea what the instructor was talking about—in fact, even the terms he used out were almost all foreign to me. And I could make no sense out of his demonstrations, though most of them were fun to watch because something unexpected usually happened. In high school, I had learned what to do in situations like this: memorize. And so memorize I did. I memorized my lecture notes. I memorized entire passages in the textbook. My head was filled with memorized material.

At the end of 2 weeks, the teaching assistant gave our section of the class a quiz. I received an F—in fact, a perfect F, because I had not answered one question correctly. Not only had I not answered the questions correctly; I couldn't even figure out what they were asking me to do. My faith in memorizing was shaken, and I decided that a new study strategy was in order. I asked the teaching assistant what I should do, and his advice was sound. "Spend some time figuring out what chemistry is all about," he suggested; "and I'll help you when you have questions."

So I set out to try to understand chemistry—its structure, its language, and its way of discovering facts. Once I had done this (it took several weeks), I began fitting things into my new framework: what the instructor was lecturing about, what I was reading in the text, and what my section was discussing.

WHAT STUDYING THE DISCIPLINES MEANS

Derek Bok, the president of Harvard University, says that college instructors are changing the way they teach:

> Earlier educators put great stock in what a student could gain by acquiring a sufficient body of information and by observing and emulating superior minds in action. Faculties today are likely to perceive a more difficult, changeful, complicated world in which there are many conflicting points of view and many questions without prospect of answers. In such an environment, knowledge alone is not enough; the ability to think clearly about complex problems becomes more and more important. A critical mind, free of dogma but nourished by humane values, may be the most important product of education in a changing, fragmented society.[1]

Thus the study of disciplines in a college curriculum—chemistry, English, biology, mathematics, physics, computer science, sociology, psychology, history, economics, foreign languages—is much more than memorizing subject matter, and this is a point I have already made in Chapter 11.

Students may still ask why they should spend precious time learning the special characteristics of each discipline, when they know that the most important immediate outcome of their efforts is the grade they receive at the end of a course. This is not the place for a debate about the importance or unimportance of grades. But from my personal experience, and from my work with several hundred students over the years, I can say that working out a strategy for studying the various disciplines not only will help you in the years ahead but will help you improve your grades tomorrow. Some people call this strategy "studying smart."

UNDERSTANDING A NEW DISCIPLINE:
BASIC QUESTIONS

When you first encounter a new discipline, no matter which one, start your study by asking and answering several basic questions:

1   What is the structure of the discipline? How is it organized?
2   What subject matter, topics, or questions does the discipline address?
3   Who are the major contributors to the discipline—such as past and contemporary researchers, scholars, and writers?

---

[1] Derek Bok, *Higher Learning,* Harvard University Press, Cambridge, Mass, 1986, p. 47.

4 What special words do writers in the discipline use?
5 How is new knowledge discovered in this discipline? What research approaches are used?

Let's look at each of these questions in turn.

What Is the Structure?

Think of studying a discipline as you would study a map before making a trip. Let us say that you want to travel from Chicago to Yellowstone Park. If you look at a map, you can see the major cities along the way and alternative routes you could take. The map certainly doesn't tell you all about the trip; in fact, a map can be quite boring. But a map does show you directions. It tells you what the major roadways are and what important places you will encounter along the way. It lets you figure out roughly how much time you will need to travel from Chicago to, say, Omaha. It tells you that you will not be traveling through Florida, nor will you see the Atlantic ocean (or any other ocean).

A map, then, is a beginning. To take this example a step further, I remember the first time I traveled to Madison, Wisconsin, where I now live. I got lost, and no matter which street I took, every few minutes I arrived again at Capitol Square, where Wisconsin's capitol building is located. What I did not know then was that downtown Madison is planned so that all the major streets radiate out from Capitol Square. Of course, there are also many shorter, connector streets (a street map of Madison would look something like a spider web); but at first I couldn't figure out which were the major streets and which were the connecting streets. This kind of experience is common when you are first becoming acquainted with a discipline: without an image of the overall structure of the discipline, you may become confused about what is and what is not important to learn.

Jerome Bruner said it this way:

Knowledge has a structure, a hierarchy, in which some of what is known is more significant than the rest of what is known about some aspect of life or nature. It is more significant because armed with the significant knowledge and armed with a theory and operations for putting the significant knowledge together and for going beyond it, one can reconstruct with reasonable approximation the less significant knowledge and the multitude of stray items that constitute the whole body of knowledge.[2]

To begin studying a discipline, therefore, you develop a mental map of

[2] Jerome S. Bruner, *The Relevance of Education,* Norton, New York, 1971, pp. 122–123.

it. Once you know the main features—the main principles of organization—you are able to fill in the gaps. For example, in *adult education,*
which is my academic area, history and philosophy of adult education,
teaching and learning strategies for adults, curriculum development, program evaluation strategies, and educational leadership would be at the
center of the map. These are the "core elements." Outward from this
center are the actual subjects to be studied, which are based on students'
interests. These include continuing professional education, international
development, leisure studies, agricultural education, adult basic education, and human resources development.

A map for *philosophy* would include (among other things) five basic
areas of study: logic (systematic argument, what's valid, what's invalid),
metaphysics (the search for essences or fundamental truths), epistemol-
ogy (what do we know and how do we know it?), aesthetics (beauty and
art), and ethics (what's right and what's wrong).

A map for *world history* might include peoples and cultures (the
Greeks, the Romans, the Germans); major wars, colonial settlements,
and immigration patterns; eras (the Middle Ages, the Renaissance, the
industrial revolution); intellectual movements (such as political philoso-
phies), their development, and their effects; and so on. World history is a
very broad subject, and what I've mentioned here is only a brief example
of what you might include in your own map of this discipline.

What Is the Subject Matter?

Once you know something about the structure of a discipline (its map),
you can begin asking about its subject matter. Of course the structure
itself will tell you something about the subject matter, and as you examine the subject matter further, you will continue to learn more about the
structure.

What is the subject matter of *economics,* for instance? Economics includes supply and demand and the relation of supply and demand to price
fluctuations; theories of competition; and the money system.

Sociology is concerned with social organization: how it develops and
what patterns it takes.

The subject matter of *botany* includes plant classification systems; the
structure, physiology, and reproduction systems of plants; and the evo-
lution of plants.

In the discipline of *building engineering,* the subject matter includes
building materials for different uses, types of structural frames, ventila-
tion and cooling systems, and principles of insulation.

Psychology includes two basic clusters of subject matter. One has to
do with physiological, chemical, and neurological structures and func-

tions that affect human behavior; the second has to do with mental states such as motivation, consciousness, and choice.

Political science is the study of systems of power and influence; it includes such concepts as force, reason, propaganda, and economic and social pressures, which help explain how people and their organizations, institutions, and governmental units influence each other.

The subject matter of *anthropology* includes physical and cultural descriptions of human groups, where they live, how they live, their languages and customs, their rituals, their laws, and their social organization.

Geography includes the study of human beings in relation to the regions in which they live; population; food supply; transportation systems; climate; and natural resources.

History is concerned with human beings in time, and especially with how people lived in the past. Its subject matter includes not only detailed information about various time periods but often carefully developed information about the context in which various events took place.

The subject matter of the *fine arts*—dance, music, literature, painting, and sculpture—includes the development of the creative spirit in human beings over time and the skills and knowledge involved in creative expression.

Who Are the Major Figures?

Knowing who did what in a discipline makes it more interesting, at least for me. I want to know who is behind a theory or idea I am studying, and what that person is or was like.

For instance, in the study of music, emphasis is almost always placed on the great composers. Most of these composers are extremely interesting: many of them (such as Mozart) were fantastically gifted child prodigies; many had dazzling careers as virtuoso instrumentalists (Mozart again, and Beethoven, and Liszt); some were charismatic conductors (Beethoven was, until he became deaf); and a remarkable number of them seem to have led very tempestuous personal lives (Mozart yet again, Liszt, Tchaikovsky, Wagner, Mahler).

In my own field, adult education, an important figure is Eduard Lindeman, who was a pioneer theorist, writer, and activist. His ideas about a life of learning, and the relation of learning to doing, came alive when I read his biography.

Learning about the major figures in a discipline can also help you understand the history and development of the discipline. Who did what, and when? For instance, in art history most instructors naturally give considerable attention to artists, and taking up artists in chronological order—Rubens (late 1500s and early 1600s), Rembrandt (early 1600s),

Monet (late 1800s), Picasso (1900s)—is one way of tracing the development of western art.

Likewise, when you study philosophy, you can often associate philosophical developments with specific people: Plato (c. 427 to c. 347 B.C.) is associated with reasoning and conceptualizing as a way of arriving at the truth; Saint Augustine (A.D. 354–430) is associated with rational defenses of Christianity; René Descartes (1596–1650) is associated with inquiry into how we know what we know; Immanuel Kant (1724–1840) is associated with major changes in nearly all branches of philosophy; William James (1842–1910) is associated with pragmatism; and John Dewey (1859–1952) is associated with the problem-solving approach to education.

What Special Terms Are Used?

The specialized terminology of a discipline is sometimes called its *jargon*, but because *jargon* has negative connotations, I generally don't use it in this context. I prefer to say *special terms, special words,* or *special language*.

In addition to learning about the structure, subject matter, and major figures of each discipline, most of us are helped greatly by systematically learning its special language. When we first encounter a new discipline, making lists of new words and their definitions is often very helpful. Many students find that this allows them to move quickly past the initial stage of confusion, which is often caused primarily by having to deal with many new words at once.

In textbooks, one often encounters three particularly important categories of special language: (1) words with multiple meanings, (2) words with specialized meanings, and (3) abbreviations. Let's briefly consider each of these.

Words with multiple meanings can be particularly difficult. You think you know what a word means, but the author of the textbook is using it in a different way. For instance, in sociology some commonly used terms are *society, institution,* and *culture*. These words are also in general use, though (we hear them all the time in everyday conversation); therefore, we must be careful to determine the meanings that sociologists have given them. Computer science gives its own different meanings to a host of common words: BASIC (a computer language), *boot* (to start up a computer), *documentation* (a written description of a computer program), and *file* (a collection of information stored by a computer) are only a few examples.

It is easy to spot *new words* when we begin studying an unfamiliar discipline. For instance, when we begin studying economics, we will confront terms such as *econometrics* (the use of computer analysis and statistical techniques to describe economic relationships in mathematical terms) and *macroeconomics* (the study of a nation's economy as a whole). In computer science, we will see terms such as *bit, byte, microprocessor, nanosecond, disk drive,* FORTRAN, *silicon chip,* and *word processing*. In the physical sciences, we see words such as *half-life, mass, quark, quantum,* and *symbiosis*. Each discipline has specialized words, and the sooner you are able to identify and define them, the sooner you will be able to study the discipline comfortably.

In many disciplines, *abbreviations* are used for common terms. In computer science, many terms are abbreviated: ROM (read-only memory), LCD (liquid crystal display), DOS (disk operating system), and CPU (central processing unit), for example. Other disciplines also use abbreviations, which may seem baffling at first but actually make communication easier and more efficient. Chemistry uses abbreviations extensively to identify elements and compounds: C = carbon, N = nitrogen, Fe = iron, NaCl = salt, and so on. In economics and business, we find CEO (chief executive officer), CPI (consumer price index), COLA (cost-of-living adjustment), FTC (Federal Trade Commission), and GAAP (general accepted accounting principles).

How Is Knowledge Developed?

Without addressing the often controversial question whether knowledge is actually created, as opposed to simply being discovered, within a discipline, one way to begin understanding a discipline is to find out how new knowledge is *added* to it. What methods and approaches are used in research and scholarship? How are these methods used? Because methods of research and scholarship vary somewhat, or considerably, from discipline to discipline, we would expect the resultant knowledge to vary—and this is indeed the case.

Broadly speaking, the physical sciences seek general or universal knowledge, whereas history seeks detailed and specific knowledge. But as Joseph Schwab says, there is considerable difference even within the sciences in how knowledge is sought:

> Biologists find it necessary or desirable to seek knowledge in bits and pieces while physicists, at the other extreme, work hard to develop broad, comprehensive theories which embrace vast ranges of subject matter.[3]

---

[3] Joseph J. Schwab, *The Structure of Knowledge and the Curriculum*, Rand McNally, Chicago, Ill., 1964, p. 21.

Knowing how a discipline seeks knowledge helps us understand what kinds of knowledge it contains (though this information should also impress on us that knowledge and the disciplines are constantly changing). Also, learning how a discipline seeks knowledge will generally lead us to its major researchers, help us learn more about its subject matter, and reveal more of its structure.

HOW DISCIPLINES CHANGE

Disciplines are not static. They do not sit there like immobile piles of information waiting for you to come along and learn about them. Just as you are constantly changing while you learn, disciplines constantly change while researchers and scholars continue to contribute to them.

Moreover, disciplines do not simply take on new knowledge in a linear, additive way. That is, disciplines are not like warehouses; they do not just receive, categorize, and store new information. Rather, just as individuals must unlearn from time to time, leaving old information behind, disciplines go through a constant process of challenging existing information—reconsidering it in light of new information that is being discovered or created.

As I explained above, disciplines have structures; and new scholarship and research from time to time challenge and change these basic structures. As Schwab points out,

> Our new knowledge of the subject, our improved techniques, and our sharpened awareness of inadequacies in our substantive structures enable us to conceive new structures more complex than the old, more adequate to the richness of the subject matter. With the advent of a new structure, the knowledge continued in the older conceptions, though "right" enough in its own terms, is rendered obsolete and replaced by a new formulation which puts old facts and new ones together in more revealing ways.[4]

There are also times when old "facts" are declared to be in error and are dropped from a discipline.

Also, as disciplines develop, new disciplines are often spawned. As new knowledge accumulates, certain substructures emerge to accommodate it. The new knowledge fits comfortably in a substructure; yet the substructure may no longer fit comfortably within the larger discipline. When this occurs, a new discipline is likely to be formed. Anatomy is an example. For many years, anatomy was part of the study of biology. But as more information about anatomy was discovered and new structures were developed, anatomy split away from biology and became an inde-

[4] Ibid., p. 28.

pendent discipline. Another example is dairy science, which was once a part of animal science, a discipline that goes back many years in American colleges and universities. Early in the twentieth century, new knowledge began accumulating about dairy cattle, and soon an independent discipline, dairy science, emerged. More recently, computer science emerged from at least two other disciplines, physics and mathematics, as new knowledge accumulated.

AN INTERDISCIPLINARY PERSPECTIVE

It certainly makes sense to learn how to study the various disciplines. But certain questions you will explore in your college studies, and in your day-to-day living, do not fit neatly within a single discipline. In fact, most problems in life cut across several disciplines. Therefore, we must learn not to wear blinders—not to expect every question on every problem that we face to fall into one discipline.

A basic point to consider is this: Disciplines are established for our convenience; they help us organize huge quantities of information. But they do not necessarily reflect the reality that exists "out there." Physics, and particularly quantum mechanics, is leading us to the realization that nature is unified.

For instance, Fritjof Capra writes,

Quantum theory... reveals a basic oneness of the universe. It shows that we cannot decompose the world into independently existing smallest units. As we penetrate into matter, nature does not show us any isolated "basic building blocks," but rather appears as a complicated web of relations between the various parts of the whole. These relations always include the observer in an essential way. The human observer constitutes the final link in the chain of observational processes, and the properties of any atomic object can be understood only in terms of the object's interaction with the observer. This means that the classical ideal of an objective description of nature is no longer valid.[5]

Capra is telling us two things: first, that the disciplines are related to each other; and second, that we cannot be detached observers when we are studying a discipline. This brings us back to a point I have made before: You, as learner, must put yourself into what you are learning.

[5] Fritjof Capra, *The Turning Point*, Bantam, New York, 1983, p. 57.

SUMMARY

- Learning techniques for studying the disciplines can help you develop an approach that will serve you long after you leave college and will also help you learn better (and thus improve your grades) now. Increasingly, the disciplines are taught not as information to be memorized, but as subject matter to be understood and applied.
- When you are studying a discipline for the first time, ask several basic questions: (1) What is the structure of the discipline? (How is it organized?) (2) What subject matter, topics, or questions does the discipline address? (3) Who are the major contributors to the discipline, such as past and present researchers, scholars, and writers? (4) What special words are used? (5) How is new knowledge discovered? (What research approaches are used?)
- Disciplines are not static; they change constantly as a result of new research and scholarship. New disciplinary structures often emerge; sometimes, new disciplines are spawned as these new structures develop.
- It often makes sense to take an interdisciplinary perspective. This strategy helps us realize that disciplines are simply convenient ways of organizing knowledge; often, we must draw on more than one discipline to answer a question or solve a problem.

PART THREE

RESOURCES FOR LEARNING

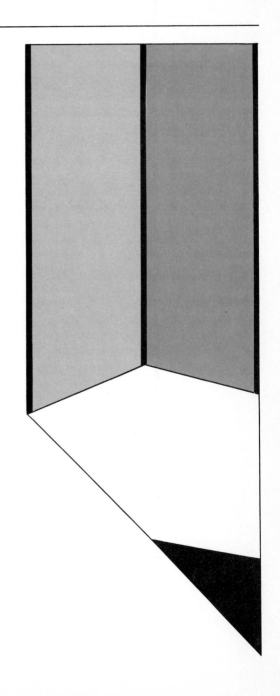

15

USING THE LIBRARY

If you are a returning student and haven't been inside a college library for several years, you are in for a surprise. The electronic library has arrived. No longer must you spend untold hours flipping through a card catalog to find a book when you know only the topic and not the title or author. No longer must you depend solely on the resources of your own college library; your library is now probably linked to national and international computer databases that already contain almost limitless information and are adding to it at a mind-boggling rate. The amount of information in the world is said to be doubling every 7 years, and much of that information is available through your college library.

This vast amount of readily available information is both an asset and a problem. You may have heard the phrases "drowning in information" and "information explosion," which imply that we actually have too much information. In most cases, though, it would be more accurate to describe the problem as having too much of the *wrong* information. We may gather facts from many sources and still lack the specific information we need. The crux of the situation is how to find the *right* information to answer a question or solve a problem.

I'll begin by describing the nature of college libraries, and then, step by step, show you how to find the information you want and need.

LIBRARIES: WHAT TO EXPECT

Contents of a Library

Following is a list of what you can generally expect to find in a college or university library. In many colleges and universities, not all of these resources will be found under the same roof; the library's contents will be distributed among several buildings on the campus. (This is particularly true of large universities.)

1 A collection of *books relating to courses taught at the college or university*. (Many of these books are kept on reserve shelves for specific courses, and students enrolled in these courses have priority in using them.)
2 A collection of *general books*, not relating specifically to courses. Examples of general books include books on broad interdisciplinary topics and classical literature.
3 *Reference books* of a general nature and reference books related to disciplines emphasized at the college or university.
4 *Periodicals and newspapers*, including current issues and bound volumes. In many libraries, older issues are on microfilm and microcards.
5 *Pamphlets and clippings.*
6 *Government publications.*
7 *Audiovisual materials:* films, slides, filmstrips, records, videotapes and audiotapes, maps, globes, etc.
8 *Microforms* such as microfilm, microcards, microprints, and microfiche.
9 *Electronic storage systems* such as CD-ROM.
10 *Archival materials* related to the institution.
11 *Old and rare books.*
12 Books for *recreational reading.*
13 *Dissertations and theses* (at institutions with graduate programs).

In addition, most libraries have extensive areas for studying, and many also have lounges.

Types of Libraries

On most campuses, as I noted above, you can expect to find more than one library, and on some large campuses you will find several, some rather general and others quite highly specialized.

There will usually be one general library that serves the entire college or university. In this library are located major references works, general collections of books, government publications, periodicals, and newspapers. If this is the only library on campus, then the other resources listed above will be located there as well.

On larger campuses, you will often find special subject libraries such as art, astronomy, biology, chemistry, geography, geology, mathematics, music, and physics. Professional schools and colleges will generally also have their own libraries. Depending on what professional schools there are on your campus, these could include agriculture, nursing, engineering, law, business, and pharmacy.

On many larger campuses, one library is generally designated as the undergraduate library. Here you will find a variety of resources, including reserve books for your courses, a recreational reading area, and study facilities.

Layout of a Library

Once you've discovered what libraries exist at your college or university and decided which of them you will be most likely to use, you should plan a tour to get acquainted with the ones you will be using. Most libraries have maps showing the location of their various areas. Generally, you can expect to find the following.

Catalog Room   The catalog room could be considered the heart of the library. In today's electronic library, card catalogs take two forms—traditional and computerized. The traditional catalog has trays of cards organized by author, title, and subject. The computerized catalog will have several computer terminals for access.

Many libraries continue to use both systems because their older books are often not put into the computerized catalogue. (For example, at the University of Wisconsin—Madison, the computer catalog generally includes only materials acquired since 1976.)

Reference Area   The reference area may be a special room or rooms, or a special area set aside for reference works such as dictionaries, encyclopedias, indexes, yearbooks, and directories. CD-ROM storage materials (when available) are generally found in the reference area, as are computer terminals linked to on-line databases which give you access to research materials located elsewhere in this country and often abroad.

Materials in the reference collection usually do not circulate: that is, you can't remove them from the library. But you will generally find an area where you can work near the reference collection.

Study or Reading Rooms   Many students find the library's reading and study rooms the best place on campus to study. In some libraries, it is possible to rent carrels, where you may keep your own study materials for regular use; but often these carrels are reserved for graduate students and faculty members.

Periodical Room   Current issues of magazines, journals, and newspapers are stored in the periodical room (or rooms).

Stacks   The stacks are areas where the library stores the major collection of books and usually the bound periodicals. You will need to find out if the stacks in your library are "open" or "closed." The term *open stacks* means that you may enter the area and find books by yourself. The term *closed stacks* means that you may not enter the area; with closed stacks, assistants will find books for you.

Because many libraries have open stacks, it is important to know how the collection is stored. Libraries generally provide guide sheets that show which categories of books are stored where.

Audiovisual Area   Audiotapes and videotapes, slides, films, and microforms are often stored in a separate audiovisual area, with the necessary equipment for viewing or listening nearby.

UNDERSTANDING THE LIBRARY: HOW INFORMATION IS ARRANGED

To find information efficiently, you'll need to understand how libraries arrange it. Below, I describe card catalogs, library classification systems, types of reference books, and computer databases.

Card Catalogs

Traditional Card Catalog   As I noted above, even though most college libraries now have computerized card catalogs, this new electronic system does not always include a library's entire collection. Thus it is still important for you to know how to use the traditional card catalog, with its trays of 3- by 5-inch cards.

Generally, you can expect to find three types of cards in a card catalog: author, title, and subject (see the illustration on the opposite page). Most publications have at least two entries in the card catalog: an entry under the author's name and an entry under the title *or* subject.

Author card   The author card is the main entry for any publication. In general, the author card shows the following information:

1   *Call number,* which indicates where the book can be found in the library.
2   *Author's full name (last name first), date of birth, and date of death* if the author is not living. The author may be an individual (who wrote the work); an individual who edited the work (as opposed to writing it); an institution or organization (such as U.S. Department of Agriculture or Green Valley Community College); a committee (such as the Committee on Adult Learning); or the title of a publication (such as National Geographic Magazine).

AGRIC
LIBRARY   Apps, Jerold W., 1934-
LB   Study skills for adults returning to
1049   school / Jerold W. Apps. —2nd ed.—
A66   New York : McGraw-Hill, c1982.
1982   xvi, 200 p. : ill. ; 23 cm.
                   Previous ed. published in 1978 as:
               Study skills for those adults returning
               to school.
                   Includes bibliographical references
               and index.

                   1. Study, Method of.   2. Adult
               education.   I. Title

AUTHOR CARD

                   Study skills for adults returning to
                       school
AGRIC
LIBRARY   Apps, Jerold W., 1934-
LB   Study skills for adults returning to
1049   school / Jerold W. Apps. —2nd ed.—
A66   New York : McGraw-Hill, c1982.
1982   xvi, 200 p. : ill. ; 23 cm.
                   Previous ed. published in 1978 as:
               Study skills for those adults returning
               to school.
                   Includes bibliographical references
               and index.

                   1. Study, Method of.   2. Adult
               education.   I. Title

TITLE CARD

                   STUDY, METHOD OF.
AGRIC
LIBRARY   Apps, Jerold W., 1934-
LB   Study skills for adults returning to
1049   school / Jerold W. Apps. —2nd ed.—
A66   New York : McGraw-Hill, c1982.
1982   xvi, 200 p. : ill. ; 23 cm.
                   Previous ed. published in 1978 as:
               Study skills for those adults returning
               to school.
                   Includes bibliographical references
               and index.

                   1. Study, Method of.   2. Adult
               education.   I. Title

SUBJECT CARD

3 *Title and subtitle* of the book.
4 *Coauthor, illustrator, or translator.*
5 *Imprint,* which includes place of publication, publisher, and date of publication.
6 *Collation,* which includes the number of pages or volumes, the illustrative materials, and the size of the book in centimeters.
7 *Series* to which the book belongs, if it is one of a series.
8 *Subjects* that are treated fully in the book.
9 *Full name and birth and death dates of the coauthor, translator, editor, and illustrator.*[1]

Title card The title card is prepared for a book that has a distinctive title. On the title card, the title of the book is typed above the author's name; the rest of the card is the same as the author card.

Subject card Generally, a subject card is prepared for each subject that is discussed fully in a book; thus the number of subject cards for a particular book will depend on the number of subjects it discusses fully. Usually, the subject is typed at the top of the card (it may be in capital letters); the rest of the card is the same as the author card.

Most students know how to find a book when they know the author and title; fewer know how to use the subject catalog to find specific authors and titles under subject-matter areas. If you a writing a paper or doing research in a subject area where you don't know any authors or titles, the subject catalog is the place to start. Also, if you find one book in the subect catalog that seems promising and go to the stacks to find it (assuming that your library has open stacks), you will probably find more books on the topic shelved nearby. It can be rewarding to spend a few minutes browsing.

Computerized Card Catalog When you use a computerized card catalog, the information you see on the computer screen will generally be the same as what you would find in a traditional card catalog. But the process of searching is somewhat different.

If you enjoy flipping through a traditional card catalog—browsing to find books by one author, for instance, or looking at information on several books catalogued under the same subject—then you may find a computerized system frustrating at first. With a computerized catalog, there are no cards to flip through, of course; and if you don't know how to operate the computer, or if you make a mistake in operating it, you will

---

[1]Adapted from Jean Key Gates, *Guide to the Use of Books and Libraries,* 4th ed. McGraw-Hill, New York, 1979, pp. 52–62. The descriptions of the title and subject cards are also based on Gates.

get nothing but a blank screen or an embarrassing beep and a message telling you to seek help.

But using a computerized catalog is not difficult. Instructions are prominently displayed; staff members will show you what to do; and once you have mastered the few simple steps, the computer catalog will save you hours of time. Also, a computerized search will usually yield more and better material.

On campuses with several libraries, all or most of the card catalogs are usually tied together in one computerized catalog. (For example, at the University of Wisconsin—Madison, it is possible to search within the collections of 24 different libraries at the same time.) And on many campuses, the library has set up computer terminals at a number of other locations, so that you can do a card-catalog search without setting foot in the library itself. On many systems, anyone with a microcomputer and a modem (a device for linking your computer to the telephone system) can telephone the computerized card catalog at any time, day or night. Some systems also tell you if a book is already checked out, and when it is due back. Of course, once you identify what you want in the catalog, you'll have to visit the library to pick it up.

To find materials in a computerized card catalog, you can follow the traditional approach of searching by title, author, or subject. You can also search for key words such as parts of a name, or words in a title or subject heading.

If you cannot find a book you want in your library's collection, contact the librarian on duty. Most college libraries are members of the Online Computer Library Center (OCLC), or a similar organization that arranges for interlibrary loans. These organizations will look for the materials you want and send them to your library. Often, you will receive the materials in a matter of days, and generally there is no cost to you.

Library Classification Systems

Library materials are generally stored according to the Dewey Decimal classification system or the Library of Congress system. Let's look at each of these.

Dewey Decimal Classification   In the Dewey Decimal system of classification, numbers are used to divide documents into general categories and then into more specific categories. The general categories are as follows:

000–099   General works: bibliographies, encyclopedias, periodicals
100–199   Philosophy: metaphysics, psychology, logic, ethics
200–299   Religion: Bible, theology, Christian churches

300–399   Social science: political science, economics, education
400–499   Philology: comparative philology, English language, various languages
500–599   Pure science: mathematics, physics, chemistry, biology
600–699   Applied science: medicine, engineering, agriculture
700–799   Arts and recreation: architecture, sculpture, painting
800–899   Literature: American literature, English literature, other literatures
900–999   History: geography, biography, ancient history, modern history[2]

Library of Congress Classification   The Library of Congress classification system uses letters of the alphabet for broad categories, as follows:

A   General works. AC, collections; AE, encyclopedias; AY, yearbooks; AZ, general history.
B   Philosophy-religion. BC, logic; BF, psychology; BL, religions.
C   History-auxiliary sciences. CB, civilization; CS, geneology; CT, biography.
D   History and topography. DA, Great Britain; DC, France; DK, Russia; DU, Australia and Oceania.
E–F   America. E, America (general) and United States (general); F, United States (local) and America except the United States.
G   Geography. GC, oceanography; GN, anthropology; GT, manners and customs; GV, sports and amusements.
H   Social sciences. HB, economic theory; HD, economic history; HE, transportation; HF, commerce; HG, finance; HM, sociology; HQ, family, marriage, home; HT, communities; HV, social pathology, philanthropy.
J   Political science. JA, general works; JO, theory of the state; JX, international law.
K   Law.
L   Education. LB, theory and practice; LC, special forms; LD, United States.
M   Music. ML, literature of music; MT, musical instruction.
N   Fine Arts. NA, architecture; NC, painting; NK, industrial arts.
P   Language and literature. PA, classical languages; PC, romance languages; PD, Teutonic languages; PR, English literature; PS, American literature.

---

[2]Clifford T. Morgan and James Deese, *How to Study*, McGraw-Hill, New York, 1969, p. 89.

Q   Science. QA, mathematics; QC, physics; QD, chemistry; QE, geology; QL, zoology; QP, physiology.

R   Medicine. RB, pathology; RE, ophthalmology; RK, dentistry; RM, therapeutics; RT, nursing.

S   Agriculture—plant and animal industry. SB, plant culture; SD, forestry; SF, animal culture; SK, hunting sports.

T   Technology. TA, engineering; TH, building construction; TK, electrical engineering; TN, mineral industries; TR, photography.

U   Military science.

V   Naval science.

Z   Bibliography and Library Science.[3]

In the Library of Congress system, numbers are used for subdivisions of these broader categories.

Reference Books

Your library's reference books are resources you will use often. Although reference librarians will help you find reference books, the sooner you learn to find them for yourself, the more efficiently you will be able to find answers to your questions.

Reference books can be divided into two broad categories: first, those that are general in scope and not limited to a specific subject; second, those that are specific to a subject area, such as history, art, science, or literature. No attempt is made here to indicate the many references available in specific subject-matter fields. But the following books do list references according to various subject fields; you will find them very helpful:

Cook, Margaret G.: *The New Library Key,* 3d. ed., H. W. Wilson, New York, 1975.

Gates, Jean Key: *Guide to the Use of Books and Libraries,* 4th ed., McGraw-Hill, New York, 1979.

McCormick, Mona: *Who-What-When-Where-How-Why Made Easy,* Popular Library, New York, 1979.

Sheehy, Eugene P.: *Guide to Reference Books,* 9th ed., American Library Association, Chicago, Ill. 1982.

The following sections describe the types of general reference books you can expect to find in a college library and list some examples of each type.

[3]Ibid., p. 90.

Dictionaries Dictionaries provide information about words: meanings, spellings, pronunciation, usage, syllabification, and derivation. Examples of *unabridged* dictionaries are:

Webster's Third New International Dictionary, Merriam, Springfield, Mass., 1981.

Funk and Wagnalls New Standard Dictionary of the English Language, Funk and Wagnalls, New York, 1963.

Oxford English Dictionary, Clarendon Press, Oxford, England, complete edition, 1933. (This classic work comes in thirteen volumes plus supplements.)

Often, a smaller "desk edition" will meet your needs; an example is:

Webster's Ninth New Collegiate Dictionary, Merriam, Springfield, Mass., 1983.

Encyclopedias Encyclopedias are concerned with many subjects and provide an overview of each topic that includes definitions, background, description, and bibliographic references. Examples are:

The Encyclopedia Americana, Americana Corporation, New York, 1979, 30 vols.

Encyclopaedia Britannica, Encyclopaedia Britannica, Chicago, Ill., 1972, 24 vols.

Indexes Indexes are guides to where information can be found. They are particularly useful for finding articles in periodicals. Examples are:

Readers' Guide to Periodical Literature, Wilson, New York, 1900– .

Book Review Digest, Wilson, New York, 1905– .

Yearbooks Yearbooks, sometimes called *annuals,* present information about the events of the past year. Examples are:

Collier's Year Book, Collier, New York, 1938– .

U.S. Bureau of the Census: *Statistical Abstract of the United States,* U.S. Government Printing Office, Washington, D.C., 1878– .

Handbooks Handbooks are small books that provide a variety of information. Sometimes they are called *manuals* or *compendiums.* Examples are:

Robert, Henry M.: *Robert's Rules of Order Newly Revised,* Scott, Foresman, Glenview, Ill., 1981.

United States Government Organization Manual, U.S. Government Printing Office, Washington, D.C., 1935– .

Almanacs   Almanacs were originally developed as a day-by-day projection of the coming year, with weather forecasts, phases of the moon, major holidays, and the like. Today, almanacs include collections of miscellaneous facts and statistical information. Examples are:

Information Please Almanac, Simon and Schuster, New York, 1947– .

The World Almanac and Book of Facts, Newspaper Enterprise Association, New York, 1868– .

Biographical Dictionaries   Biographical dictionaries provide short articles about the lives of individuals, arranged alphabetically according to surnames. Examples are:

The International Who's Who, 47 eds., Europa and Allen and Unwin, London, 1935– .

Who's Who in America, Marquis—Who's Who, Chicago, Ill., 1899– .

Directories   Directories list names and addresses of persons, organizations, agencies, institutions, and the like. For organizations, they may also include purposes, names of officers, and people to contact. Examples of directories are:

Directory of American Scholars, 7th ed., Bowker, New York, 1978, 4 vols.

National Referral Center for Science and Technology: *A Directory of Information Resources in the United States,* U.S. Government Printing Office, Washington, D.C., 1974.

Atlases   An atlas is a bound collection of maps, which may also include pictures, tables, and diagrams. Examples are:

National Geographic Atlas of the World, 5th ed., National Geographic Society, Washington, D.C., 1983.

Rand McNally Cosmopolitan World Atlas, Rand McNally, Chicago, Ill., 1987.

Gazetteers   Gazetteers provide lists of place names, arranged alphabetically, with some information about each place, including its location and historical or descriptive material. Examples are:

Seltzer, L. E. (ed.): *The Columbia Lippincott Gazetteer of the World,* Columbia, New York, 1962.

Webster's New Geographical Dictionary, Merriam, Springfield, Mass., 1977.

Bibliographies   Bibliographies list books and other materials on the same topic. They include author, title, publisher, number of pages, and often price. Sometimes they also include a brief description of what each listing contains. Examples are:

The Bibliographic Index, Wilson, New York, 1938– . (This contains a listing of all current bibliographies, including those published in books, pamphlets, and periodical articles.)[4]

Courtney, Winifred F. (ed.): *The Reader's Adviser and Bookman's Manual,* 11th ed., Bowker, New York, 1960, 2 vols.

Database Searches

On-Line Databases   Although college libraries contain a great deal of information, modern libraries are portals to even more through on-line computer databases.

Terminology of on-line databases   Before discussing some of the advantages and disadvantages of on-line database searches, let's explore some terms and definitions.

Database: A database is a collection of documents—journal articles, monographs, research reports, newspaper articles, lists of books, and the like. Generally, these documents are electronically stored at a central computing center and available to users' computers via telephone.

On-line: The term *on-line* describes a computer data search conducted via telephone. Charges are generally based on the amount of on-line time that is used and on a varying fee (depending on length of citation and database) for documents listed.

Database vendor: A company that stores electronic databases. Examples are Dialog and BRS.

Bibliographic citation: A bibliographic database generally includes a bibliographic citation and a list of "keywords" (see below). The bibliographic citation includes article title, author's name, and relevant information about the source of publication.

Keywords: Sometimes called *indexing terms* or *descriptors,* keywords describe content, issues, topics, or concepts covered in the specific bibliographic item. Most databases follow a "controlled vocabulary" approach; that is, only words or numbers (codes) listed in the database thesaurus are used as keywords. For comprehensive computer database searching, it is more efficient to consult a copy of the thesaurus for that database, where key search terms will be listed.

---

[4]Gates, op. cit., p. 124.

Abstract: A short summary of the information in an article. Usually, the abstract appears after the bibliographic citation and the list of keywords. A good abstract will often provide the specific information you want, so that you do not need to find the article itself.

Full-text format: This term is used when a database contains a complete copy of the source material. Generally it indicates that a complete magazine, newspaper, or journal article is available on-line.

Printout: A computer-printed record of your search. You have the option of saving your material on a computer disk, seeing it on screen but not saving it, or printing it on paper. If you save it on a computer disk, you can later print it on paper.

Advantages and disadvantages of on-line databases On-line databases have some important advantages. Nearly unlimited information is available and can be obtained in a relatively short period of time—15 to 20 minutes. This information may be physically located thousands of miles away, but it is readily accessible. Information can be obtained using a variety of access points such as author, title, and keywords. Most databases are kept up-to-date frequently; some are updated daily. Thus the most recent information is available. The cost of searching is relatively low, particularly when you consider the value of your time, and the ease with which you can obtain information that might otherwise be available only by mail, or not at all. It is possible to subscribe to a computer database service and have access to huge amounts of data at home, but for this you need a computer, a modem (for the telephone hookup), and the appropriate software; you also need to become proficient in database searching, or the cost will be high for the amount of information you receive. Students usually can simply use the services for computer database searching available at their libraries. Expert help is on hand, and the service is free or very inexpensive.

There are some disadvantages to on-line databases, however. For one thing, it is sometimes not possible to search for materials produced before 1970 (this varies from database to database). When early material is listed, abstracts are generally not available. Second, the most comprehensive databases are in the applied and pure sciences, medicine, agriculture, social sciences, and education; few databases exist for the humanities or the arts. Third, a certain amount of skill is necessary to conduct a search. Even if you are working with an expert reference librarian, you must have a rather precise idea of what you are looking for in order to make most efficient and effective use of an on-line search.

CD-ROM Databases CD-ROM stands for "compact disk, read-only memory." It is a technology for storing vast amounts of information in a very small space. For example, one CD-ROM disk which measures 4.72 inches (12 centimeters) in diameter and weighs little more than half an ounce can store 220,000 pages of text.

How CD-ROM databases work   A CD-ROM disk is made of polycarbonate plastic, sealed with a transparent plastic coating and a reflective aluminum base. The disk is read with a CD-ROM drive or player which uses a low-power laser beam. Nothing actually touches the disk surface; this allows for nearly endless use without wear.

To retrieve data stored on a CD-ROM disk, you need a microcomputer, a CD-ROM drive, and the necessary software. Once the information is retrieved from the CD-ROM disk and stored in the computer, it may be printed as is or incorporated with other written materials you may be creating on your computer.

At this writing, most CD-ROM equipment is available only in libraries and in businesses where the disks are used to store routine information (such as lists of automotive parts). In libraries, CD-ROM equipment is increasingly used to store databases such as the ERIC (Educational Resources Information Center) bibliographic database, *Psychological Abstracts, Dissertation Abstracts,* and reference works such as *Books in Print. Grolier's Electronic Encyclopedia* was the first encyclopedia to be converted to CD-ROM application.

Advantages and disadvantages of CD-ROMs   The advantages of the CD-ROM system for students—and many others who need to obtain information quickly—are several. In an on-line database search, the database may actually be thousands of miles away, but a CD-ROM disk is right there in front of you. Also, with an on-line search there is usually both a charge for the telephone and a charge for the actual time you spend searching. But a CD-ROM disk has been purchased outright by the library, and the cost of using it is minimal. Thus in most libraries, students are encouraged to perform CD-ROM searches themselves, without the intervention of a reference librarian. And a CD-ROM search may take only a few minutes, as opposed to the hours you might spend rummaging through materials in a traditional card catalog and the stacks.

As with on-line database searches, the more carefully you have planned your search and the more precisely you know what you are looking for, the more successful your CD-ROM search will be. If you don't know exactly what you are looking for, a CD-ROM will not provide much useful information.

FINDING INFORMATION: HOW TO CONDUCT A SEARCH

In this section, you'll find guidelines for conducting an information search. Most of these are general principles which will be applicable no matter whether you are using a traditional card catalog, a computerized card catalog, an on-line database, or a CD-ROM database; but some are more specific.

A few comments are in order before we turn to these step-by-step guidelines, however. First, remember that invariably, planning before a search will save you many hours of time and considerable frustration. Second, remember that the new technologies are only tools, which you must wield. That is, you are in charge; as exciting as an electronic technology may sound, its performance will not impress you—and it may even make your work more troublesome and complicated—unless you know exactly what you want it to do and how to tell it what to do. Third, remember that what we are considering here is how to find information— just that and no more. No method of finding information, new or traditional, will write a paper for you.

Step 1: Select a Topic

For most students, selecting a topic means finding a subject for a term paper or a class assignment. For graduate students, this step may be related to a review of literature for a research project that will ultimately become part of a thesis or dissertation.

When selecting a topic, ask yourself several questions: Is this topic of sufficient interest to sustain my motivation through the research and writing phases of the work? Do I have sufficient time to do the necessary research for this topic as I have defined it, or should I consider narrowing the topic? Is my topic so new or so specialized that sufficient research material may not be available?

Step 2: Obtain Preliminary Information

In step 2, do a topic check. Consult an encyclopedia, your textbooks, a periodical index, and perhaps *Books in Print* to obtain some preliminary information about your topic. On note cards, jot down terms, concepts, authors' names, and references.

Step 3: Refine Your Topic

In step 3, make some preliminary decisions about your topic. Can you find enough material to cover the topic in the time you have? Or, on the other hand, is there too much material for your topic? At this point, you will probably narrow or broaden your topic.

In my experience, most students tend to begin with too broad a topic. Thus step 3 should usually mean narrowing the topic in some way. This may be done by giving the topic a particular focus or a particular point of view. For example, if your original topic was the misuse of insecticides in agriculture, you would soon discover that this topic is extremely broad. To narrow it, you could focus on insecticide residues in groundwater. To narrow it further, you could focus geographically: you could examine insecticide residues in groundwater in, say, vegetable-growing areas of the United States.

Step 4: Develop a Topic Statement

For step 4, state in one or two sentences what you expect your paper to be about. This is your topic statement. Using your statement as a guide, you should next formulate a series of questions that you will try to answer.

Once you are researching and writing your paper, you may find that you want to revise your topic statement. But starting with a topic sentence, before you begin extensive research or the actual writing, will help provide a clear direction for your work.

Step 5: Develop a List of Terms

Construct a list of words that are related to your topic, and thus to what you will be looking for in your research. The words can be descriptors (keywords), authors, titles, or years. When making up a list of words, include plural and variant forms, for example, *school, schools, schooling.*

In the example above, terms might include *pesticides, residues,* and *groundwater.* If you searched for any of these terms, you would of course find considerable material; but what you really want is a combination of all three terms—that is, *pesticide residues in groundwater.* Combining terms in this way will enable you to exclude vast amounts of information from your search.

The system of using terms in relation to each other is called *Boolean logic.* Boolean logic can help you considerably when you began searching in an electronic (computerized) card catalog, an on-line database, or a CD-ROM database.

Boolean logic uses the words *or, and,* and *not* in particular ways. For instance, if you are searching in an electronic card catalog for information about pesticide residues and you ask the computer to search for pesticides *or* residues, it will retrieve every book that includes the topic "pesticides" and any book that includes the topic "residues" and books about both topics. This would not be helpful: it would give you too much unrelated information. But if you ask the computer to search for pesticides *and* residues, it will search only for books in which both terms occur. And if you ask the computer to search for pesticides *and* residues

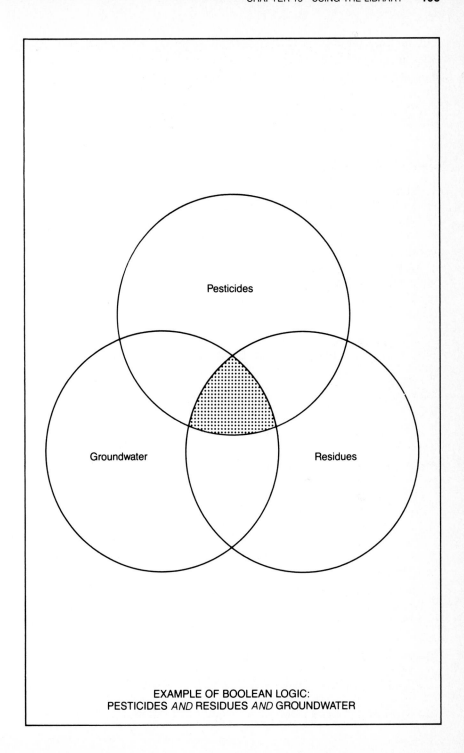

EXAMPLE OF BOOLEAN LOGIC:
PESTICIDES *AND* RESIDUES *AND* GROUNDWATER

but *not*, say, "food," it will exclude all references to food. Here, a good strategy would be to search for pesticides *and* residues *and* groundwater. The computer would search only for occurrences of all three terms at once. The illustration on the preceding page makes this search strategy clearer: when you combine the three terms, what will turn up in your search is whatever falls into the area where the circles overlap.

Step 6: Refer to the Traditional Card Catalog

It is often a good idea to begin your search with the library's traditional card catalog. You may be more comfortable using it, and the kind of "browsing" it allows may be very effective. Moreover, as noted above, it is sometimes the best way to find valuable material that was produced before about 1970.

The preliminary information you obtained in step 2 has probably yielded some names of authors and some titles that can serve as a starting place. Find these materials and consult their bibliographies for additional sources to pursue.

Step 7: Refer to the Electronic Card Catalog

If your library has an electronic card catalog, do a search in it, using your keywords. If you have never used a computerized card catalog, first read the posted instructions. Then try a search. If you have difficulty, ask the librarian for help.

Step 8: Make an On-Line Data Search

If you believe that information you are seeking is available in a database, work with the reference librarian to make an on-line data search.

Up to this point, your search will have incurred no costs. But at many colleges and universities, you will pay a nominal fee for an on-line search—generally based on the actual time on-line, though sometimes you will pay a flat fee. When making an on-line database search, therefore, it is extremely important to know what you are seeking. If you don't, you will pay for material that is not exactly what you are looking for, or perhaps isn't what you are looking for at all.

Step 9: Make a CD-ROM Data Search

If the nature of your topic is such that journal articles and other materials are likely to be stored in a CD-ROM database, you will want to make a CD-ROM search. You can find out from the librarian what databases are available on CD-ROM before beginning a search. As with a search in a computerized card catalog, use keywords, follow the posted instructions for using the machinery, and ask the staff for help if you run into difficulties.

A CD-ROM search will generally produce bibliographic information and abstracts of articles (this is also true of an on-line search). You must then search out the complete sources if, on the basis of title, abstracts, etc., an entry appears promising for your project.

Step 10: Review Your Information

Finally, review what you have collected. Does it provide a reasonable selection of materials for your project? Or is the list of materials so long that you will not have time to find and work through all of it? If the list seems too long, do you want to focus your work more narrowly? The list may also be so short that you believe you couldn't write a comprehensive paper on the basis of it. In that case, you may want to add to your keywords and do some more searching.

SUMMARY

- The modern college or university library contains an enormous amount of information and has electronic access to even more. It is important to understand how libraries work in order to find, amid all the information available, the *right* information to answer a question or solve a problem.
- A college or university library usually contains books related to specific courses, general books, reference books, periodicals and newspapers, pamphlets and clippings, government publications, audiovisual materials, microforms, electronic storage systems, archives, old and rare books, recreational reading materials, and dissertations and theses (if the institution has a graduate program). These may be housed in several different buildings.
- A campus usually has one general library, and often special subject libraries.
- Students should become familiar with the layout of each library they expect to use. Generally, a library will have a catalog room, one or more reference areas, study and reading rooms, periodical rooms, stacks, and an audiovisual area.
- Although most college libraries now have computerized, or electronic, card catalogs, it is still important to know how to use a traditional card catalog, in which author, title, and subject cards are stored in trays.

- A computerized card catalog provides essentially the same information as a traditional catalog, but that information is displayed on a computer screen, and the process of searching for it is somewhat different. Electronic catalogs can save you time and usually yield more and better materials than traditional catalogs.
- Materials in the library are usually stored according to one of two classification systems: Dewey Decimal classification or Library of Congress classification.
- The library's reference books are important resources. General reference books found in most libraries include dictionaries, encyclopedias, indexes, yearbooks, handbooks, almanacs, biographical dictionaries, directories, atlases, gazetteers, and bibliographies.
- Through on-line databases and CD-ROM databases, libraries become portals for almost unlimited materials in addition to their own holdings.
- To conduct an effective information search, follow ten steps: (1) select a topic; (2) obtain some preliminary information about it; (3) refine your topic (usually by narrowing it); (4) formulate a topic statement; (5) draw up a list of terms related to your topic; (6) consult the traditional card catalog; (7) consult the electronic card catalog; (8) make an on-line data search; (9) make a CD-ROM data search; and (10) review your information.

16

FINDING
LEARNING RESOURCES

At first glance, a college or university may seem cold, frightening, and confusing. But help is generally close at hand. When you have a question or problem—whether it's finding out the requirements of your major, transferring credits, applying for a student loan, or locating reference material for a term paper—someone is available to assist you.

The key is learning what resources are available on your campus and how to use them. Using resources effectively takes some effort, some practice, and perhaps some luck, but after a few weeks most students know where the resources are and what shortcuts will make these resources more usable.

SOURCES OF INFORMATION
AND HELP ON CAMPUS

Where to Start

When you have a problem—or, better, even before you have a problem—the place to start is your campus's *resource directory*. It may have some other name, but people will know what you are talking about when you ask for it. At the University of Wisconsin—Madison, our resource directory is called "Wheat and Chaff." It tells students where to find out about university procedures and guidelines, housing, student organizations, health services, financial aid, and much more.

Many campuses also have an *information desk,* booth, or office—a place to go when you don't know where to go. In fact, if you don't even know where to find the resource directory, you could start with the information desk. Generally, people staffing such a desk can help you with questions like "What is it?" "Where do I find it?" "When will it happen?" and "Who does it?"—questions that you are sure to have, no matter whether you are in college for the first time or are returning after several years away.

It is easy to hurry past one of the most useful sources of information on campus: the *bulletin board.* Most campuses have bulletin boards inside buildings, outside on kiosks at busy locations, near classroom doors, and in housing units. Here you can find out about music groups, films, outside lecturers, and student organizations.

Most colleges and universities also have a *college newspaper* in which campus events are regularly listed, along with other valuable information (where to find the best pizza in town; who wants a ride to Washington, D.C.).

On some campuses, the administration publishes an "official" *newsletter* or newspaper for faculty and staff members and students. It lists campus events, describes new policies, and has feature articles about various (usually) interesting happenings on campus.

Don't overlook one very obvious source of information—the public *telephone directory.* Here you can find out about restaurants, theaters, and favorite gathering places.

Many colleges and universities also have their own *telephone services.* Students can dial a campus number, often 24 hours a day, and listen to a cassette on a specific topic. These tapes cover such topics as what majors are offered in a college, studying abroad, tuition, financial aid, parking, child care, housing, legal issues, health and nutrition, veterans' benefits, and special programs for returning students.

Dean's Office

Visit the dean's office if you have questions about curriculum: "Will my courses at X University be transferred into my program here?" "Is advanced chemistry recommended?" The dean's office also keeps a file of information on loans and scholarships, internships (opportunities for students to work in an area they are studying, usually part time), and job-placement services for graduating students. If you need tutoring in a course, or if you are having other study problems, the dean's office knows where to refer you.

Many deans' offices also provide services to minority students, including information about program planning, registration, curriculum requirements, and personal issues. And they refer students to other campus offices for assistance with such matters as financial aid and housing, and for the special support programs that are available on many campuses.

Advisers

Academic advisers are often underused, but they can be a gold mine of information. Advising varies from college to college. You may have been assigned an adviser who will work with you personally during your college years. (This is almost always the case for graduate students and often true for undergraduates as well.) Or you may have access to a faculty advising service.

In either case, the academic advisers are available to discuss degree requirements, requirements for specific majors or fields of study, and course planning, including detailed sequencing of courses to meet degree requirements. Academic advisers are also available when there are problems—courses that give you particular difficulty, examination strategies that baffle you, and the like. If the advisers don't know the answer to your question, they generally know who does.

Course Instructors

Questions about material being covered in a specific course should be taken up with the course instructor. Sometimes it is not possible to raise such a question during the regular class period. If that is the case, talk with the instructor after class or make an appointment to talk with him or her at some other time. Most instructors welcome the opportunity to talk with students about questions that grow out of their classes, yet many students are reluctant to talk with instructors outside of class.

The professional thing to do is to ask the instructor for an office appointment, or to call the instructor's office (generally the syllabus will include the instructor's telephone number) and make an appointment. Then, be sure to keep the appointment.

Use common sense, too. If your question can possibly be answered simply by consulting the textbook or talking with another student, do this first. But don't hesitate to consult your instructor if a question remains unanswered.

Other Faculty Members

Faculty members who are not your own course instructors will help you if you seek them out. If you are writing a paper and know that an authority on the topic works on the campus, make an appointment with him or her, or (if that is not convenient) use the telephone for a brief interview.

Don't hesitate to contact instructors at other colleges and universities who have information you need. Write to them, call them, or visit them if possible. Most academics are flattered to be sought out and eager to assist someone working in their field.

As is true with all "resource people," the more specific your questions are, and the more sharply focused your ideas are, the more help you are likely to get. You may not be received well if you ask a vague, general question because you haven't taken the time to think through your project or to be specific. For example, if you came to me and asked me to tell you "about adult and continuing education," you would receive only questions in response. I would need to know what specifically interested you in this broad field of study, which ranges from life-span development research to the relationship between nutrition and learning.

Tutoring Centers

Many campuses have volunteer tutoring programs run by students. Their emphasis is on "peer education"—students helping students. Generally, help is provided (free of charge) for a variety of courses, but particularly those at the introductory and intermediate level.

Tutoring services take a variety of forms. A student may come to a center with a particular question or problem, and a single session may provide the answer. Or a student may come weekly for ongoing one-to-one tutoring for a particular course. Or small groups may meet to discuss a subject with an experienced tutor.

Many tutoring centers also offer English as a second language (ESL) for international students and Americans whose first language is not English. The emphasis is commonly on conversational English and pronunciation; writing is usually covered in a writing laboratory (see below).

Writing Laboratories

Writing laboratories are found on many campuses; they may be "free-standing" or set up in conjunction with other student services. Writing lab instructors usually offer short, noncredit classes and workshops on planning and organizing papers; improving writing style; taking essay examinations; and writing research papers, reports in the sciences, book reviews, and cover letters and résumés. Often, writing assignments you are working on for your courses will be used as examples in these laboratories.

Study-Skills Workshops

Topics emphasized at study-skills workshops include how to read a textbook, how to plan a study schedule, how to prepare for and take an exam, and how to write academic papers—many of the topics covered in this book. Instructors are available to work with students individually or in groups.

Many college students today take part in study-skills programs whether or not they are having problems. Students with average or even above-average study skills can increase their skills considerably by enrolling in these programs. The programs are not designed only for those who experience difficulty with some aspect of studying.

"Test Anxiety" Programs

Examinations are a problem for many students. I've discovered in my research that returning students, who may not have taken an academic examination for years, develop many fears about upcoming exams. And many younger students, even though they have taken examination continually for 12 or years more, still approach an exam with sweaty palms and twinges of panic.

A "test anxiety" program focuses on helping students develop a positive attitude toward examinations and hone their test-taking skills. The program may include exercises for relaxing, staying calm, and controlling fear.

Computer Centers

Today, many students are required to use computers in some facet of their college work, and many want to use word processors to make their papers and other written assignments easier.

Campuses often have a variety of computer centers where students have access to computers for writing and other projects. Instructors are generally available to help them operate the machines. Many computer centers also offer short courses and workshops on certain types of microcomputer software (such as word-processing, spreadsheet, and statistical analysis programs), as well as information about computer operating systems.

Counseling Centers

Every campus has at least one counseling center designed to help students with whatever problems they are facing, including feelings of inadequacy, marital difficulties, problems with family relationships and relationships with friends and "significant others," academic work, test anxiety, vocational planning, alcohol and drug abuse, and the like. Counseling centers always maintain confidentiality; no records can be released without a student's permission.

Religious Counseling

Most colleges and universities have religious organizations on campus, or easy access to neighborhood organizations. Such religious centers have experienced staffs, prepared to deal with a wide range of problems: depression, personal relationships, and so on.

Centers for Returning Students

Almost every campus has a center for returning students, a place where these students can gather and find help with a number of issues. The centers are often staffed by counselors who are themselves older returning students.

Such a center typically offers educational and vocational counseling for adults who are considering returning to school or changing careers, assistance with registration procedures, financial aid, and information about child care. Many centers for returning students also offer study-skills workshops which take up overcoming test anxiety, learning how to concentrate, managing time, and dealing with role conflicts (an important issue for students who are also spouses, parents, workers, and community members).

In addition to these functions, centers for returning students serve as referral offices for any problem they cannot directly solve.

College Bookstores

College bookstores not only serve as places where you can buy textbooks, general books, and various types of supplies; they also can be a source of up-to-date information about new books available on a host of topics. Also, since most college bookstores are organized according to subject-matter areas (education, philosophy, psychology, sociology, history, business, science, etc.), by browsing through a bookstore you can often identify books you may want to buy later, or check out of the library.

You can also learn about books that instructors recommend for courses you are considering taking. Leafing through a suggested textbook can tell you a considerable amount about the course itself.

PERSONAL RESOURCES

At any college or university, the students themselves are an important resource—one that is too often overlooked. Possibly the most neglected resource of all is you yourself. Let's consider how you and your fellow students can be effective personal resources.

You and Your Experiences

You and your own experiences are among the most valuable resources you have. Often, you'll encounter a question in your reading, or in a class, that you've dealt with sometime during your life—perhaps you ran into something similar at work or while traveling. Unfortunately, however, some students have the mistaken notion that their own experiences don't count or don't represent potential answers to academic questions. It's important to remember that your life experience *does* count and very often can be relevant to your studies.

Older returning students have a particular advantage here, simply because they have lived longer and have accumulated more experience. But for younger and older students alike, putting your college studies into the framework of your life experiences—and using your experiences to help you understand new information, concepts, and theories—can make learning challenging, exciting, and more real to you.

Other Students

If you are a resident student, you will soon come to know many other students through contacts in classes, in discussion groups, and in your dormitory. But if you are commuting to campus (and particularly if you are a returning student commuting from home and perhaps working as well), getting to know other students may be more difficult. In fact, you may need to make a point of meeting other students before or after class.

Strike up a conversation with other students during a break, or before and after a lecture. Suggest going out for coffee after class with two or three other students. It's a good chance to discuss the lecture you've just heard, and to begin establishing a student network that can pay off in many ways. Returning students may want to join appropriate organizations: single-parent groups, or returning-student groups, or perhaps (if they are graduate students) their department's graduate-student organization—most departments have them.

What can you gain from contacts with other students, beside the fact that these social exchanges are interesting and worthwhile in themselves?

For one thing, your fellow students' diversity will help broaden your perspective: some will be your own age, some younger, and some older, for example; and they will come from many different backgrounds and be pursuing many different goals.

Also, students can be a good source of information. For instance, ask several students about courses you plan to take. They can tell you much more about instructors, course requirements, and examinations than you can learn from the college bulletin or even from a syllabus. This "inside information" is invaluable for planning your curriculum.

Furthermore, as I discussed in Chapter 6, meeting with a group of classmates can help greatly in preparing for examinations. Of course, you will have to prepare on your own as well; but other students can be "sounding boards" for your ideas, and you can compare your understanding of concepts and theories with theirs. Some students may have considerably more experience in certain areas than you do, and they can help by providing additional background information.

Two cautionary points are in order here. First, it is easy for student encounters to degenerate into gripe sessions. This tendency can be overcome, however. For example, to make group work most effective, the students in the group should plan an agenda, deciding what questions or issues they will discuss and policing each other to make sure they stay on the topic; they can also assign individual work to each member, which will be reported back to the group for discussion.

Second, in some academic settings, students unfortunately develop a competitive rather than a cooperative attitude toward each other. To move past such competition, a few students must sometimes take the initiative—by organizing a student group, for instance. So much can be gained when students work together on common problems and questions that it is depressing when students believe that helping another student will somehow lessen their own ability to achieve.

COMMUNITY RESOURCES

Resources in the community can also be very helpful. For instance, if you are writing a paper for a course, you can often obtain practical information about the topic if you talk with a working professional. If your paper is on, say, the professional education of engineers, you might talk with someone in a local engineering firm. If you have a project related to social work, talking with a community social worker can give you practical insights and lead you to other resources. If you are studying personnel practices followed in business, talking with the personnel director of a local company will give you invaluable information.

The kind of information available in the community is often an important addition to the information you obtain from the library and from computerized data searches. Sometimes, we overlook information in the community, or believe that it is not as important as what we get from the library. Don't forget that for many of your class projects, community resources can provide the most powerful of all the information you collect.

SUMMARY

- Colleges and universities provide a host of resources to help you with your studies, with practical issues of college life, and with personal problems. Most schools publish a directory which lists resources; this is obviously the place to start if you have a question. Important resources on campus include the dean's office, academic advisers, course instructors, and a variety of centers such as counseling services and writing laboratories. The college bookstore is also a useful resource.
- An often overlooked resource is your own experience. The experiences of other students can also be helpful, and knowing other students is likely to be invaluable.
- Agencies, institutions, and businesses in the community can also be valuable resources for your learning.

PART FOUR

DEVELOPING LIFE SKILLS

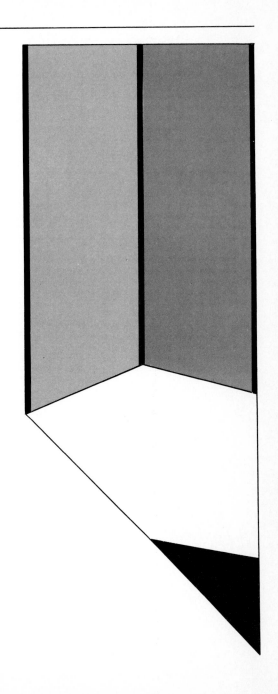

17

MANAGING YOUR TIME

Students mention no other block to learning more often than insufficient time. It is understandable. To do college work successfully, you must juggle many activities. Some students are working part time or full time, and this requires skillful time management. Some students are married and some have children; their time can be strained to the extreme.

In one of my research projects with returning students, I interviewed older students about what they found to be blocks to learning. Many told me about problems with time. For instance, one student said:

> I won't have time till the end of the semester. I'm not sure I can get everything done. I'm not sure I will meet my responsibilities to the people at work, or to myself at school, or to my husband....I am trying to do too much; I really don't know where or if I could eliminate anything. There's nothing I could eliminate. I couldn't drop a course, because the department wouldn't let me. I couldn't cut my hours back at work. They are already cut back so far, and I have to work to make some money. What's really sliding is home. I don't do any cooking, and I don't do any cleaning.... You just keep going.... It's like a train I saw once in a movie that just slid through to no end. You just slide right up to the end of the semester and hope that when you hit the last day or the last exam, you can walk away.

TIME-STEALERS

We all have mental "time thieves." They lurk in the shadows of our minds, and when we least expect it, they sneak out and snatch away valuable minutes—sometimes hours. What are these time-stealers?

Procrastination

I once heard a story about a man who attended a workshop on how to overcome procrastination. When he came home, his wife asked him if had gotten any ideas about how to solve his problem. He said he surely had. "What are you going to do then, Charles?" "I'm going to think about it," he replied.

Each of us pushes aside tasks until this afternoon, until tomorrow, until next week. Soon, there may be a logjam of postponed projects, and panic sets in because deadlines are approaching. When this happens, we have lost control of our time.

I believe that all of us procrastinate to some extent. The issue is how much we procrastinate and how seriously procrastination affects our use of time. If you have a serious problem because of procrastination, the time-savers and time-makers outlined later in this chapter can help you.

A very common form of procrastination is working too close to deadlines. When we habitually do this, work piles up, and we labor frantically to finish it on time. We often delude ourselves with the thought that we do our best work under these circumstances. It may be true for some people, but not for many. Most of us need time to revise and polish our work, and that is not possible in a frantic all-night session immediately before a deadline.

Unclear Priorities

Although we may be busy—extremely busy—we may actually be working on the most insignificant of the tasks we must complete. Spending vast amounts of time on minor tasks can steal valuable time from tasks which are more important.

No one else can tell you which of your own everyday tasks are most important. But you can ask yourself some questions that will help you to identify the important things. For each task you face, ask yourself four questions:

1 *What would happen if I ignored this altogether?* You might be surprised at how often it makes little difference whether a task is completed or not.
2 *Could this be postponed so that something more important could take its place?* Often, a task can be completed at some time in the future rather than right away.
3 *Could I combine this with another task?* Combining two or more tasks can save time.
4 *Am I concentrating on this because it is really important, or simply because I enjoy it?* We don't want to eliminate things we enjoy, of

course, but some of them might better become leisure-time activities so that they will not compete with more important tasks for our time.

Daydreaming

Summer breezes and days at the beach, snowcapped mountains and flower-lined hiking trails, quaint cabins in the woods, time with a special person—these and hundreds of other thoughts sneak into our consciousness and snatch away valuable time. In Chapter 18, on concentration, I outline some approaches for overcoming daydreaming.

Frustration and Anxiety

"I won't do well on this test." "Why did I ever take this course? I don't have the background for it." "I'm going to run out of money before the end of the semester." "I wish I could understand what my instructor is talking about. Most of the time I'm lost." Such thoughts are common— and they are time-stealers. Frustration and worry also leave us with a sense of inadequacy and often with actual physical symptoms. They not only rob us of valuable time but make us feel miserable as well.

TIME-SAVERS

Now that I've described how we lose time, or have it snatched away from us, let's look at the positive side. You can do several things to save time—in effect, to arrest the time thieves in your life.

Time Inventory

A "time inventory" is a record of how you actually spend your time. To start a time inventory, keep an exact record of what you do from the time when you get up in the morning until you go to bed at night, for 1 week. (Use the time inventory worksheet shown in the illustration on page 212.) Record your work hours if you have a job. Write down the time you spend commuting to work and to classes. Write down the time you spend eating. Record the time you spend with your family and the time you spend with your friends.

When you have done this for 1 week, you should begin to see certain patterns in how you use time. Then, you can begin to question your use of time and the priorities you are giving to your activities. In particular, have you set aside enough time for study?

	Sunday	Monday	Tuesday	Wednesday	Thursday	Friday	Saturday
6:00 A.M.							
7:00 A.M.							
8:00 A.M.							
9:00 A.M.							
10:00 A.M.							
11:00 A.M.							
12:00 NOON							
1:00 P.M.							
2:00 P.M.							
3:00 P.M.							
4:00 P.M.							
5:00 P.M.							
6:00 P.M.							
7:00 P.M.							
8:00 P.M.							
9:00 P.M.							
10:00 P.M.							
11:00 P.M.							
12:00 MIDNIGHT							

TIME INVENTORY WORKSHEET

	Sunday	Monday	Tuesday	Wednesday	Thursday	Friday	Saturday
6:00 A.M.							
7:00 A.M.							
8:00 A.M.							
9:00 A.M.							
10:00 A.M.							
11:00 A.M.							
12:00 NOON							
1:00 P.M.							
2:00 P.M.							
3:00 P.M.							
4:00 P.M.							
5:00 P.M.							
6:00 P.M.							
7:00 P.M.							
8:00 P.M.							
9:00 P.M.							
10:00 P.M.							
11:00 P.M.							
12:00 MIDNIGHT							

WEEKLY TIME PLAN

Weekly Time Plan

When you have completed your time inventory and have made some decisions about how you can improve your use of time, draw up a weekly time plan which will allow sufficient time for study. (Use the weekly planning form shown in the illustration on page 213.) As you develop your time plan, you should keep a few important considerations in mind.

First, *be realistic* about planning study time. Remember that it is generally better to study for, say, 2 hours every day than just once a week for a whole day or twice a week for half a day. Most people accomplish more with several shorter study periods than with one or two long sessions. Remember also that you should plan time for family, friends, and leisure activities. If you are living at home—and especially if you have a spouse or children—let your family in on your time plan. The time you have set aside for study should be "protected"; it is your time, a time when you are not to be disturbed.

Second, along with planning must go *discipline*. If you have planned 1 hour of study time each day at 5 A.M., then you must discipline yourself to get up every morning and actually study at that time. You may find that you carry on some interesting conversations with yourself until you get into a routine of daily study; one part of you will insist, for instance, that you owe yourself another hour of sleep and that you don't really need to get up to study, while another part of you argues that you must stick to your plan.

Professional writers, like students, must struggle with the problem of disciplining themselves and sticking to a schedule if they are going to be productive. Many professional writers write every day, whether they feel like writing or not. They do not wait for inspiration, as some people believe. They sit in front of the typewriter or word processor and write, as painful as it may be. This approach is also appropriate for students. Whether you feel like it or not, you must stick to your plan. In the long run, it is the hours you spend studying each day that will determine your success as a student. Although some students manage to pass examinations by cramming at the last minute, this is not the most productive way to learn. Day-by-day, ordinary, disciplined study will help you learn more and keep up with your assignments, and it will also provide you with what you need to pass examinations.

Third, *break up blocks of study time.* If you find that you have 2- or 3-hour blocks of study time, try to subdivide them in some way. John Muir, a famous naturalist who was also an inventor, devised a special study desk for his own use. When he worked at this desk, every 50 minutes a gadget connected to a clock would pick up the book he was studying, remove it, and set another in front of him. Muir's theory was that he should not work on any one topic for longer than 1 hour at a time. His theory makes sense. After 50 minutes or 1 hour of study in one subject, turn to another subject; or at least give yourself a 10- or 15-minute break before continuing. You will be fresher and more productive.

Monthly Calendar

Keeping a monthly calender helps you put all your academic tasks into perspective. Use a large calendar with enough space for written entries on each date. Note the dates of forthcoming examinations; note due dates for papers; and so on.

If you are already keeping a month-by-month family calendar, it is a simple matter to add entries related to your college work. But be sure to use different colors of ink to set off academic activities from dentist appointments, car pools, and the like.

"To-Do" List

Another technique for managing time and setting priorities is a daily "to-do" list. A to-do list includes all the things you want to accomplish in one day—personal and family activities as well tasks at work and school. Put an asterisk in front of items that are of high priority. When a task is completed, cross it off. If a task is not completed, enter it on the next day's to-do list.

Some people find a weekly to-do list more convenient than a daily list. Most people find it useful to write the daily or weekly list on note cards, or in a notebook small enough to carry in a pocket, backpack, or handbag. Then, the cards or notebook can be used to record new items that they learn about during the course of a day.

Saying No

Learning how to say "no" is a problem for all of us. We are asked to serve on committees, participate in social events, travel, help organize activities, and so on—the list is unending. I am not suggesting that you turn down every request that comes along. But before you say "yes," find out, if you can, how much time an activity will take. With this information, you can begin to make an informed decision about whether or not you want to do it.

A common problem for new college students is becoming involved in far too many activities outside of classes—activities that take an enormous amount of time and will ultimately destroy the most carefully conceived time-management plan. You will of course want to become involved in some out-of-class activities—I am not advocating a hermit-like existence for students. But say "no" if you decide that a particular activity will take too much of your time.

TIME-MAKERS

You can make more time in three ways: first, by learning how to work more efficiently; second, by using your spare moments effectively; third, by "storing time." Let's look at each of these.

Working More Efficiently

Throughout this book, I emphasize ways to be more efficient and effective as a student. These include improving your reading, writing, and note-taking skills; learning how to study the different disciplines; and using resources productively.

Another way to be more efficient is to "work fresh." Trying to study when you are tired is inefficient. Sometimes, of course, you have no choice; other necessities in your life have taken up your time, and you cannot study until these activities are completed. But whenever possible, you should plan to study when you are relaxed and refreshed. It is particularly important to tackle difficult study tasks when you are fresh. The difficult tasks will seem even harder if you come to them after a long day of other activities, when you are already tired.

To help yourself "work fresh," you should plan to take breaks. Apply John Muir's theory and study each subject no more than 1 hour at a stretch. Or take a 15-minute break after each hour of work.

Improving your concentration will also improve your efficiency. A concentrated hour of study is worth 3 hours of on-again, off-again concentration. Study Chapter 19, on concentration techniques, and remember that you cannot study efficiently without a high degree of concentration. The two go hand in hand.

Using Spare Moments Effectively

We all have little "extra" pieces of time in our lives, which we tend to ignore. These small blocks of time often come unexpectedly: your instructor is 10 minutes late; your bus is 20 minutes late; you have to wait 30 minutes in a dentist's office; you finish one CD-ROM data search and have to wait 15 minutes before starting another. We can "make time" by using these snippets.

There are many techniques for using spare moments. For example, make a habit of carrying note cards. When you're waiting for a bus, or waiting to see your adviser—whenever you have 5 minutes or so—think about what you are studying and note the important points. Another good way to make time is to carry one or more textbooks with you. When you have a spare moment, start reading. These short reading sessions cannot take the place of more concentrated study periods, but they add up (three 5-minute study periods every day for 5 days equals 1 hour and 15 minutes that would otherwise have been wasted).

Storing Time

Time cannot actually be stored, because it never stops; we all know this. But we can in effect store time by keeping notes and developing reference files.

One technique many busy people use is to take notes when something significant flashes into their minds as they are doing other things. When your reading triggers a thought, jot it down; you may later find it useful. Get into the habit of carrying a small notebook or note cards, to capture your fleeting thoughts and to record names, book titles, and ideas you come across during the day.

Another way of storing time is to develop a filing system for your class notes, reference materials, and the like. Many of us lose an inordinate amount of time merely trying to find things. We know we have something; we've seen it recently; but when we need it, we can't find it. A simple filing system—labeled manila folders kept in an inexpensive filing cabinet (it can be cardboard)—will help you find material quickly. Your records are your "stored time." But if you can't retrieve them, another time-stealer is at work.

SUMMARY

- Not having enough time to finish everything is a common problem for college students, no matter if they are older returning students or younger students just out of high school.
- Time-stealers snatch away many of our precious hours. These time thieves include procrastination, unclear priorities, daydreaming, and frustration and anxiety.
- Ways to save time include keeping a time inventory, developing a weekly time plan, keeping a monthly calendar, drawing up daily or weekly "to-do" lists, and learning to say "no."
- You can make more time by learning how to use time more efficiently, by using the spare moments in your life more effectively, and by "storing" time. Effective use of notes and a carefully developed filing system, to let you find material that you know you have, are useful ways to store time.

18

DEVELOPING CONCENTRATION TECHNIQUES

Almost all of us are constantly interrupted and distracted. The telephone rings; someone knocks at the door; a television set assails us; loud music bombards us. In this regard, college is no different from any other area of life; in fact, interruptions and distractions at college may even be greater than elsewhere. Nevertheless, to meet your study goals, you must learn how to concentrate in the midst of all this.

Concentration isn't necessarily difficult. All of us manage to concentrate on things that interest us. At a football game, we generally have no trouble concentrating on the action. A good movie commands our attention. We have little difficulty concentrating when we're working on a hobby or playing a game. But we tend to have difficulty concentrating on things that are new to us and on things that we may (at least initially) consider boring. And for some of us, studying falls into one or both of these categories.

External and internal distractions can destroy your concentration. External distractions include television, radio, stereo systems, friends who want to talk, and family members who want your attention. Internal distractions may be more subtle, and they are often more powerful. Your concerns about your own ability as a student may distract you. If you are a returning student, you may worry about whether you made the right decision in returning to school, and about how you will meet all your personal and academic obligations; these thoughts may weaken your concentration. You may also find yourself daydreaming—about the midterm break, about a special person, about your summer vacation—and thoughts like these can derail your concentration.

Following are some tips for improving your concentration. Concentration is a skill, and—like other study skills—it can be developed to a high level. But certain principles must be followed, and practice is important.

PREPARING TO STUDY: LEARNING TO CONCENTRATE

Learn to Relax

A growing body of research suggests that relaxation helps concentration and can increase your overall success as a student. Relaxation can help rid your mind of conflicting thoughts and relieve some of the physical stress that may make concentration difficult.

I'll share two relaxation exercises. One is essentially physical, the other mental. Try each to see which one works best for you; some people prefer mental relaxation techniques and others prefer physical techniques.

A Technique for Physical Relaxation   Find a chair that is comfortable but not so comfortable that you will fall asleep in it. Sit up straight and close your eyes. For each of the following exercises, tense the indicated muscles for a count of 7 and then relax for a count of 7, breathing deeply. Go from tension to relaxation slowly, allowing yourself to experience the change fully.

1 Tense the muscles in your toes.
2 Raise your heels until your calves are tense.
3 With your feet firmly on the floor, and about 12 inches apart, tense the muscles in your thighs.
4 Pull in your stomach.
5 Straighten and tense your arms.
6 Bend your elbows and tense your biceps.
7 Tense the muscles across the top of your shoulders.
8 Clinch the muscles in your jaw.
9 Wrinkle your forehead.

When you have completed these exercises, immediately start studying.

A Technique for Mental Relaxation   Once again, find a comfortable chair. Sit up straight with your feet on the floor and your arms at your side or folded on your lap. Close your eyes and breath deeply once or twice.

Then think about the space within your big toe, allowing no other thoughts to interfere with that single thought. Once you are able to do that, think of the space within your ankles, within calves, thighs, buttocks, stomach, chest, shoulders, neck, and head. Then think about your personal space within all the space of the universe.

When you have moved from toes to head to universe, open your eyes and immediately begin studying. At first, this process may take 15 minutes or so. After you have done it a few times, you will be able to relax in 5 minutes or even less.

Other Relaxation Techniques   The methods above are only two examples of relaxation techniques. Perhaps you have others that work as well; for instance, some people find a long walk or a run a good way to relax before studying. What technique you use isn't important. What is important is being relaxed when you start to study.

Shelia Ostrander and Lynn Schroeder suggest that music can help people concentrate and thus help them learn:

> The idea that music can affect your body and mind certainly isn't new. For centuries, people have been lullabying babies to sleep. For centuries, people sang sea chanties and harvesting songs to ease their labor. For centuries, from Asia to the Middle East to South America, people have used music to carry them into unusual states of consciousness.[1]

But according to Ostrander and Schroeder, not just any music will do. They believe that music by seventeenth- and eighteenth-century composers such as Bach, Vivaldi, Telemann, Corelli, and Handel—that is, baroque music—works best. According to their research, the most effective rhythm is sixty beats per minute, which is like a slow human pulse; your body will listen to such music and will tend to follow the beat:

> Your body relaxes and you mind becomes alert in this most simple of all forms of relaxation. You don't have to tell a muscle to relax, you don't have to concentrate or even say a mantra. All you have to do is be with the music.[2]

If you try this musical approach to relaxation, remember to use the recommended kind of music. If you're not familiar with baroque music, you'll find it very different from the popular music that you may be used to hearing when you study; but popular music is a distraction for many students.

Develop Study Goals

Developing study goals is another concentration technique. How does this work?

---

[1] Shelia Ostrander and Lynn Schroeder, *Super-Learning*, Dell, New York, 1979, p. 73.
[2] Ibid., pp. 74–75.

Let's be specific. Let's say your sociology assignment is to read, before the end of the week, 50 pages in your textbook and another 50 pages in a book on reserve at the library. That is, you have 100 pages of reading in sociology alone. You also have readings and other assignments in your other courses.

The principle is this: *Set study goals by breaking each task down into subunits.* Here, divide the 100 pages of reading for sociology by 6, if you are studying 6 days a week. This yields something less than 17 pages a day—a manageable goal as long as you don't skip too many days. (This principle can be applied in various ways; for mathematics problems, for example, you could assign yourself so many problems per hour.)

Our principle also has a corollary: *Keep a record as you accomplish your goals.* For instance, write in your sociology notebook—perhaps in a special section you've created—"Monday, 20 pages," "Tuesday, 15 pages," and so on.

By establishing study goals, you are developing "pressure points": to meet each goal, you must concentrate. And by recording your accomplishment of these goals, you not only keep track of your work but also reward yourself for concentrating.

Establish Regular Times for Study

Concentration seems to become easier if you can study at the same time each day. Studying history at, say, 8 P.M. every day will usually result in better concentration than studying it at 8 P.M. one day and 7 A.M. another day and noon another day—or, worse, studying it only when you have a few spare minutes. Mapping out a study schedule that complements your class schedule and takes your other responsibilities into account is generally the way to ensure concentration and get the most done.

Establish a Regular Place for Study

A regular place for study also improves concentration. If you live in a college dormitory, establish a place in your room that will be used solely for studying. This will probably be your desk and the area around it. Once you've established a study area, don't use it for recreational reading, or for making social telephone calls. If your desk is your study area, use it for that purpose and that purpose alone. Then, when you sit down at your desk, you know you are there to study, not for any other reason, and you are already beginning to concentrate.

If you are living at home and commuting to campus, you will also need a special study place. We've all heard of students who push aside the dirty dishes on the kitchen table and do their studying there, in the midst of a hubbub of family activities. But it's a rare person who can maintain concentration under these circumstances. If you don't have a whole room to use for studying, set aside a corner of a bedroom or the basement—any place that can be separated from the rest of the household. Designating a special place for studying works the same way at home as in a dormitory: it improves the psychology of concentration ("When I'm here, I study"). Moreover, if you are living with your family or others, it sends the message that when you are in your special place, you are not to be bothered.

To make your study area more conducive to concentration, have a comfortable chair, but not a big easy chair in which you could easily drop off to sleep. Minimize distractions; for example, don't put your desk in front of a window, where you could glance up and see something interesting that would divert you from your work.

Adequate lighting is essential. According to Walter Pauk, the quality of light is of crucial importance:

> Researchers report that poor lighting can cause eye strain, general tension, headaches, and sleepiness. Worst of all, these irritations interfere with concentration.[3]

Pauk says that a good study light should not create glare: the bulb should be covered with a shade, and you should avoid a shiny desk surface, which would reflect light. Also, rid your desk of contrasting light and dark areas, since areas of light and shadow in your field of vision can be extremely tiring. To avoid this, you may need a floor lamp plus a desk lamp, or a ceiling light which provides general lighting for the area. Pauk also recommends that you avoid all flickering light. An incandescent light with a lose connection will flicker; so will a fluorescent lamp with one bulb burning out. Don't use a one-tube fluorescent lamp at all, as it is impossible to eliminate all flicker.[4]

As far as lighting is concerned, personal preferences should also be considered, particularly when you are deciding between a fluorescent desk lamp and a lamp with an ordinary incandescent bulbs. (I have a fluorescent ceiling light and a desk lamp with a regular 60-watt soft bulb. I find that the incandescent bulb reduces the harshness of the fluorescent light.) The choice is yours. The important thing is to have sufficient light, without glare or shadows.

---

[3] Walter Pauk, *How to Study in College*, 3d ed., Houghton Mifflin, Boston, Mass., 1984, p. 62.
[4] Ibid., pp. 61–62.

Maintain Your Health

Keeping healthy is also important for concentration, since without good health, concentration is difficult. If you are not feeling well, if you have headaches, or if you are chronically tired, you will find it hard to study.

I discuss health more fully in Chapter 20; here, I'll point out only that eating well, having regular patterns of sleeping, and exercising regularly are essential to good health.

WHILE YOU ARE STUDYING: TIPS FOR CONCENTRATING

Resist Daydreaming

After external distractions, the next most serious challenge to concentration is daydreaming. As I said in Chapter 17, we all do it. Daydreaming is fun; it's a diversion when we're in situations that do not interest us. We daydream when we're driving, when we're waiting for a bus, or when we're at a boring party. All that is natural and common, and fairly harmless. But if we daydream while we are studying, we lose our concentration and accomplish little.

You've probably often noticed that when you are reading, you suddenly realize that while your eyes have been moving along the page, your mind has been somewhere else—you've been thinking about something entirely different, such as what you'll eat for dinner or some new clothes you want to buy. You don't know when you began this little mental diversion, but you do know that you can't remember one word of what you have read for a page or more.

One way to handle this kind of daydreaming is to make a check mark in the margin every time you catch yourself thinking about something that is not related to what you are reading. How many check marks do you have per page? Simply recording your diversions will help stop daydreaming while you read.

In Chapter 7, I gave a number of tips for improving your reading skills. Using these tips will also help you to concentrate and avoid daydreaming.

Shape and Control Your Study Sessions

You will concentrate better if you shape and control your study sessions.

For example, how do you warm up for a study session? Most of us find the first 15 or 20 minutes the most difficult part of each session. One technique for getting started quickly is to stop each study session in the middle of something. If you are reading a textbook chapter, read all but the last page. If you are writing a term paper, stop in the middle of a sentence. Then, when you sit down to work again, you will know exactly what to do.

Restrain yourself from such diversionary tactics as sharpening your pencils, clearing your desk, and arranging and rearranging your textbooks. These are avoidance techniques that keep you away from your work. Instead, try one of the relaxation techniques I described earlier in this chapter, to clear your mind and prepare yourself for the study session.

Don't get involved in a serious discussion just before a study session. Particularly, avoid heated arguments about sex, politics, and religion. These topics are perennial favorites for ongoing discussions, probably because they lead to more and more questions and are issues that will never be settled. There is certainly nothing wrong with a good healthy discussion of an interesting topic, no matter what the outcome. But don't be drawn into one just before a planned study session; the questions that emerged from the discussion will continue to swirl around in your head, and concentration will be next to impossible.

For some people, wearing a special sweater or hat—something they wear only when studying—helps to establish a mood for study. Also, wearing a special article of clothing can tell others that you aren't to be bothered now.

Take a 10-minute break every hour when you are studying, and plan to do something special during the break—take a short walk; make a telephone call; close your eyes for a few minutes. The break can be your reward for 50 minutes of concentrated work.

Try Alternative Approaches to Study

Sometimes a change from your usual pattern of studying can aid concentration. Just as a vacation can improve your efficiency when you return to work, trying different study approaches can help you maintain concentration when you return to your usual approach.

For instance, if you study alone most of the time—reading, writing, jotting down notes, and thinking—occasionally you may want to study with three or four others who are enrolled in the same course. Their questions may stimulate you, and their perspectives on the course topics may surprise you. Most important, group study can provide variety. (However, as I've noted elsewhere, group study cannot replace individual work. Ultimately, you must do much of your studying by yourself.)

Increasingly, courses are being offered in multiple formats. An instructor lectures to a group in person, and his or her presentation is videotaped or audiotaped for students who can't be present in the lecture hall. If you were present for the original lecture, you might find it valuable to watch the video or listen to the audio as well. A second experience with the lecture may give you some new insights—and it may also help you focus more specifically on your lecture notes, the textbook, and other readings. And again, this kind of variety will help you concentrate when you are studying by yourself.

Sometimes reading beyond an assignment can provide useful variety. This is particularly so if you are having difficulty understanding—or even concentrating on—the assigned materials. You can ask your instructor for a list of additional readings; or you can look for additional readings on your own in the library, using the search techniques outlined in Chapter 15.

Develop the Ability to Study in Unusual Places

Once you have developed concentration skills, you should be able to study almost anywhere. True, it is easier to study at the same time and in the same place, as I explained above. But during the day, you will often find little "time windows" when, if you are prepared, you can do additional studying. For instance, as I described in Chapter 17, you can study while waiting for a bus, or waiting in a dentist's office.

To take advantage of these opportunities, which can amount to several hours over the course of a few weeks, try to carry a textbook with you at all times, for those moments when you can flip it open and read. Also, carry a small notebook or note cards for jotting down some of your thoughts. You can reflect on a lecture or even begin outlining a paper you know you must write within a few weeks.

Once you are used to doing this sort of thing, you'll discover that you are able to blot out all the background noise around you, attend to the task at hand, and accomplish much. But it does take some practice. Because I travel considerably, I have learned to do much of my work (which includes writing and reading) in airports. I've learned not to notice the sounds and bustle of people all around me, and I would lose many hours of valuable time if I were not able to concentrate on my work in the midst of noise and confusion.

DISCIPLINE AND CONCENTRATION

I believe that discipline and concentration are closely allied: to discipline yourself so that you can work according to a schedule, you must of necessity concentrate during your working sessions. In other words, discipline enhances concentration, and concentration enhances discipline.

Moreover, concentration and discipline together will produce another benefit. If you are able to hone your concentration skills to a point where your disciplined schedule works well, then you will have more free time for the leisure activities you enjoy. By disciplining yourself and developing your concentration skills, you enable yourself to accomplish much in a relatively short time. Thus you are able to plan for more free time in your schedule.

SUMMARY

- Most of us have trouble concentrating because of external and internal distractions. External distractions include noise and interruptions; internal distractions include worrying and daydreaming.
- Learning to relax is often a good first step in learning to concentrate. Concentration can also be improved by developing specific study goals, establishing a regular time and a regular place for study, and maintaining your health.
- While you are actually studying, you can improve your concentration by avoiding daydreaming and by shaping and controlling your study sessions.
- Concentration may also be enhanced by trying alternative study approaches, such as group work. Learning how to study in unusual places—when you are waiting for something or someone, for example—can add considerably to your overall study time.
- Developing a disciplined approach to study is closely allied with improving concentration skills.

19

MANAGING STRESS

Ask any group of college students whether stress is a part of their lives and you'll see an immediate nodding of heads. A few years ago, as part of a research project, a colleague and I asked older returning students about problems they were facing; 90 percent reported "increase in stress" as a barrier to their learning. In a series of interviews, we asked these students to describe the nature of the stress they were experiencing. Typical responses were, "The stresses at school are different from the stresses I felt in my job"; and, "Tests and examinations are stressful. I wasn't evaluated like that in my job....I could come home from work, not worry about it, and do something else. At school I bring everything home with me. I have all these stresses on my mind constantly."[1]

Ellen Ostrow and her associates conducted a research project with a random sample of students at the University of Utah, young and old, undergraduate and graduate. Stressful life events that these students identified included financial difficulties (48 percent), academic difficulties (40 percent), and conflicts in relationships (36 percent). More women (40 percent) than men (32 percent) reported personal relationships, family conflicts, and terminations of relationships as contributors to stress.[2]

[1] From Daniele Flannery and Jerold Apps, *Characteristics and Problems of Older Returning Students*, College of Agricultural and Life Sciences (Research Report), Madison, Wis., 1987, p. 8.

[2] Ellen Ostrow et al., "Adjustment of Women on Campus: Effects of Stressful Life Events, Social Support, and Personal Competencies," in Stevan E. Hobfoll, *Stress, Social Support, and Women*, Hemisphere, Washington, D.C., 1986, p. 35.

Another researcher, James H. Humphrey, asked several hundred students to finish the sentence "Stress is..." in 25 words or less. He then identified the words these students used most often in their sentences. *Pressure* appeared in more than 40 percent of the responses; *tension* appeared in 23 percent; *frustration* and *strain* each appeared in 13 percent; *anxiety* and *emotion* were used in slightly less than 5 percent.[3]

Obviously, college students experience considerable stress.

WHAT IS STRESS?

Definition of Stress

Girdano and Everly define stress as "strain, pressure, or force on a system."[4] Stress is generally associated with some change caused by an event, an object, or another person. Such a change becomes stressful when a person reacts to it physically or mentally. Some of these physical and mental reactions may be short-lived, but too often the effects of stress accumulate and the results are serious and debilitating.

Symptoms of Stress

You are about to take a major examination in a course that is difficult for you. The exam begins in 30 minutes. Your heart is pounding, your respiration rate has increased, and (though you may not be aware of it) the pupils of your eyes are dilated. The palms of your hands are perspiring, and your stomach feels knotted. Your mouth is dry, and you have difficulty swallowing. After the exam, many of the symptoms disappear, but not all. Your heartbeat, respiration rate, and pupils return to normal. But the muscle tension generated by the stressful situation doesn't go away so quickly. Your stomach may still feel upset, and you may have a severe headache brought on by muscle tension. These are rather typical reactions to a single, identifiable and highly stressful event.

We also face less easily identifiable stressors, which may not generate such dramatic immediate responses but can have devastating results over time. Examples include stress that results from personal relationships which aren't working (difficulties with a spouse, a boss, or a friend), worries about finances, anxiety about completing a degree program, and concern for one's children. All these are stressors, too, but they are of a more continuing nature. Symptoms of longer-term stress include nervous

---

[3] James H. Humphrey, *Profiles in Stress*, AMS Press, New York, 1986, pp. 103–106.
[4] Daniel A. Girdano and George S. Everly, *Controlling Stress and Tension: A Holistic Approach*, Prentice Hall, Englewood Cliffs, N.J., 1979, p. 5.

tics or muscle spasms, twitching of the eyelids, pain in the lower back, abdominal pains, periodic indigestion, frequent colds, insomnia, itchiness, and frequent headaches. Even more serious physical problems can also develop, such as hypertension, ulcers, heart disease, spastic colon, acne, rashes, and infections.

In my own research with adult returning students, described above,[5] 45 percent of the students said that they were less healthy after returning to school. Students made comments like these:

> When I came back to school, I experienced a lot of health problems. Apparently, it was a shock to my system. I went through a traumatic time. I was on medication, and I had infections I couldn't get rid of. The doctor suggested that it was due to stress.

> My health changed after I returned to school. I was tired, but I couldn't sleep, especially on Sunday nights. I would lie in bed and think about work and school and how I was going to fit it all in.

Stress also affects us psychologically:

> People under stress tend to walk faster, talk faster, even breathe faster....Cognitive processing is disrupted....Normal patterns of organization can be changed by stress. A usually neat and well organized person can become disorganized and untidy under stress conditions.[6]

Persons under stress will often pace the floor, crack their knuckles, or bite their lips. In some cases, stress affects our ability to remember—we become confused about details, and sometimes we have trouble remembering the names of people we encounter, even though we may have known them for a long time. Stress can also affect the emotions; it can produce "...sudden outbursts of anger or joy, or sharp changes in mood toward either depression or hyperactivity."[7]

WHAT CAUSES STRESS?

Exams, money, personal relationships, schedules, family responsibilities, someone smoking near you, too many people living in too small an area—all kinds of factors, large and small, can cause stress. Even positive events in our life can sometimes cause stress.

In the early 1960s, Thomas H. Holmes and Richard H. Rahe developed a Social Readjustment Rating Scale (SRRS),[8] which was based on

---

[5] Flannery and Apps, op. cit., p. 89.
[6] Martin Shaffer, *Life after Stress*, Plenum, New York, 1982, pp. 23–24.
[7] Ibid., p. 24.
[8] Thomas H. Holmes and Richard H. Rahe, "The Social Readjustment Rating Scale," *Journal of Psychosomatic Research*, No. 11, 1967, pp. 213–218.

the premise that any change in our lives, whether it is desirable or undesirable, contributes to stress. Negative changes are generally more stressful because they tend to be disruptive for longer periods of time; but positive changes, which we don't at first associate with stress, more often catch us off guard. Holmes and Rahe calculated point values for various life events, which suggest that some events are potentially and measureably more stressful than others. Death of a spouse, the event considered most stressful, was given a point value of 100. The next most stressful event, divorce, had a value of 73 points. The first year and the final year in college each had 63 points. Death of a close friend had 40 points. Repeated arguments with a roommate also had 40 points. Problems with an instructor, an outstanding personal achievement, failing a course, and taking final exams all had 25 points. Family reunions, and changes in eating habits had 15 points each.[9]

To understand all these different kinds of stressors, it is helpful to categorize them. Girdano and Everly's classification is a useful one, for example. They describe three broad categories of stressors: psychosocial, bioecological, and personality-related.[10] Let's look at these.

Psychosocial Stressors

Psychosocial stressors include problems having to do with *adapting to change*. To take a very simple example, if you are an older returning student, the modern electronic card catalog in the library can be a source of stress until you learn to use it.

Frustration is another psychosocial stressor. Registration seems to take forever. You've waited 2 weeks for an appointment with your academic advisor. The bursar's office seems to have no record of your scholarship. Situations like these are all frustrating, and thus they contribute to stress.

Overload is also an important psychosocial stressor. You are expected to do more than you have time to do—or more than your ability and skills allow. Your course assignments are piling up. Exams loom on the horizon. Your boss at work wants more from you. Your spouse says that you are neglectful. All these are stressful situations.

On the other hand, *"underload"* can be a psychosocial stressor. If you don't have enough to do, if you feel lonely and left out, or if you simply feel bored with college, these feelings will contribute to stress.

[9] Holmes and Rahe, cited in Daniel Girdano and George Everly, *Controlling Stress and Tension,* Prentice-Hall, Englewood Cliff, N.J., pp. 55–57.
[10] Ibid., pp. 54–117.

Bioecological Stressors

Girdano and Everly discuss three forms of bioecological stress: stress related to *biological rhythms, nutritional habits,* and *noise pollution.*[11]

Most of us are aware of our body's natural time rhythms—when we eat, when we sleep, when we are most creative. The menstrual cycle is an example of a natural time rhythm involving hormonal, structural, and functional changes. Jet lag, the syndrome we experience after rapidly crossing time zones, is an example of what can occur when we disrupt our natural rhythms.

Sensible eating habits contribute to healthful living; no one has to tell us that. But not everyone is aware that poor eating habits can contribute to stress. For instance, let's consider caffeine, a powerful amphetamine-like stimulant found in coffee, tea, and cola drinks. Too much caffeine—more than, say, four cups of coffee a day—can cause anxiety, inability to concentrate, and irregular heartbeat; it can also irritate the stomach lining and thus may lead to digestive disorders. Vitamin deficiencies are another nutritional factor that can contribute to stress; Girdano and Everly say that vitamin depletion is characteristic of a "stress-prone" diet. They note:

> Especially during stressful times, high levels of certain vitamins are needed to maintain properly functioning nervous and endocrine systems: These are vitamin C and the vitamins of the B complex, particularly Vitamin B1 (thiamine), B2 (riboflavin), niacin, B5 (pantothenic acid), B6 (pyridoxine hydrochloride), and choline.[12]

Nicotine, alcohol, and drugs are not exactly "nutritional habits," of course; but they do involve consumption by the body and should therefore be mentioned here. Many people believe that smoking "calms their nerves" or helps them relax. Research has shown, however, that it has the opposite effect, because nicotine acts as a stimulant. Smoking, chewing tobacco, and inhaling other people's smoke affect the nervous system much as caffeine does, causing stress responses. (I need not describe all the other health problems associated with smoking; most people are well aware of them.) Abuse of alcohol, prescription drugs, and the various illegal recreational drugs also contributes to stress, often in profound and extremely debilitating ways.

Girdano and Everly's third type of bioecological stress is noise pollution. College students don't need to be reminded that noise can be stressful; in Chapter 18, for example, we saw how noise can impair concentration.

---

[11] Ibid., pp. 76–103.
[12] Ibid., p. 91.

(Readers who want to learn more about noise as a stressor will find Girdano and Everly's book an interesting source of information.)

Personality Stressors

In addition to psychosocial and bioecological stressors, Girdano and Everly discuss personality-related stressors. Your self-concept (how you see yourself) and your personality type (your temperament) are important factors affecting stress.

It's not hard to find illustrations of the relationship between stress and self-concept. For instance, people who consider themselves victims and believe that the world is out to get them usually fare less well in stressful situations than people who believe that they have some control over stressors. To put it another way, if you believe that you are a failure and helpless, you will have more difficulty coping with stress than you would if you felt more positive about yourself. Also, feelings of incompetence and inadequacy may themselves become stressors—particularly if you worry a great deal about your shortcomings. (I'll say more about this when I discuss ways of coping with stress.)

Your personality type can also contribute to stress and make management of stress more difficult. In fact, there seems to be such a thing as a "stress-prone" personality. Following is a profile of the stress-prone type; check yourself against it to see how closely it resembles you.

1 *You overplan each day.* Your "to-do" list has more projects than you can accomplish, and you have a constant feeling of inadequacy because you are always behind. You have a great sense of urgency; *speed* is your guiding word. You want to do as much as possible as quickly as possible.

2 *You attempt several projects at the same time.* You eat, read, and talk all at once. When you talk with someone, you don't really listen, because you are planning the next activity. You talk quickly and often take over conversations. You are not a "good listener."

3 *You need to win.* When you don't win—at a game, at a sociology quiz, etc.—you are agitated and unhappy. For you, winning is an end in itself.

4 *You crave recognition.* Your concern for recognition pervades everything you do. You strive for visible signs of success—accumulation of possessions, for example. If you are working, you try to earn as much money as possible. On the surface, you appear confident and self-assured, but underneath you feel insecure and have a constant need to prove yourself. You are highly dependent on what others think of you, and give little attention to what you think of yourself. A "job

well done'' is not enough for you; the external recognition associated with completing a job is more important.

5 *You feel guilty when you take time to relax.* Even when you are playing, you are not relaxed. You want to talk about your courses and your instructors. Your schooling is never really out of your thoughts, no matter what you are doing. Seldom will you do simple things for the sheer enjoyment of doing them—watching a sunset, hiking along a rock-strewn shore, listening to a bird sing. You believe that all your waking moments must be spend on ''important things''—being a successful student, a superparent, an irreplaceable employee.

6 *You cannot tolerate delays or interruptions.* You have little patience with anyone who can't complete a task as quickly as you can. You are enraged if you are behind a slow-moving car and can't pass it. When talking to someone, you often interrupt to finish the other person's sentence. Waiting in lines nearly destroys you.

7 *You tend to take on too many projects.* When someone asks you to volunteer, you do. You take the maximum course load. And you often feel fragmented and besieged by deadlines. When your many projects pile up, you begin to make errors, and then you become upset with yourself. In effect, you have become your own worst enemy.

8 *You are known as a ''workaholic.''* You tend to neglect any aspect of your life that is not associated with your major responsibilities.[13]

How many of these descriptions fit you? If several or most of them do, you are probably stress-prone, and the stressors in your life are probably causing difficulty.

You may want to argue that many of these characteristics seem to be applauded by our society. Don't many of the people who succeed in business, and in college, display them? I would raise two points in reply. First, these ''outstanding'' people are living with so much stress that we can only imagine what they have sacrificed, physically and mentally. And second, isn't it possible to accomplish much, accomplish it well, and yet have inner peace?

COPING WITH STRESS

By now it should be very clear that we all face stress in many forms and many situations. Some stress can be avoided; but much stress is an inevitable part of life, and we must learn how to manage it. In this section, you'll find a chart for assessing your own stress level and some specific

---

[13] Adapted from Rosalind Forbes, *Life Stress,* Doubleday, Garden City, N.Y., 1979, pp. 35–42.

guidelines for managing stress. I'll also describe how college students cope with stress.

Stress Assessment

The first step in managing stress is to make a "stress assessment" that will identify the stressors in your life and how they affect you. Following is an assessment form.

STRESS ASSESSMENT CHECKLIST

Environmental stressors	Yes	No
1 I am experiencing troubled personal relationships (with my spouse, boss, family, friends, etc.).	____	____
2 I have gone through one or more major life changes in the past year (a move, starting college, marriage or divorce, a new job, death of a loved one).	____	____
3 I am often frustrated by bureaucracy, by rules, and by requirements.	____	____
4 I have problems with adapting to change (such as learning to use a computer or to study from a videotape).	____	____
5 I often feel overloaded and unable to do what is expected of me.	____	____
6 Too often I feel trapped; I feel that I lack the power to make decisions affecting my life.	____	____

Personal stressors	Yes	No
1 My diet is often inadequate.	____	____
2 I seldom get enough sleep.	____	____
3 I don't consider my natural time rhythms.	____	____
4 I smoke.	____	____
5 Alcohol, drugs, or both are sometimes a problem for me.	____	____
6 I drink more than four cups of coffee a day (or the equivalent of other caffeine-containing substances).	____	____
7 I have difficulty managing my time.	____	____
8 I can't concentrate on one activity or project for an extended period of time.	____	____
9 I often have negative feelings about myself.	____	____
10 I have many of the characteristics of the stress-prone personality (overplanning, a need to win, craving for recognition, competitiveness, inability to relax, addiction to work).	____	____
11 My friends tell me that I don't know how to relax.	____	____
12 I often wonder if my life has any meaning.	____	____
13 I have few or no hobbies, and few interests other than work, school, and family life.	____	____
14 I seldom have time to exercise.	____	____

STRESS ASSESSMENT CHECKLIST (*Continued*)

Indicators of stress	Recently	Not recently
1 Headaches.	——	——
2 Lower back pain.	——	——
3 Insomnia.	——	——
4 Sweating.	——	——
5 Stomach problems.	——	——
6 Loss of appetite.	——	——
7 Dizziness.	——	——
8 Depression.	——	——
9 Panicky feeling.	——	——
10 Irritability.	——	——
11 Worrying.	——	——
12 Temporary losses of memory.	——	——
13 Eye or muscle tics.	——	——

Fill out the stress assessment checklist and count the number of "yeses" in the first two categories and the number of times you checked "recently" for the "indicators of stress." If you have a large number of "yeses" and several checks under "recently," you are experiencing considerable stress.

To further analyze your personal stress, list specific instances of stress you experienced during the past week, indicating what happened before and after each stressful event and what physical signs of stress you showed. Then search for patterns of stress. For instance, if you are a returning student, did you experience stress on Sunday night? Did you experience stress before an examination? Examinations are obviously stressful; but remember that some of the stress in your life may be more subtle. For example, if you live in a large dormitory, and you come from a rural area where you grew up with relative peace and quiet, the noise in the dorm may affect you more than you realize.

Tips for Managing Stress

Here are some practical suggestions you can follow for managing stress. Try them to see which ones work best for you.

Think Positively   Think positively about yourself. Throughout this book, I have promoted the idea that you should take charge of your learning. Likewise, you should take charge of the other events in your life.

How you view the stress in your life is often the key to how well you are able to manage it. For example, if you go into an exam well prepared and confident that you will do your best, some of the stress will disappear. If you learn how to manage your time and how to concentrate, and if you develop solid study skills, you are helping to build your self-confidence; and self-confidence reduces stress.

When you are feeling down, or unsure of yourself, review some of your recent accomplishments. Put them in writing if necessary. Nothing bolsters self-confidence more than reviewing the important things you have accomplished. In fact, when you are facing a particularly challenging project, it's helpful to review other challenging projects you've completed and say to yourself, "I've handled projects just as tough as this one."

Don't expect stress to disappear entirely, however. It won't—nor should it. A certain amount of stress is a good thing; it provides challenges and makes life more interesting.

Eat Well   Make sure that you have an adequate diet which includes eating breakfast. (See Chapter 20 for tips about nutrition.)

Get Enough Sleep   Be sure that you get sufficient sleep, since lack of sleep upsets our time rhythms and fatigue is itself a stressor. (Chapter 20 has more on the importance of sleep.)

Learn to Relax   It's important to relax, and to know how to relax. We've already seen that inability to relax is a characteristic of the stress-prone personality. Furthermore,

> Recent research has demonstrated the preventative power of relaxation. In one study, it was found that college students who napped or relaxed daily for up to 20 minutes during the daytime had significantly fewer illnesses than those who did not rest.... Relaxation is a potent antidote to the ravages of stress.[14]

For two specific—and easy—relaxation techniques, refer to Chapter 18. Other relaxation techniques include meditation and massage.

If you believe that relaxation takes too much time—time you don't have—you should realize that a great deal of relaxation can be accomplished in very little time. The relaxation techniques I describe in Chapter 18, for instance, take less time than a coffee break.

Spend Some Time Alone   Solitude—sitting quietly or walking by yourself—can be a very effective way to relax and to cope with stress, particularly if you are constantly surrounded by other people and interacting with them. (This is of course the typical situation for college students.)

[14] Martin Shaffer, *Life after Stress,* Plenum, New York, 1982, p. 59.

Develop Leisure-Time Activities Cultivate some leisure activities—reading, music, hiking, biking, photography, or whatever interests you. Look into clubs on your campus that bring together students with common leisure interests. (One of the most popular on my campus, called Hoofers, is for sailboat enthusiasts, hikers, campers, and canoeists.)

Take Time Off Take mini-vacations to relieve stress. For instance, do something special on a Sunday afternoon. Take a weekend off and travel to a place that interests you. New places, new people, and new activities can do much to reduce stress.

Laugh Laugh, out loud, several times a day. Dr. Joel Goodman, a "laugh specialist," says, "People who laugh...last."[15] Goodman says that humor and a good laugh can do much to rid people of anxiety and let them see the funny side of their lives. And there is scientific evidence that laughter is important for good health:

> Laughter releases endorphins, which are natural pain killers. A good hearty laugh exercises internal organs like the diaphragm, thorax, abdomen, heart and lungs, providing a mini-workout.[16]

Do Things for Others By doing something for someone else, you can take your mind off a stressful situation of your own. If you help someone else deal with stress, you will often find that your stress has been relieved as well.

Discuss Your Problems Talk with someone about your problems. In our research, older returning students often told us that when they began talking with other returning students, they were surprised that everyone had similar problems. They also told us that as they talked about their problems, they began to feel much better and often found relatively easy solutions. As a result, their stress subsided.

In some colleges and universities, student groups or clubs are organized to provide an opportunity for students to talk with each other. But you don't need a formal organization; talk with someone who'll listen, and you'll be surprised at how much better you feel.

How College Students Cope with Stress

James Humphrey conducted research with a large number of college students to find out how they dealt with stress. He was surprised to learn

---

[15] Leslie Zganjar, "Go Ahead, Laugh, It'll Do You Good," *Wisconsin State Journal,* Monday, May 9, 1988, p. 1c.
[16] Ibid.

that almost one-third of the students in his study were at a loss; this group said that they often simply tried to forget about the stresses they felt or decided to "grin and bear it."

But many of Humphrey's respondents did have ways of coping with stress. One-fifth of the students used physical exercise to reduce stress—jogging, biking, weight lifting, etc. Another fifth said that they used recreational activities such as reading, sports, games, and so on. Fifteen percent talked things over with others: classmates, girlfriends or boyfriends, instructors, administrators, counselors, and parents and other relatives. Ten percent used alcohol or drugs, prescription and nonprescription. Three percent said that setting priorities, organizing a daily routine, and planning ahead helped reduce stress. Two percent used meditation and reported great success with it. One percent used specific relaxation techniques.[17]

CONSTRUCTIVE STRESS: ARE YOU A STRESS SEEKER?

Not all stress is bad. There is such a thing as "constructive stress," and the right amount of constructive stress can challenge us, motivate us, help us think more clearly, and enable us to see many tasks through to their end.

Some people not only can cope with stress but actually thrive on it and seek it out. Perhaps you are one of these people. Rosalind Forbes says that stress seekers have the following ten characteristics:

1 *They constantly seek self-improvement.* Stress seekers are never satisfied with what they have accomplished but always want to improve on their last performance.
2 *They tend to procrastinate.* They claim that the added pressure of working against a tight deadline helps them do their best work in a short time.
3 *They tend to seek out the unusual* and are bored with tasks that are easy or secure. An executive who has reached the top and then abruptly changes careers, saying that he or she needs a new challenge, may be a stress seeker.
4 *They view obstacles as challenges.* A businessperson who goes bankrupt and then immediately starts over again is an example.
5 *They pursue active recreation.* Stress seekers are not content to read a book or watch a movie; they prefer to climb mountains, canoe over rapids, or camp out.

[17] James H. Humphrey, *A Textbook of Stress for College Students,* Thomas, Springfield, Ill., 1982, pp. 69–78.

6 *They actively search out stressful situations.* Stress seekers are eager to get into situations that most of us would avoid—skydiving, or joining a mercenary force in a distant civil war.

7 *They look for novelty* in what they do. Routine nine-to-five jobs bore them.

8 *They choose activities which energize and exhilarate them.* Usually, a certain amount of risk is also associated with what stress seekers choose (see item 10).

9 *Their major accomplishments are usually prompted by stress.* Many famous novelists, poets, and songwriters claim that they did their best work in extremely stressful situations, and that the stress prompted them to do their best.

10 *They are risk takers.* Though the risks are carefully calculated, they are nevertheless real. In a risky situation, the fear generally associated with the risk adds to the stress. Stress seekers, surprisingly, often experience a kind of euphoria during this kind of activity. Free-fall parachutists and mountain climbers are examples.[18]

Are you a stress seeker? Are you sometimes a stress seeker and sometimes not? What defines stress seekers is searching out stress and gaining from it. They are in control and can choose to have additional stress or not to have it. In everyday life, we usually don't have the choice of accepting or rejecting stress; it is there, and we must cope with it. And for most of us, less stress is better than more.

SUMMARY

- Stress—strain or pressure generally associated with change—is a fact of life for college students.
- Symptoms of stress include sweaty palms, pounding heart, dry mouth, memory lapses, and dilation of the pupils of the eyes. After a stressful event passes, these symptoms usually disappear.
- If stress continues over a prolonged period of time, and it is not managed well, more serious symptoms can develop, including ulcers, hypertension, spastic colon, rashes, and infections.
- Many factors, major and minor, can cause stress. Holmes and Rahe developed a well-known stress rating scale, based on the premise that both positive and negative changes in our lives contribute to stress.
- Girdano and Everly identified three broad categories of stressors: psychosocial, bioecological, and personality-related.
- Psychosocial stressors include adaptation to change, frustration, over-

---

[18] Rosalind Forbes, *Life Stress*, Doubleday, Garden City, N.Y., 1979, pp. 145–150.

load, and "underload." For many college students, overload is a major source of stress; they have more to do than they think they can do
in the time available. On the other hand, students who have too little
to do at college, feel left out of things, or are simply bored will also
experience stress.

- Bioecological stressors include disruptions of our natural time
  rhythms, poor nutritional habits (such as overuse of caffeine and lack
  of vitamins), smoking, drinking, drug abuse, and noise.
- Personality-related stressors have to do with self-concept and personality type. A poor self-concept makes it difficult to cope with stress,
  and some personalities seem to be more stress-prone than others.
  Characteristics of the stress-prone personality include overplanning,
  undertaking too many projects, needing to win, craving recognition,
  being unable to relax, being unable to tolerate delay or frustration,
  and being a "workaholic."
- The first step in coping with stress is a stress analysis to identify environmental stressors, personal stressors, and symptoms of stress in
  your own life.
- Guidelines for managing stress include thinking positively, eating
  well, getting enough sleep, learning to relax, spending time alone, developing leisure activities, taking time off, laughing, and discussing
  your problems with others.
- Although some college students seem to have no way of coping with
  stress except ignoring it or simply putting up with it and some turn to
  drugs or alcohol, others report that they can reduce stress by exercise, recreational activities, talking things over, setting priorities,
  meditating, and using relaxation techniques.
- Some stress is constructive, and some people are stress seekers who
  thrive on stress and actively search it out.

20

KEEPING HEALTHY

Our health is so easy to take for granted that we often overlook relatively simple ways of keeping ourselves fit and feeling well. We all know that good health is essential for many things we do, and most of us are aware that it helps us cope with stress and improves our concentration. But we are sometimes careless about maintaining our health.

In recent years, a "wellness movement" has developed in the health professions: they are concentrating on prevention rather than treatment. This means that the responsibility for good health falls on each of us, and that health ought be viewed in context with the rest of our lives:

> Health, according to the Hippocratic writings, requires a state of balance among environmental influences, ways of life, and the various components of human nature.[1]

How we live our lives, how much stress we face, and what kinds of tasks we take on all affect our health. Conversely, our state of health affects our ability to face stress and take on tasks. In other words, there is an interaction between our health and how we live our lives: each depends on and affects the other.

In this chapter, I'll share some tips for keeping healthy. I'll begin with nutrition and then talk about sleep, drugs, and exercise.

---

[1] Fritjof Capra, *The Turning Point*, Bantam, New York, 1982, p. 311.

NUTRITION

What to Eat and What Not to Eat: Guidelines for Good Health

Make sure that your diet is adequate and that it includes breakfast. The Department of Agriculture and the Department of Health and Human Services recommend the following.

Eat a Variety of Food   Each day, eat a selection of different foods, including:

Fruits

Vegetables

Whole-grain and enriched breads and other products made from grains

Milk, cheese, yogurt, and other products made from milk

Meats, poultry, fish, eggs, and dried beans and peas

To Maintain a Desirable Weight, Don't Overeat   Adjust the number and size of portions of food (and beverages) so that you can reach and stay at your desirable body weight. To help control overeating, eat slowly, take smaller portions, and don't take second portions.

To lose weight:

Eat a variety of foods that are low in calories and high in nutrients.

Eat more fruits, vegetables, and whole grains.

Eat less fat and fatty foods.

Eat less sugar and sweets.

Drink less of alcoholic beverages.

Increase your physical activity.

Moderate Your Intake of Fats, Saturated Fats, and Cholesterol   To cut down on fats and cholesterol, do the following:

Choose lean meat, fish, poultry and dry beans and peas as protein sources.

Use skim or low-fat milk and milk products.

Moderate your intake of egg yolks and organ meats.

Limit your intake of fats and oils, especially those high in saturated fat, such as butter, cream, lard, heavily hydrogenated fats (some margarines), shortenings, and foods containing palm oil and coconut oil.

Trim fat off meats.

Broil, bake, or boil rather than fry.

Moderate your intake of foods that contain fat, such as breaded and deep-fried foods.

Read labels carefully to determine both amount and type of fat present in foods.

Eat Enough Starch and Fiber   Choose foods that are good sources of fiber and starch, such as whole-grain breads and cereals, fruits, vegetables, and dry beans and peas. Also, substitute starchy foods for foods containing large amounts of fats and sugars.

Moderate Your Intake of Sugar   Use less of all sugars and foods containing large amounts of sugar, including white sugar, brown sugar, raw sugar, honey, and syrups. (Examples include soft drinks, candies, cakes, and cookies.)

Remember that *how often* you eat sugar and sugar-containing foods is as important for dental health as *how much* sugar you eat. Avoid eating sweets between meals.

Read food labels for clues about sugar content. If the word *sugar, sucrose, glucose, maltose, dextrose, lactose, fructose,* or *syrups* appears first on a label, the product contains a large amount of sugar. Eat fruits processed without syrup or with light rather than heavy syrup—or, of course, eat fresh fruits.

Moderate Your Intake of Sodium   To cut down on sodium:

Learn to enjoy the flavors of unsalted foods.

Cook without salt or with very little salt.

Try flavoring foods with herbs, spices, and lemon juice instead of salt.

Add little or no salt to food at the table.

Limit your intake of salty foods such as potato chips, pretzels, salted nuts and popcorn, condiments (soy sauce, steak sauce, garlic salt), pickled foods, cured meats, some cheeses, and some canned vegetables and soups.

Read food labels carefully to determine how much sodium prepared foods contain.

Use low-sodium products, when they are available, instead of products with higher sodium content.

Drink Little or No Alcohol   If you drink alcoholic beverages, do so in moderation. Alcoholic beverages are high in calories and low in nutrients. Also, remember that 12 ounces of regular beer, 5 ounces of wine, and 1½ ounces of distilled spirits all contain about the same amount of alcohol.[2]

Additional Concerns about Nutrition

Fast Foods   You leave your job, jump into your car, drive to the campus, look for a parking place, and discover you have just 15 minutes before class starts—and you haven't eaten. What are you likely to eat? A quick hamburger and a side order of fries washed down with a large soda would be typical, but decidedly not good for you.

Julie Dockendorff, a clinical nutritionist at University of Wisconsin Hospital and Clinics says:

> If you chow down on fast food, break the burger-and-fries habit. Many fast foods are packed with fat and sodium—bad news for your heart, blood pressure, and waistline.[3]

There are fast-food alternatives to burgers and fries. Try the salad bar, but don't cover your lettuce with heavy dressings or bacon bits—and avoid salads that are swimming in mayonnaise. Pizza is another good choice.

Avoid deep-fried foods; they contain a heavy load of fat, which is bad for your health and your waistline.

You don't have to skip dessert. Try frozen yogurt; many brands are much lower in calories than ice cream, and most are low in fat. Even better, try fresh fruit.

If you know you won't have time for even a fast-food place or a snack bar on campus, pack a lunch or a snack: fruit, muffins, fruit juice, yogurt, and the like. These foods are both portable and nutritious. But avoid having a candy bar as a snack. You do get a quick "sugar rush" from candy, but it is soon followed by a "down" which leaves you feeling even more fatigued. If you crave a sweet snack, try an apple or some dried fruit. If you want a snack but it doesn't have to be sweet, take some nuts. Fruits and nuts won't put you on a "sugar roller coaster" the way candy bars do.

Caffeine   Although there have been a number of studies on the effects of caffeine, no link between caffeine and cancer or heart attacks has been

---

[2] U.S. Department of Agriculture, U.S. Department of Health and Human Services, *Dietary Guidelines for Americans*, Home and Garden Bulletin No. 232, U.S. Government Printing Office, Washington, D.C., 1985.

[3] Kristin Visser, "A Healthy Appetite," *Isthmus*, February 26, 1988, p. 2.

established. Still, consumption of caffeine—particularly in coffee— remains a controversial issue. In Chapter 19, for example, we saw that caffeine can be a stressor.

Two or three cups of coffee, or even four, can give you a lift to start the day. But more than four cups can turn your alertness into nervousness, anxiety, and irritability—and even into an upset stomach. If you drink one of the colas, Mountain Dew, or Dr. Pepper as well as coffee, you may well have an overload of caffeine. And if you get a headache and take a couple of Anacin or Excedrin tablets, you've made matters even worse: these painkillers contain large amounts of caffeine.

Try alternatives—fruit juices, low-fat milk, and caffeine-free soft drinks such as 7-up, Fresca, and Sprite.

SLEEP

Students are notorious for existing on little sleep. The students who stay up all night to study for exams are legion; maybe you are one of them. Most students would be much better off if they closed their books and got 6 or 7 hours of sleep; but all-night cramming is unfortunately a way of life on many campuses.

Sleep is essential to good health, and to your success as a student. Once or twice a semester you can get away with no sleep in 24 hours or even more, but then your body will tell you, ''Give me some rest, or I'll do something terrible to you.''

Martin Shaffer points out:

> For sleep to be functional, it must be full, relaxed, continuous, and long enough. Most people need from 6 to 8 hours of full sleep to function optimally....The amount of sleep that each person needs is influenced by many factors. The degree of relaxation versus tension, what we ate, what we did physically, and what we did to achieve resolution of psychological conflicts, and the events we are about to face the next day, as well as the type of bed and the room temperature, can influence the depth of sleep.[4]

DRUGS

Nicotine

There is little more to be said on the subject of nicotine. By now, everyone knows that smoking tobacco is dangerous—as is chewing tobacco. If you don't smoke or chew, don't start. If you do smoke or chew, stop. Period.

---

[4] Martin Shaffer, *Life after Stress*, Plenum, New York, 1982, p. 93.

Alcohol and Illegal Drugs

I mentioned above that alcohol adds calories to your diet without providing any nutrients, but this is probably its least harmful effect. The dangers of alcohol and other drugs are generally well known. Addiction is devastating to physical and mental health, to work, and to relationships with family and friends.

Drinking and drug abuse are problems students can't ignore. Every campus provides information about dealing with alcohol and drug problems, as well as support groups and other educational programs.

EXERCISE

Students, particularly full-time students, sit for hours—in lecture halls, in libraries, in front of computer screens. Not surprisingly, their neck and shoulder muscles often begin to tighten, so that a dull headache develops. Gravity is at work, pulling the head and shoulders forward and making the back suffer.

Stand up occasionally and move. Play a game of basketball, jog, lift weights, do exercises, or—best of all—walk.

Our society has forgotten how to walk. We complain if we have to walk two blocks to buy a newspaper or cross the campus to get from one classroom to another. Try climbing out of bed in the morning and walking 1 mile, no matter what the weather. A friend who has walked for years told me once, "Walking gets everything working." Indeed it does. The heart starts pumping blood throughout the system. Those little aches and pains that most of us have in the morning—there will be more as you grow older—often disappear after a little activity. And, perhaps most important, your brain will receive a dose of oxygen to clear it and get it started for a day of thought. Another excellent time to walk is at midday, and still another is in the evening.

We need about the equivalent of a 4-mile walk each day to keep the body systems, particularly the heart, in good condition. If you don't have time to do all that walking at once, make up for it during the day: use the stairs instead of the elevator; let the bus go without you and walk to class; and so on.

You don't need a whole lot of equipment for walking. But if you want to impress your friends, you can buy one of the color-coordinated walking outfits now on the market. As for me, I wear an old pair of blue jeans and any old shirt I can find. I do have good shoes—my one piece of special walking equipment.

How fast should you walk? That's up to you. A brisk walk will do more for you than a stroll. But if you're only up to strolling, then stroll.

And don't carry a stopwatch and try to better your walking time each day. Enjoy yourself.

SUMMARY

- Today, health professionals think in terms of prevention rather than cure, emphasize individuals' responsibility for their own health, and see health in the context of life as a whole. How we live affects our health, and our health affects how we live.
- Guidelines for good nutrition include eating a variety of healthful foods; maintaining a desirable weight by eating moderately; cutting back on fats and cholesterol, sugar, and sodium; drinking little or no alcohol; substituting nutritious foods for fast foods and sugary snacks; and being careful not to consume too much caffeine.
- Sleep is essential to good health, and students should try to break away from the pattern of skipping sleep.
- Drugs—nicotine, alcohol, and the illegal drugs—are obviously a threat to health. Don't smoke or chew tobacco; don't ignore the danger of drug abuse and alcoholism.
- Students, because they must sit so much, are especially in need of exercise. Walking may well be the best exercise of all.

PART FIVE

RETURNING TO SCHOOL

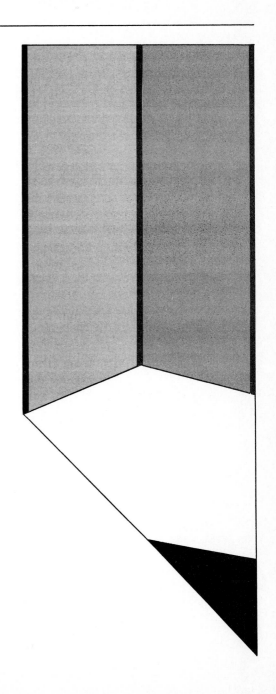

21

THE RETURNING
STUDENT

This chapter is written especially for those of you who are returning to school after several years away. To be sure, the entire book was written with you in mind. For one thing, many of the suggestions for improving study skills will be as useful to you as they are to younger students who have just completed high school; in my research with returning students, I have learned that some have difficulty with basic study skills such as reading, writing, note-taking, and examinations. Also, many returning students, like younger students, have problems concentrating, managing their time, and coping with stress. But older returning students do face some special issues and challenges.

ADJUSTING TO COLLEGE:
ISSUES FOR RETURNING STUDENTS

In my research, the vast majority of returning students told me that it took them about a semester to adjust to study and to student life. Some were able to make the adjustment in 1 month or so, but some took well over 1 year—and all of them said that some degree of adjustment was involved, that it took time to begin thinking and working as students again.

Some of the problems these returning students faced were of course no different from problems encountered by younger students; but some of their concerns were substantially different.

For example, one returning student told me:

When I arrived in Madison, my most distressing problem was trying to find an apartment with the Sunday ads and a map of the city: every street I wanted seemed to be one way in the wrong direction. Running a close second was trying to find buildings on campus. And it took me 1 month to work up enough courage to search for something in Memorial Library. My son encouraged me to use it and assured me that the tales of students who disappeared into the stacks, never to be heard of again, were just local folklore.

Another returning student said:

As an adult, I am sometimes distracted from my studies by concerns about money and by domestic problems that drift through my mind as I try to work on something like statistics, which for me requires total concentration. The figures I am dealing with may represent the association between poverty rates and crime rates in neighborhoods; but my mind skips to other figures, like my complicated, goofed-up joint income tax return with my estranged (and solvent) husband. Sometimes when I study, I think about my adult sons and wonder if they are safe. In a way, these distractions may be no worse than the ones I had when I was 17 at Penn State University. Then, I was distracted by wondering whether or not I'd be invited to a fraternity party; when I was invited, I was distracted by thoughts of what I ought to wear. As I look back, these seem like small concerns, but at the time they did take my mind away from my assignments. In this regard, I think adult and younger learners are not very different. But today the importance of my problems and decisions seems very great. It is as though I have no room for error any more, and that is a heavy strain.

Still another returning student said:

What probably would have helped me most is the information that readjustment to the academic situation is a problem experienced by many returning students and is not unique to myself. Knowing this might have helped to relieve some of the frustration I felt.

Let's consider several issues of concern to returning students.

Overcoming Negative Attitudes toward Formal Education

Not everything in my elementary and secondary schooling evokes pleasant memories. My guess is that it is the same with you. Returning students often bring excess baggage in the form of bad memories.

You may remember long, boring hours spent behind a desk on warm spring days. You may recall cool, crisp fall afternoons when a walk in the woods, or any outdoor activity, would have been more pleasant than the schoolroom. You may remember teachers who insisted on directing all of your learning, so that you had little if any freedom to do what you wanted to do or learn what you wanted to learn. And you probably remember examinations—the very thought of them may bring back feelings of terror—when you sweated through hours of preparation and then (too often, perhaps) found that the exam bore little resemblance to what you had studied.

And you probably also remember teachers who told some children that they were "not students" and probably never would be—that they should seek some work for which study would not be important. This is not only cruel but untrue. It is obvious today that all of us will be students all our lives. Many of us will spend some time in schools and colleges as adults, and almost all of us will be involved in on-the-job training and study programs, or in home study programs we put together for ourselves, or in noncredit classes and courses. There is no such thing as "not being a student": whether we realize it or not, we are and must be learning throughout our lives. We are always students.

What happened to us in elementary and high school, and perhaps in college at an earlier time, has a great affect on our attitude toward learning in college today. The challenge is not to let negative memories get in the way of our present learning.

Admissions and Registration

During the last decade or so, colleges and universities have greatly improved their policies and procedures to make admission easier and more humane for returning students; but you may still run into problems.

Recently, I learned about a school whose admission procedures sounded as if they hadn't been changed since the 1950s. A man with a Ph.D. in engineering wanted to enroll in this college to earn credits in some subjects that had changed since he had completed his graduate work. He filled out the registration form until he came to a line that said, "Provide recommendation from high school principal." The engineer asked the admissions clerk if he could substitute his doctoral major professor. "Indeed not," the clerk said; "a requirement is a requirement." The engineer pointed out that he had done his high school work 25 years ago and that the principal was long dead. "A rule is a rule," said the clerk. "If we made an exception, everyone would want an exception." I never heard if the engineer was eventually admitted or not.

Cases like this are the exception rather than the rule today. If you do have problems with admissions, though, two approaches generally work well: first, be patient; and second, be assertive. Many rules governing admission and registration have been changed as returning students have quietly but effectively challenged them.

One common problem with admissions is transferring credits from other institutions. It is not unusual for a returning student to have a semester of credits from college A, perhaps two courses from college B, and another semester's work from college C—and then to enroll in college D to complete a degree. Moving from college to college is becoming quite typical, since people's jobs move them from place to place. Therefore, whenever you leave a college, be sure to collect the transcripts of your work there. Also, keep a copy of the college catalog in which the courses are described. Admissions offices can decide more easily about transfers of credits and about content areas that have already been covered when they have access to more than just a course name and number.

Another problem for many returning students has to do with "equivalency credits"—that is, credits for experience. Returning adults have experience from their work, from their communities, and from their social life; but colleges and universities often ignore these experiences when considering students for admission. As a result, many returning students are required to take college-level courses in subjects where they already have the content and skills on the basis of their life experiences. In determining required courses, colleges and universities need to work out systems for recognizing the life experiences of returning students—and some are now doing so.

The Curriculum: Learning Opportunities

With regard to the curriculum itself, there are several potential problem areas: What opportunities are available? How are they made available? When are they available? What is their actual content?

On many college and university campuses, as I noted in Chapter 13, most educational opportunities take the form of traditional courses, taught by an instructor or a teaching assistant who relies primarily on lectures. Such courses meet for a 50-minute period two or three times a week, or sometimes for a 100-minute period once a week. But as returning students make up an increasingly larger proportion of the students on campus, many new formats are evolving, including evening courses that meet once a week, weekend courses, and courses offered through electronic media that allow students to remain home. One of the questions you'll want to ask about any college you are considering is when and in what format it offers courses.

For many college majors, most of the curriculum—the courses you take—will be dictated by degree requirements. This too can be a problem, since returning students often want some say in what they will study and some flexibility in the curriculum. Be sure to examine the course requirements for the major you are considering. If you are frustrated by lack of flexibility, you may want to choose a different major. Or you may want to check to see if some adjustment of the requirements is possible, despite what the published materials may indicate.

Relationships with Instructors

A decade ago, I often heard returning students complain about their instructors. Today, as more and more instructors have had experience working with returning students, many of these complaints have disappeared—but some college instructors still do not understand returning students. Instructors who have spent most of their time with younger students may be unaware that the older returning student has some different characteristics and needs.

Many instructors consider a college education a "preparation for life": one goes to college and then enters adulthood and the world of work. Returning students, though, may have already spent considerable time as adults and workers, and they may be preparing not for "life" but for a different *kind* of life—a new career, for example—or simply for an improved life. Many women return to school after their children are grown, so that they can pursue a new career outside the home; many returning students are interested primarily in improving careers they've pursued for years.

For some instructors, returning students are a source of uneasiness. One returning student said:

> Several of my professors are younger than I am. They completed their graduate work without ever working outside the confines of the university. I am a threat to them, both because I am older and because I have had several years of experience in areas we are studying in class. How much better it would be if the professor would relax a little and allow (even encourage) students who have experiences that are relevant to the content of the course to share them. This would make a richer experience for everyone. We wouldn't lose any respect for the professors and their position—quite the contrary. I think many students would admire a professor who was smart enough to draw on the experiences of students to bring theory and practice together. Isn't relating theory and practice to each other one of the reasons many of us are studying at the university?

Another problem that sometimes gets in the way of a good relationship between returning students and their instructors is the mistaken notion that returning students are not "serious students." Apparently, the successful integration of thousands of veterans into colleges and universities at the end of World War II, and again after the war in Viet Nam, has been forgotten. These veterans were serious students: they studied hard, and they did well. Likewise, today's returning students are serious students. They have goals and aspirations, and they see attending college as one way of accomplishing them.

Technology

As I have discussed elsewhere (see Chapters 13 and 15), technology is a part of the college experience that can create problems, perhaps especially for the returning student.

For instance, if you have been away from school for more than 5 years, the new electronic card catalog at the library will probably baffle you at first. You may remember thumbing through a traditional card catalog to find a book you wanted to check out; this is still possible (at least in part) in many libraries—but now you can also find a book by calling up title, author, or topic on a computer terminal. This new process is somewhat more complicated than the old version, and it entails learning some basic procedures. (I remember vividly the first time I used our computerized card catalog. I tried to follow the directions carefully, glancing around from time to time to see if anyone was watching me, but what I most feared happened before long: the machine "froze," beeped loudly, and announced in large letters on the screen, ASK LIBRARY ASSISTANT FOR HELP. This story has a happy ending, though: I did ask for help; a very pleasant and helpful assistant showed me the error of my ways; and soon I was back on track, happily foraging through the computerized catalog with nary a beep.) In Chapter 15, I examine in detail how to use a computerized card catalog, as well as how to use the on-line data searches that are now a part of the modern college library.

Many college courses also use technology as adjuncts to instruction. Some courses are available entirely on videotape or audiotape, to be seen or heard at the student's convenience. Some are offered via computer. Many combine face-to-face instruction, videotape, audiotape, and computerized instruction. All this has implications for study skills. Traditional skills—how to listen, how to read—are still important. But these skills may need to be adapted, and some new skills are needed as well. What is the best way to learn when your course is on videotape, or on "real-time" television (meaning that you and perhaps hundreds of others are watching it at the same time, and you can't "back up" as you can with a videotape), or on audiotape, or on a computer?

In Chapter 13, I discuss learning with electronic media and share some guidelines.

The Returning Student's Family

One way in which returning students differ from younger students is that when an adult who has been out of school for several years decides to return, usually the entire family is directly involved. It is true that younger students often depend partly or completely on their families for financial support. But with returning students, a family's involvement is often more than just financial.

Time is one important family issue. When a parent decides to return to school, for example, there is obviously less time for spouse and children.

The family's attitude can also be an issue. In one of several surveys of returning students, I asked about problems these students faced. One student wrote,

> I had the disadvantage of not having moral support from anyone. My family and friends thought it was pretty ridiculous for me to go back to school. I already had a master's degree; why didn't I just go to work? And after several semesters back in school, I still don't feel completely "legitimate."

For returning students, the support of the immediate family—particularly a married student's spouse—can be essential to success. If your family is bombarding you with comments about how foolish you are to return to school, you must be of a strong mind to not let these comments affect your own attitude toward study and learning. There is always a tendency to believe that maybe these people are right, that maybe you shouldn't be going off on this adventure of once more becoming a student.

One way to overcome a negative attitude on the part of your family is to involve family members in what you are doing. Take them to the campus. Show your children the classrooms; they will be interested to see where mom or dad goes to school. Take your spouse to social activities so that he or she can meet other students. Share your excitement about what you are learning; get your family involved in debates and discussions you are having with other students.

As a returning student, one thing I myself learned immediately was that I was not the only one in college: although I was the only one attending classes, indirectly my wife and my three children were also enrolled.

A POSITIVE NOTE

About 15 years ago, when I first began working with returning students—and with the colleges and universities where they were enrolled—I saw many problems. Since then, most colleges and universities have changed. In fact, at some schools great changes have occurred, and major steps are being taken to make the college experience better for returning students. Other colleges and universities have made more modest changes.

Many problems still exist, of course. But as one returning student told me,

> Sure, there are going to be problems along the way, and certainly some disillusionments. But think of all the rewards—getting your brain into gear again,

having the stimulation of contact with fellow students and instructors, seeing an A on a paper you've worked hard on, and feeling that you're accomplishing a personal goal.

SUMMARY

- Many of the problems returning students face are similar to those encountered by younger students: developing basic study skills, concentrating, managing time, and dealing with stress. But returning students do have some special problems and concerns as they adjust, or readjust, to college life.
- Many returning students have had bad experiences with schooling; their memories of elementary school, high school, and previous college work may be negative. Overcoming a negative attitude toward formal education can be an issue for these students.
- Some returning students encounter problems with admissions and registration, though many colleges and universities are improving in this regard. Patience and assertiveness are important in dealing with admissions problems.
- The curriculum may be a problem for returning students, particularly if all the courses offered are in a traditional format or if degree requirements are inflexible.
- Today, more and more college instructors have had experience with returning students; but some instructors see college only as a "preparation for life" and thus may not understand returning students who are in school for other purposes, such as changing careers or progressing in well-established careers. And some instructors feel threatened by returning students, or have the mistaken idea that returning students are not "serious."
- For some returning students, adjusting to new technology becomes a problem: the library's electronic card catalog and electronic adjuncts to instruction are examples.
- The returning student's family is also an important concern. When an adult returns to school, the entire family is involved.
- In general, the college experience has improved, and continues to improve, for returning students; and most returning students say that the advantages of being in school far outweigh any problems they face.

22

THE GRADUATE STUDENT

In this chapter, I share some ideas that graduate students have found helpful as they decided on and began graduate programs. The first section of the chapter focuses choosing a graduate program; subsequent sections focus on planning the graduate program and doing graduate work. The final section is a profile of the successful graduate student.

Though I refer to master's degrees and doctoral degrees in this discussion, not every graduate school offers both—many offer graduate degrees only at the master's level. Different graduate programs offer a variety of master's degrees, including master of arts (M.A.), master of science (M.S.), master of business administration (M.B.A.), master of music (M.M.), master of fine arts (M.F.A.), and master of social work (M.S.W.). Doctorates also take various forms. The doctor of philosophy (Ph.D.) is the basic research degree offered by many graduate programs. Depending on the school, professional doctorates may also be taken in education (Ed.D.), veterinary medicine (D.V.M.), medicine (M.D.), and so on.

CHOOSING A GRADUATE DEGREE PROGRAM: QUESTIONS TO ASK

There are several factors to be considered in choosing a graduate degree program: the quality of the program, the focus of the department, entrance and degree requirements, curriculum, faculty, students, career opportunities, departmental decision making, and financial aid. It's useful to think of these in terms of a series of questions to be asked and answered. Let's look at each of them in turn.

Is the Program of High Quality?

You can assess the quality of a degree program in several ways. Start with the *faculty*. Do the faculty members have national and international reputations? How do they compare with faculties of similar programs at other institutions? Are they in demand as consultants and speakers at national meetings? What is their publication record? Have they written books and research articles that are seen as major contributions to the field? Is the faculty large enough to provide a "critical mass?" Only one or two faculty members in a program may simply not provide enough expertise to make the quality of the program high (there are of course exceptions to this rule).

Then, consider the *students* in the program. Are there enough graduate students in the program to provide interaction and excitement? Where do the students come from? Many programs have international students who add an important dimension.

Also, consider the program's *facilities*. Do the support services and facilities for the department seem to be adequate? Is there word-processing equipment for the secretarial staff? Is there adequate office space for instructors? Is the support staff large enough?

Finally, consider the *library*. Is the library's collection sufficient for the area in which you are interested?

What Is the Focus of the Department?

It's important to determine the focus of a graduate program. For example, if you are seeking admission to a psychology program, is the department's focus primarily clinical or experimental? If it is a history department you are considering, what areas of history are emphasized—American, European, middle eastern, women, etc.? In almost every graduate department, one or more areas are usually given more emphasis than others. What are they, and are they the areas that interest you?

Does the department have an undergraduate program (most do); and if so, how are its resources distributed between its graduate and undergraduate efforts?

What Are the Entrance Requirements?

A program's entrance requirements are another consideration. Most graduate programs review all or most of the following when considering a student for graduate work:

Undergraduate grade-point average (often, the requirement is 2.75 or above, on a 4-point system)

Score on the Graduate Record Examination (GRE)

Score on the Miller Analogies Test

Letters of recommendation from persons who know the applicant's academic potential

Grades on postbachelor's work

Test of writing ability (this is required for certain Ph.D. programs in the social sciences)

Returning students who finished their undergraduate programs 10 or more years ago often have inadequate undergraduate grade-point averages. There are two common reasons for this. First, grading may have been more rigorous when they were in school. Second, some returning students may not have taken their undergraduate work seriously enough, and this is reflected in lower grade-point averages. If your undergraduate average is too low, find out whether the graduate school will allow you to enter on academic probation or enroll as a special student until you are able to establish a record of successful graduate work.

What Are the Program's Requirements?

Requirements will of course vary from program to program, but most graduate programs have several requirements in common.

Most programs require that you maintain an average of B or better in your graduate courses. Many, particularly at the doctoral level, require some periods of full-time study. If you are working full time and also have other commitments, this last requirement may be difficult for you to meet. But in some programs, particularly those with many returning students, there are several different ways to fulfill the full-time-study requirement. Often, for instance, you can do 2 to 4 weeks of full-time study several times during the program, and many people can attend classes full-time for 2 weeks although a semester of full-time work would be out of the question.

Is a minor required? Many graduate programs, particularly those at the doctoral level, require students to have a concentration of course work (a minor) in an area other than their major. This requirement, usually about 10 to 12 semester credits, is determined by the department in which the student wishes to minor. Many graduate schools also allow students who want a broader minor to do their minor course work in more than one department.

What are the research requirements? At most institutions, a graduate degree—particularly a Ph.D.—is a research degree. And even if a graduate program does not actually emphasize research (as is true of certain professional master's degree programs), some research is still required. At the doctoral level, the research requirement usually includes courses in statistics, computer science, and research methods; and completion of a dissertation. The *dissertation* is a report of original research completed by the student and is usually seen as the capstone of the student's doctoral program. At many graduate institutions, students invest more time in carrying out and reporting research than they do in course work.

What comprehensive examinations are required? One important difference between an undergraduate and a graduate degree is the increased emphasis on analysis and integration in graduate programs. Comprehensive examinations are designed to measure the extent to which graduate students are able to analyze and integrate what they have been studying. At the master's level, an oral or a written examination is usually required at the end of the program. At the doctoral level, a comprehensive examination—which is usually called a *preliminary examination*—is given when the student's course work for the program is completed. A student is not officially admitted as a doctoral candidate until he or she has passed a comprehensive examination in the major field.

Besides passing a comprehensive examination, a doctoral student is required to defend a dissertation in a final oral examination. This is usually a 2-hour examination in which the student meets with a graduate committee, made up of three to seven faculty members.

What Is the Curriculum for the Degree?

What courses are required for the degree, and what courses are electives? To what extent can courses be taken outside the department? Do you have a say as to which courses you will take, or is the entire curriculum prescribed? To what extent is the graduate program (the courses you take) the result of discussion between you and your major professor? When courses are selected, to what extent are your previous courses and your other experiences considered? This is particularly important if you are a returning student and have done many things since completing your undergraduate degree.

How Are the Courses Offered?

Increasingly, graduate students—particularly returning graduate students—are working either full time or part time and thus may not be able to attend courses offered at traditional times (such as three times a week at 1:20 P.M.) It's therefore important to find out how courses are offered.

Ask which courses (if any) are available in the late afternoon or evening, which are available on weekends, and which are taught off campus. Also, ask whether any of the courses are available on videotape or in other electronic forms for studying at home, at your own speed.

If your area of study is one where employment requires practical experience, ask whether internships are available. Such practical experience on the job with supervision, as you are studying, will often make a difference when you complete your degree and are looking for a job.

How Are Major Professors Selected?

Whether you are a master's or a doctoral candidate, you will work closely with your major professor. You need to find out how this person is selected and whether you will have any voice in the selection.

In many departments, a temporary adviser is assigned to all new graduate students. After a time—up to 1 semester—a permanent assignment is made. You should have an opportunity to select your major professor, as you will spend many hours working with this person, particularly if you are a doctoral student. The temporary-adviser concept is helpful, for it gives you time to get to know the faculty in the department before selecting a permanent major professor.

Under certain circumstances, you may want to select your permanent major professor before enrolling in a graduate program; for example, you may know a professor in your field of interest whom you respect and with whom you want to do your graduate work. But consider the practical problem of workload: the professor of your choice may not have time to add one more graduate student to an already heavy advising load.

What Are the Characteristics of the Students?

One of the greatest resources available to any graduate student is the other students enrolled in the program. Before entering a program, ask to meet some of the graduate students who are already there. What are their interests? What kinds of research projects are they pursuing? What are their attitudes toward their graduate programs and toward the department? What are their attitudes toward the faculty? What are their backgrounds? What are their career goals? Do they appear to be helping each other in courses and research projects? Is there a graduate student organization? Such an organization can be of help when you have academic questions and can also be of help psychologically throughout a graduate program.

What Career Opportunities Exist?

Career opportunities are a very important consideration. Ask the person you talk with in the department to describe the positions its graduates have recently taken. Do the graduates seem to have difficulty finding positions? Ask for the names of recent graduates whom you may contact for additional information about how well their careers were served by their graduate program.

Are Graduate Students Involved in Departmental Decision Making?

Do graduate students have a voice in departmental decision making? Do they serve on the department's committees, such as the graduate admissions committee, the graduate programs committee, and the examinations committee? Do they have a voice in deciding what new courses will be offered by the department and which courses will be eliminated? Do they have a say in deciding what adjustments can be made in degree requirements? Do they have some input with regard to the department's admissions requirements? Are they asked to help evaluate the faculty? The extent to which graduate students are involved in departmental decisions and policies is a significant factor in choosing a graduate program.

What Financial Aid Is Available?

Most adults returning to school (and many other students as well, of course) need financial assistance.

In most graduate departments, three kinds of assistantships are available: research assistantships, project assistantships, and teaching assistantships. Each of these generally requires 20 hours of work per week. As the title suggests, a *research assistant* assists a faculty member with research. Usually, the student is also able to do personal research as part of the assistantship; thus an assistantship provides not only general financial help but also funding for the research required by the degree program. A *project assistant* may work for the departmental secretary, being responsible for various administrative tasks, or may assist with any of a variety of programs conducted by the department. A *teaching assistant* works closely with a course instructor, helping with the planning and carrying out of a course, including the administration and grading of examinations. Teaching assistantships involve responsibility for conducting discussion sections of a lecture course and perhaps even giving an occasional lecture in the absence of the instructor. Not only do assistantships provide financial help; they also provide an internship experience that is of great value to most students. Working side by side with a faculty member on a research project or with an instructor teaching a course provides a learning opportunity very different from lectures, discussions, and so on.

Also available to many graduate students are scholarships, fellowships, and loans. Inquire at the graduate school where you enroll for more information about these forms of financial aid.

PLANNING A GRADUATE STUDY PROGRAM: USEFUL TIPS

In planning a program of graduate study, the first important step is to *have a clear idea of your overall study goals*. You should be able to answer two questions: (1) Why are you pursuing a graduate degree? (2) What do you hope to do when you complete your degree? Many returning graduate students are seeking advancement in their present careers or are changing careers. A few have enrolled in graduate degree programs for general self-improvement, with no particular career plans in mind. Students who are going into graduate school directly from undergraduate programs usually see graduate work as an extension of their undergraduate work.

Once you know your overall goals, the next step is to *decide how to meet your goals*. Here, the question you should be able to answer is: How, specifically, do you plan to accomplish your study goals? For most graduate programs, the core learning opportunities are courses and research, supplemented by independent work, internships, and the like. As an example of the planning process, let's look briefly at courses.

Selecting courses for a graduate program (if you have enrolled in a program where you can choose at least some of your courses) can be trying. One potential problem is finding out about the content of courses. Start with the graduate catalog, which lists all the courses offered, but be careful. Courses change over the years as different instructors teach them, and even when the same instructors teach them; and often the descriptions in graduate catalogs have not kept up with the actual content of courses. One way to learn about the content of a course is to contact the instructor who teaches it and ask for a copy of the course outline. Another way is to talk with students who have recently taken the course; they not only can tell you about the content but can also give you an evaluation of the quality of the course and the instructor. You can also learn about course content by discussing courses with your major professor, though he or she cannot have as much information as students who have recently taken a particular course or the instructor who teaches it.

A second area of concern in deciding on courses is finding out when the courses are offered. Often, one course is a prerequisite for another. You need to know the semesters when courses are offered in order to plan courses in sequence.

A third area of concern in deciding on courses is ensuring that there will be a close relationship between your course work and the research project that you will pursue (assuming that you are taking a degree for which a research project is required). The more closely your course work relates to your research interests, the easier the research will be.

DOING GRADUATE WORK: GUIDELINES FOR STUDENTS

In this section, I'll take up three important aspects of doing graduate work: first, preparing a research proposal; second, planning the research itself; and third, taking graduate examinations.

Preparing a Research Proposal

In most graduate departments, you must submit a research proposal as a preparation for conducting research. The research proposal is simply a written plan of what you will study and how you will conduct the research activity from its beginning to its conclusion.

Many graduate students have ideas for research topics when they begin their graduate program, but few have worked out the details. Some graduate students are recruited by faculty members to work on specific research projects; some students indicate their interests by applying for such projects. Other graduate students, particularly returning students, may have a general area of interest for research but no specific topic in mind. As you decide on a topic, remember that because you will spend many months on your research project, from the development of the proposal to the writing of the thesis or dissertation, the topic you select should be of considerable interest to you.

Research proposals vary somewhat from topic to topic, but most graduate research proposals have the basic components discussed in the following sections. (Be sure to check with your graduate department to see if it has a standard outline to follow in preparing research proposals.)

Introduction In the introduction to a research proposal, in one or two general paragraphs, indicate the nature of the research problem and the objectives of the research. This allows the reader to put the entire research project into perspective.

Review of the Literature The "literature review," as the term implies, briefly describes the literature related to your research area. To obtain a list of related literature, conduct a library search; you may want to do a computer data search to find information about other research in your area of interest. From your graduate course work, you may also have learned about background information and other research.

Statement of the Problem   In your research proposal, state as clearly as you can the specific problem to be investigated. Often, the best way to summarize this section is by formulating a series of questions.

Theoretical Framework   A theoretical framework is given for research projects that grow out of existing theory. In your framework, present a clear description of the theory, along with a discussion of how your research project relates to it. For instance, your research may set out to test a theory or some portion of a theory. Or you may have taken a particular theory as a guide to organizing the elements of your research; here you are not testing the theory but using it as a road map for conducting your research.

Significance of the Study   In the research proposal, state the significance of your study; that is, indicate what you believe will be its theoretical and practical contributions.

Definition of Terms   Clarifying your terminology is an important part of your research proposal. Define the significant concepts and unfamiliar terms used in the study.

Objectives   Objectives are statements indicating what you intend to accomplish with your research. You may want to write a general, overall objective followed by specific objectives. For instance, if you are conducting research in the social sciences, an example overall objective might read, "To determine the relationship between formal educational levels of a sample of 45-year-olds and their attitudes toward using computers." A specific objective for this study could be, "To determine the attitude of 45-year-old urban women with college degrees toward using computers as word processors."

Hypotheses   Hypotheses are statements of what you expect to find in your research study. In some types of research, you write hypotheses and then attempt to falsify them through your research. For instance, a hypothesis might read, "In 45-year-olds, there is no relationship between formal educational level and attitude toward using computers." Not every research project includes hypotheses; particularly, explorative and descriptive research may not use hypotheses.

Methodology   In the "methodology" section of a research proposal, you describe how you will carry out your research. Describe each phase of your intended project. For instance, the first phase might be identification of a research sample from which you will obtain data. The second phase could be selection or development of research instruments to collect the data you need. The third phase might be the actual data collection. Succeeding phases would involve data analysis and the writing of the research report. Sometimes it is useful to write the methodological section as a time line: you intend to accomplish x by January 15, y by April 1, and z by June 1 (or the like).

Bibliography In the bibliography, list the writings you used in the development of the research proposal.

Note: Useful References Following are references that describe the development of a research proposal in considerably more depth; they also cover the process of planning a research project, which I'll discuss below.

Borg, W. R., and M. D. Gall: *Educational Research,* 4th ed., Longman, New York, 1983.

Kerlinger, F. N.: *Foundations of Behavioral Thought,* 2d ed., Holt, Rinehart, and Winston, New York, 1983.

Miles, Matthew B., and A. Michael Huberman: *Qualitative Data Analysis: A Sourcebook of New Methods,* Sage, Beverly Hills, Calif., 1984.

Van Dalen, Deobold: *Understanding Educational Research,* 4th ed., McGraw-Hill, New York, 1979.

Planning Research

Following are tips that graduate students have found useful in planning their research.

Scope of the Research Use common sense when considering the scope of graduate research. Many students come up with ideas for research projects that would take 5 years and $1 million dollars to complete. An important aspect of selecting a research project is being realistic about how much time and money you have for it.

Often your major professor, who has worked with many students and many research projects, can help you make realistic plans for your research. Other students who are in the midst of their own research or have nearly completed it can help you assess your ideas in terms of actually carrying out the research.

Collaboration When you are conducting research, collaboration—teaming up with other graduate students—can provide dividends. In fact, the opportunity for team research is a fringe benefit of getting to know other graduate students in your department and learning about their research interests.

In *team research*, two or more graduate students work together on the same large research project. Each student identifies an aspect of the research that he or she will work on, but of course this individual work is related to the larger project. Often funded research projects under the direction of one or more faculty members are carried out this way.

Many benefits can result from such collaborative efforts, including psychological benefits. When students experience problems with their individual research (as most do), they have someone with whom they can share their concerns; and when a project is going well, they have someone with whom they can share their joy. Interaction resulting from both positive and negative situations can maintain students' motivation for a research project.

Use of Existing Data   Although you may use some existing data in your research, you should not simply accept it without careful consideration.

Often, particularly if a department has several ongoing research projects, "leftover" data will be available for students to use. There are times when using such data can be an extremely efficient and inexpensive way to develop a research project. But in some circumstances doing this can be dangerous: the student may be lulled by the availability of data and may fail to think about the research problem. In effect, such a student begins a research project with answers for which there are no questions. If a student's research problem can be answered with available data, the student should by all means use them. But it is important to begin the development of a research proposal with a problem or question rather than with data in search of a problem.

Pitfalls in Project Design   Two common sources of problems in planning research are inappropriate instruments and inappropriate approaches. As a general rule, avoid designing a research project around a favorite research instrument or a favored approach.

Occasionally, a graduate student will discover a research instrument— such as an interview schedule—that has considerable appeal and will then design a research proposal based on that instrument. This is an error, unless of course the purpose of the student's research is to refine and further develop the research instrument. Beginning a research project with a specific instrument in mind creates problems similar to those created by beginning with available data.

Some graduate students begin planning a research project with a specific approach in mind. For instance, they may want to do only experimental research, or they may be interested in ethnography or survey research. These students are beginning at the wrong place. The nature of the research problem will often suggest the most appropriate research approaches to follow; therefore, the place to start is the research problem.

Taking Graduate Examinations

In addition to the examinations that are part of course work, graduate students usually also take comprehensive examinations, and if they conduct research, they take examinations where they defend it.

Comprehensive Examinations   As their name suggests, comprehensive examinations measure the extent to which you are able to integrate into a whole the material you have studied during your graduate program.

Understanding comprehensives   In a master's program, the comprehensive examination usually comes at the end of the program. In a doctoral program, the comprehensive examination, usually referred to as the *preliminary examination*, comes at the end of the course work. Thus for most doctoral students, the preliminary examination is taken about halfway through the doctoral program, since considerable time is usually necessary to complete the research requirement of the program after the course work has been completed.

Comprehensive examinations take several forms. They may be open-book take-home examinations with a deadline of, say, 5 days for completion. They may be sit-down, classroom-type examinations in which you write for 4 hours or sometimes much more (say, 16 hours over 2 days) without notes or references. Often, a comprehensive examination is oral: the student is examined by a graduate committee for 2 to 4 hours. It is not unusual for the comprehensive examination to be some combination of these forms. For example, the examination may have a take-home section which is followed by an oral section.

In some graduate departments, students have a choice about which form of comprehensive examination they will take. And in some departments, the student and the student's graduate committee decide together on the form of the comprehensive examination.

Preparing for and taking comprehensive examinations   The discussions of essay and oral examinations in Chapter 6 include some guidelines that apply to comprehensive examinations. Following are additional tips that graduate students have found helpful.

1   When reviewing materials presented in graduate course work, *concentrate on the big ideas or major concepts*. Write the big ideas as headings on note cards (which will be filed according to these head-

ings), and for each heading write supporting information that may have been presented in several courses.

2 *Avoid extensive reading* during the review process. Extensive reading at this stage can be more confusing than enlightening. As you prepare for comprehensive examinations, you should be more concerned about integrating what you have learned so far. Often, additional details obtained from reading at this point will get in the way of this integration process.

3 For many fields of study, particularly in the social sciences, another useful approach is to *identify major issues, determine your own position* on these issues, and *note the evidence you would use to support your position.*

4 It can be extremely useful to *study with other students* who are also preparing for comprehensives. This process works best when students give each other assignments to lead discussions and raise questions.

5 Even if you do some group study, be sure to *study and review alone.* Often, group study will help you identify areas where you need to do more thinking on your own.

6 *Begin reviewing early.* Start the review process well ahead of the time when you will take the examination. At the doctoral level, many students begin their review 6 months before comprehensives. At the master's level, this time is shorter—say, 2 months. But in either case reviewing for comprehensive examinations cannot be accomplished in a week.

7 During the review process, *study old examinations.* Write practice answers to examination questions and then let your fellow students evaluate your answers.

8 *Make certain that the practice answers you prepare are your own,* not quotations from books and other authorities you have read. Students taking comprehensive examinations often string together quotation after quotation without demonstrating any real ability to integrate ideas; this is a serious shortcoming. Sometimes, students who are reviewing for comprehensives do not even seem to understand the difference between quoting authorities to answer questions and quoting authorities to support their own answers. Faculty members who evaluate comprehensive examinations are concerned first with the student's ability to answer questions and take positions and only second with the student's ability to cite authorities.

9 For a written comprehensive, *follow the suggestions in Chapter 6 for writing essay examinations.* Spend 10 percent or more of the examination time outlining and planning your answers.

10   For an oral comprehensive, *refer to the section on oral examinations in Chapter 6* for suggestions.

Research Defense Examinations   At both the master's and the doctoral levels, students who have done research as part of the degree program are usually required to defend their research in a final oral examination. For most graduate students, this oral defense of a thesis or dissertation is the culmination of the graduate program, the last activity before the degree is granted.

Some students find the oral examination an extremely stressful situation and become very anxious about the graduate committee's questions and their own ability to answer them. Obviously, the examination is not to be taken lightly: there are will be, say, five people asking in-depth questions about your research for at least 1 hour and probably 2 hours. Often, though, the extreme anxiety experienced by some students is unfounded.

Let's look at the situation. You are a graduate student and researcher and have worked on your research project for a considerable time—at least 2 years, or longer if you are a Ph.D. candidate. You know more about your research than any member of your examining committee. You've done the background reading; you've studied related research. You know how you conducted the research, and you know this better than anyone else because you are the one who actually did it. You have every reason to go into an oral examination with confidence—not arrogance, of course, but certainly confidence.

Also, you've already spent many hours working with individual members of your dissertation committee and with the entire committee. The committee members probably raised many questions while you worked on your paper, and you tried to satisfy their concerns. Thus when you come to the oral examination, you should be reasonably assured that at least those members of the committee with whom you have worked most closely, particularly your major professor, will be in agreement with you and on your side.

The final oral examination is not designed to fail students. After a major professor and a graduate committee have spent months or years working with a student, they don't want the student to fail. What your major professor and the committee do want is for you to have produced as good a research study as possible, and for you to have learned as much as possible about the process of doing research. Often during the final oral you'll receive additional suggestions for improving your thesis or dissertation. These suggestions should not be taken as indicating that you have failed, but simply as comments on shortcomings that could befall any researcher. The committee—if it operates as most such committees do—is a group of professionals helping one of their peers to polish his or her research.

THE SUCCESSFUL GRADUATE STUDENT: A PROFILE

What makes a successful graduate student? Following are some practical suggestions that, in my experience, effective graduate students seem to follow.

Successful graduate students...

Keep their priorities straight. They set aside time to spend with their families and friends. They find time for recreation and relaxation no matter how busy their academic schedules are. They tell themselves that there is life after graduate work, as there was before, and that though graduate work is important, other things in life continue to be important as well.

Are realistic about how much they can accomplish. They realize that they could probably try to do more—take more courses, add more dimensions to their research, etc.—but they decide to do the very best they can with a realistic work schedule.

Avoid a narrow perspective. It is easy, in graduate work, to spend so much time with an increasingly narrow topic that one loses sight of the bigger picture. Successful graduate students are specialists with a context—that is, they know where and how their speciality fits into a broader picture. They read, study, and take courses that challenge them beyond their area of specialization.

Take time to reflect. With all the responsibilities of being a graduate student—often combined with earning a living, caring for a family, and maintaining community interests—there is scarcely a moment to draw a deep breath. But successful graduate students manage their time so that they have at least half an hour or so each day to reflect on what they are doing and what it all means. Some take a long walk at sunset; some have a quiet time in the early morning. Where and when they reflect is not important as long as they do reflect, preferably each day. Without time for reflection, the ever-busy, ever-hurrying, even-pressured graduate student begins to feel caught up in a current, always at the mercy of uncontrollable forces.

SUMMARY

- In choosing a graduate degree program, it is helpful to ask several questions: Is the program of high quality? What is the focus of the department? What are the entrance requirements? What are the program's requirements? What is the curriculum for the degree? How are the courses offered? How are major professors selected? What are the characteristics of other students in the program? What career opportunities exist for graduates? Do graduate students have a voice in departmental decision making? What financial aid is available?

- When planning your graduate program, begin by focusing on your study goals and career plans. Then concentrate on how you can best meet these goals and plans through your graduate work.
- Graduate research often begins with a research proposal. A research proposal usually consists of: (1) introduction, (2) review of the literature (3) statement of the problem, (4) theoretical framework, (5) significance of the study, (6) definition of terms, (7) objectives, (8) hypotheses, (9) methodology, (10) bibliography.
- In planning the research itself, be realistic about its scope, don't overlook opportunities to collaborate with other students, be careful about using existing data, and resist the temptation to design a project around a favorite research instrument or approach.
- Graduate students take two types of examinations beyond those that are part of regular courses: comprehensive examinations and research defense examinations. As with course examinations, certain skills are necessary in preparing for and taking these examinations.
- Successful graduate students keep their priorities straight, are realistic about how much they can accomplish, avoid a narrow perspective, and take time to reflect.

GLOSSARY

DEFINITIONS OF
IMPORTANT TERMS

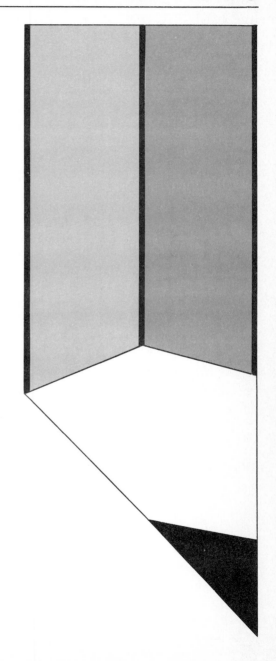

ADMINISTRATIVE STAFF

Titles Most Often Used, in Order of Rank

1 *President, chancellor, provost.* In some university systems, the president heads up the entire system, and chancellors or provosts head up individual campuses.
2 *Vice president, vice chancellor.*
3 *Dean.* The highest-ranking official in a school or college. A university made up of several schools and colleges will thus have several deans.
4 *Departmental chairperson.* The highest-ranking official in a university department.

Other Administrative Titles

Bursar. Responsible for collecting tuition and fees from students.

Dean of students. Responsible for the well-being of all students on a campus. Functions include counseling, job placement, financial aids, and many others.

Registrar. Administrator responsible for supervising admissions, enrollments, grade records, and transcripts.

ORGANIZATIONS

College. An independent institution that grants degrees; or a unit within a university (such as College of Letters and Science or College of Engineering). Headed by a dean.

Department. One of several units within a college or school. Usually organized by disciplines—history department, English department, psychology department, and so on. Administered by a departmental chairperson or sometimes a departmental head.

Division. A cluster of departments with some subject commonality—social studies division, physical sciences division, humanities division.

School. Generally, a subunit within a college, such as a school of music within a College of Letters and Science. Sometimes, a freestanding unit organized like a college.

INSTRUCTIONAL STAFF

Faculty

The instructional staff consists of the following, in descending order of professional advancement. Generally, all are referred to as *faculty members,* and collectively they are called *the faculty:*

1 *Professor (full professor).* The highest level for a faculty member. The term is also commonly used in communication to refer to associate and assistant professors.
2 *Associate professor.*
3 *Assistant professor.* The entry-level position for faculty members at most institutions. Generally, an assistant professor has 6 years to earn tenure and become a permanent member of the faculty.
4 *Instructor.* This term can also be used for any faculty member when rank is unspecified.
5 *Lecturer.* Usually a temporary position.

Other Instructional Titles

Adjunct. This term is often used to designate part-time instructional staff members, as in "adjunct professor."

Adviser. Any instructional staff member assigned to work with a student in planning study schedules.

Major professor. An instructional staff member, usually an assistant professor or above, assigned to a graduate student to assist with study schedules and supervise the student's research project.

ACADEMIC PROGRAMS

Academic year. Usually, the months from September through May, broken into two semesters or three quarters. Many institutions also offer accelerated and weekend programs, along with a variety of summer school formats—1-week, 3-week, 4-week, 8-week.

Accreditation. Official recognition by a regional, state, or other organization empowered to evaluate the quality of an institution's academic programs.

Add/drop. A procedure a student uses to take on more courses or quit courses after an academic term has begun.

Audit. To attend a course without receiving credit. Requirements such as examinations are usually waived, and an audited course does not count toward degree requirements.

Bulletin or catalog. The institution's publication which lists degrees and courses offered, general admission requirements, resources, services, and other information.

Class. Classes may take several forms: lecture, small-group discussion, laboratory, studio, etc. With electronic communications, increasingly classes are being offered via television and interactive computers.

Class schedule. The courses in which a student is enrolled and the times when they meet.

Credit (credit hour). Amount of academic award allotted to each course or other organized learning format completed. Courses generally earn 1, 2, 3, 4, and sometimes as much as 5 credits, depending on the number of hours they meet per week. To receive a degree, a specified number of credits is required.

Curriculum. A group of courses, both required and optional, needed to complete a degree.

Degrees. Depending on the college or university, three general categories of degrees are offered: (1) *Bachelor's degree,* generally a bachelor of science (B.S.) or bachelor of art (B.A.), though there are many others. (2) *Graduate academic degree,* such as master of arts (M.A.), master of science (M.S.), and doctor of philosophy (Ph.D.). (3) *Graduate professional degree,* such as master of fine arts (M.F.A.), master of social work (M.S.W.), doctor of education (Ed.D.), and doctor of medicine (M.D.) (there are many others).

Elective. A course a student may take which is not required, but generally counts toward the total degree credit requirements.

Grade point average. A number obtained by dividing the total number of grade points earned by the total number of credits attempted. Usually expressed on a scale of 1 to 4, where A = 4.0 and D = 1.0.

Incomplete. A grade received at the end of a semester when not all the requirements for a course have been met. Sometimes "incomplete" (I) becomes a failing grade (F), if the requirements for the course are not met within a reasonable time.

Independent study. Work on a particular learning project under the direction of a faculty member who is knowledgeable in the area. The student works alone.

Internship. A way of earning academic credit while working in a job setting similar to the one for which the student is preparing. For example, a student studying agriculture may enroll in a summer internship where she or he works on a farm.

Major. A student's primary focus of activity. The major can be a single discipline (English, history) or a combination of disciplines (water resources, governmental policy studies).

Minor. A student's secondary concentration of activity.

Pass/fail. In some courses, students can choose to receive only a passing or a failing grade instead of a letter grade.

Probation (academic probation). When a student's overall grade point average slips below the school standard, the student may be placed on academic probation for a given length of time in order to bring up his or her grades. Dismissal may result if grades are not brought up to the school's standard.

Study abroad. An arrangement whereby a student completes part of his or her academic program in another country.

Syllabus (course outline). A list of topics, requirements, grading procedures, readings, and information about a course.

Timetable. A listing of all courses offered on a campus during a given semester or quarter, where and when they are offered, the number of credits, and who teaches them. Invaluable for planning a class schedule.

Transcript. The student's official record of courses taken, with grades, credits, and grade point average.

FINANCIAL AID

Assistantships (teaching, research, and project). Assistantships generally require half-time work while the student studies full-time. (See below.)

Fellowships. Fellowships usually do not require work; they are gifts of money to students, generally to support graduate study. Often an exemplary academic record is required for eligibility for a fellowship.

Scholarships. Gifts of money to undergraduate students. Some scholarships are based on financial need; many are based on previous academic achievement. Other restrictions are sometimes applied (for example, the student may have to be from a certain area of the country or be preparing for a particular field of work.)

Student loans. Loans are available to both undergraduate and graduate students with limited financial means.

Veterans' educational benefits. For military veterans; also, sometimes for surviving spouses and children of veterans.

Work-study programs. Needy students are given opportunities to work for pay, often on a task unrelated to their degree program.

STUDENTS

Alumnus (plural: alumni). A graduate of a college or university.The feminine forms *alumna* and (plural) *alumnae* are used less and less these days.

Graduate student. A student who has completed an undergraduate degree and is now working on a graduate degree.

Nontraditional student (returning student, adult student): These terms refer to students age 25 and older, most of whom are returning to school after several years away.

Part-time student. A student taking a minimum of 1 or 2 credits, but less than a full-time load. At many institutions a full-time load for an undergraduate student is 12 credits; for a graduate student, it is 9 credits.

Project assistant. A graduate student with a part-time position (usually half-time) as an assistant to a faculty member on an assortment of special activities (such as organizing conferences and assisting with computer work).

Research assistant. A graduate student with a part-time position (usually half-time) as an assistant to a faculty researcher.

Special student (nonmatriculated student). A student who is enrolled in courses but is not working for a degree. Often, returning students come back to school as special students before beginning to work for a degree.

Traditional student. This term refers to students who have entered a college or university directly from high school.

Teaching assistant (TA). A graduate student with a part-time position as a teacher in a college or university.

Undergraduate student. A student working on a bachelor's degree.

WRITING ASSIGNMENTS

Critical review. A paper in which you analyze and criticize a book, an article, a research report, a film, a speech, computer software, a videotape program, an audiotape program, or some other form of communication.

Essay. A paper in which you argue a point of view, perhaps one side of a contemporary issue.

Research report. An account of research activity you conducted. It usually includes a description of the research problem, approach, findings, conclusions, and implications.

Report. A description of an experiment or some activity that you observed or participated in.

Term paper. A documented piece of writing that explores a topic in depth.

Theme. A short paper (usually part of an English course), designed to improve your writing skills.

Thesis or dissertation. Usually, a requirement for graduate students, although a senior thesis is required for some undergraduate majors. Theses or dissertations take the form of comprehensive research reports but are longer and more complex than a research report. Generally, the dissertation is associated with requirements for a doctoral degree.

INDEX

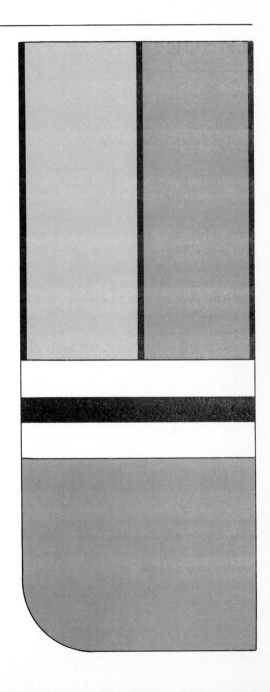

Note: Page numbers in *italic* indicate glossary entries.